TIN-GLAZED TILES FROM LONDON

Published by Museum of London Archaeology

A CIP catalogue record for this book is available from the British Library

Design and production by Tracy Wellman

Reprographics by Andy Chopping

Copy editing by Wendy Sherlock

Managing Editor Sue Hirst/Susan M Wright

Printed in the United Kingdom by Henry Ling Ltd at the Dorset Press, an ISO 14001 certified printer

FSC Mixed Sources
Product group from well-managed forests and other controlled sources
www.fsc.org Cert no. SA-COC-001860
© 1996 Forest Stewardship Council

Front cover: tiles from design catalogue, left to right: top row – **154**, **328**, **470**; middle row – **129**, **296**, **239**; bottom row – **171**, **429**, **83**

Back cover: tiles from design catalogue, left to right: top row – **149**, **339**, **60**; bottom row – **188**, **414**

TIN-GLAZED TILES FROM LONDON

IAN M BETTS AND ROSEMARY I WEINSTEIN

WITH CONTRIBUTIONS BY ANTHONY RAY AND MICHAEL J HUGHES

CONTRIBUTORS

PRINCIPAL AUTHORS
Ian M Betts and Rosemary I Weinstein

SPANISH TILES
†Anthony Ray

SCIENTIFIC ANALYSIS
Michael J Hughes

PHOTOGRAPHY
Ian Betts, Andy Chopping, Maggie Cox, Torla Evans, Richard Stroud and David Tait

GRAPHICS
Carlos Lemos

EDITOR
Wendy Sherlock

CONTENTS

SUMMARY vii

ACKNOWLEDGEMENTS viii

1 INTRODUCTION 1

Structure of this volume 2

Textual conventions used in this volume 2

Research archives 3

2 THE MANUFACTURE OF TIN-GLAZED TILES 4

3 EARLY TIN-GLAZED TILES (*c* 1500–1666) 8

Spanish tiles (Seville) 8

Flemish tiles 11

English tiles 13

Dutch tiles 19

Location and decorative use 20

4 LATER TIN-GLAZED TILES (1666–*c* 1930) 27

London tiles 27

Liverpool tiles 34

Dutch tiles 34

Location and decorative use 38

5 SCIENTIFIC ANALYSIS 44

Introduction 44

Neutron activation analysis of Antwerp-produced tiles 44

Inductively coupled plasma analysis of London-produced tiles 48

6 GAZETTEER OF TIN-GLAZED TILES IN LONDON BUILDINGS 51

City of London and immediate hinterland buildings 52

Greater London area buildings 67

7 DESIGN CATALOGUE 85

Attribution 85

Dating 85

Catalogue entries 86

Early tile designs (*c* 1500–1666) 88

Later tile designs (1666–*c* 1930) 130

FRENCH, DUTCH AND GERMAN SUMMARIES 199

BIBLIOGRAPHY 203

INDEX 212

SUMMARY

Tin-glazed tiles from London looks at the rich diversity of decorative tile designs used in the capital over 400 years. Starting with Moorish- and Renaissance-style designs from Spain, the book traces the importation of decorative tiles from Spain and the Low Countries through to their eventual manufacture in London itself. The early tiles formed spectacular multicoloured floor patterns. Later, tiles were used as a decorative wall covering, particularly around fireplace surrounds. These tiles often have the blue on white designs traditionally associated with the town of Delft in Holland.

Many of the tin-glazed tile designs from London are illustrated and discussed in this book for the first time. Large numbers of wall and floor tiles have been found in the London area over the last 50 years and it is these which form the basis of the illustrated catalogue of individual design types. The volume begins with an overview of the methods of tin-glazed tile manufacture (Chapter 2). It then looks at the introduction and use of tin-glazed floor tiles (Chapter 3) imported from Seville in Spain in the early 16th century and later imports from Belgium (Flanders) in the mid 16th century. Production started in London in 1571. These floor tiles have a wide range of colourful geometric and floral designs. Animals and birds set in circular borders were particularly popular with Londoners during the late 16th to early 17th century.

The use of tin-glazed wall tiles which first arrived in London from the Netherlands in the 1630s is discussed (Chapter 4). Many wall tiles used in London are Dutch, despite production of such tiles in London between 1676 and *c* 1800. These wall tiles again have a wide range of designs, from biblical scenes and mythological figures to sailing ships, landscapes, birds, animals and flowers. More spectacular still are the large tile pictures made from up to 66 individual tiles. Fourteen tin glaze pothouses in the London area are known to have manufactured tiles alongside tin-glazed pottery. When production ceased at the end of the 18th century, the demand for tin-glazed wall tiles was met by the Dutch who continued to supply the London area with decorative wall tiles into the early years of the 20th century. The results are presented (Chapter 5) of scientific analysis carried out to determine the place of production of ten tin-glazed tiles found in London.

The latter part of the book (Chapter 6) looks in more detail at buildings in the London area known to have tin-glazed floor and wall tiles. These are mainly Dutch tiles but there are English examples from London and from Liverpool. A catalogue of over 500 tiles illustrating the wide range of floor and wall tile designs found in London forms the final section (Chapter 7).

ACKNOWLEDGEMENTS

This volume has been produced with financial support from City of London Archaeological Trust (CoLAT), English Heritage, the Guild of Arts Scholars, Dealers & Collectors, Jonathan Horne, the Marc Fitch Fund, London Archaeologist, Museum of London (MOL) and the Society for Post-Medieval Archaeology. To all of these sponsors we express our sincere thanks. The photographs are by MOL Archaeology and MOL unless stated otherwise, whilst conservation work prior to photography was undertaken at MOL by Jill Barnard, Rose Johnson and Robert Payton. The authors also wish to thank Liberty Store and The National Trust for giving permission for use of images taken on their property and Jan Pluis for permission to reproduce previously published tile designs. Other images are with kind permission of English Heritage, Historic Royal Palaces and Linley Sambourne House, London, UK/The Bridgeman Art Library. The quotation on page 1 is from *The murder room*, copyright P D James, 2004, by permission of Greene and Heaton Ltd. The project was managed at MOL Archaeology by David Bowsher and Peter Rowsome.

The authors are very grateful for the assistance of Lynn Pearson of the Tiles and Architectural Cerāmics Society and the Survey of London who provided details of tiles in London buildings, and to the following for additional information and/or access to material: Al-Furqan Islamic Heritage Foundation; Sue Barber; Chris Blanchett; British Museum; Carshalton Water Tower & Historic Garden Trust; Jon Cotton; The Grail Centre; Hendon & District Archaeological Society; The Historic Dockyard Chatham; L-P: Archaeology; North London Collegiate School; Laura O'Shea; Pre-Construct Archaeology Ltd; Susan Pringle; Royal Borough of Kensington and Chelsea; Ruislip, Northwood & Eastcote Local History Society; Saffron Walden Museum, Essex; St Andrew Holborn; St Bartholomew's Hospital Archives and Museum; St George the Martyr church, Borough High Street; St Philomena's School, Carshalton; Andrew Skelton; South London Gallery; Dora Thornton; Wandsworth Museum; Westminster Synagogue; Timothy Wilson. Hazel Forsyth, Jonathan Horne, Hans van Lemmen and Terence P Smith kindly commented on draft versions of the text.

The summary was translated into Dutch by Hans van Lemmen. The index was compiled by Susan Vaughan.

Dedicated to the memory of Jonathan Horne, expert in English ceramics, who died on 25 June 2010

1 INTRODUCTION

> It was unostentatiously comfortable without being cluttered, over-prettified or self-consciously feminine. The fireplace was the original Victorian with a blue Delft tile surround and an ornamental iron hood.
>
> *The murder room*, P D James

The 16th century marked the introduction into Britain of vibrant multicoloured tiles with a wide range of decorative motifs painted on a white background. These new products were called tin-glazed earthenware, also popularly known as delftware after the town of Delft in the Netherlands (in the modern Netherlands province of South Holland), where the industry developed rapidly in the 17th century.

Using a wide variety of tiles from the Museum of London (MOL) collections, it is possible to trace the introduction of tin-glazed floor tiles from Valencia and Seville, in Spain, and Antwerp, in what is now Belgium, in the first half of the 16th century, to their imitation by local London potters at Aldgate in the City of London from 1571 and later at various pothouses located south of the Thames during the early–mid 17th century. The various stylistic designs can be shown to be associated with individual pothouses, and many new attributions made as a result of these discoveries.

The year 1666, that of the Great Fire of London (which destroyed some two-thirds of the City), provides a useful cut-off point between the earlier period, when the manufacture of floor tiles predominates, and the later period, when thinner tiles suitable for mounting on walls were manufactured in London.

Tiles used for wall decoration appear much earlier in the Netherlands, from around the 1580s (Schaap 1984, 20). Dutch interiors were transformed as a result of this innovation, providing colourful, easy to clean, surfaces and protection from damp. Used in England from the 1630s, the blue on white colours of these Dutch wall tiles were inspired by Chinese blue and white porcelain, which was gaining rapid popularity in the Netherlands and elsewhere in northern Europe from the 1620s (Black 2001, 67).

Despite the immense popularity of Dutch wall tiles among the well-to-do middle class, London potters experienced major technical difficulties in the production of such tiles. Seeing a gap in the London market, one potter, Jan Ariens van Hamme, left Delft and established a pothouse for the manufacture of wall tiles at Copthall, Lambeth, in 1676.

London-made tiles of the period 1680–1700 are few and copy the corner motifs and subject matter of their Dutch rivals. Dutch imports of this period show scenes of children playing, ships, cavaliers, flowers, mythological figures and landscapes painted in blue on white with spider head (also referred to in print as spiders head) and barred ox-head corner motifs.

By the mid 18th century, London tile manufacture was more efficiently organised and had come into its own artistically, as the products of the well-known Southwark and Lambeth pothouses demonstrate: these pothouses included Bear Garden, Gravel Lane, Montague Close and Pickleherring in Southwark and Copthall, Lambeth High Street, Glasshouse Street, Norfolk House and Vauxhall in Lambeth. Mortlake in Richmond upon Thames (Surrey), Isleworth in Hounslow (Middlesex) and Glasshouse Street in Lambeth were the only London tin glaze pothouses to survive into the 19th century; a fourth, Vauxhall, barely survived into that century, closing in 1802 (Britton 1987, 66). Few, if any, tiles were made during this period, with the exception of a series of very unusual decorative mosaic tiles probably made at Glasshouse Street (**480**). The end of tin-glazed production in London came with the closure of Glasshouse Street in 1846, although Dutch tiles continued to be imported into London until the early 20th century.

STRUCTURE OF THIS VOLUME

This volume begins with an overview in Chapter 2 of the manufacturing stages and techniques involved in the production of tin-glazed tiles in London. Chapter 3 covers the development of tin-glazed tile production from *c* 1500 to 1666 in Seville, Antwerp and centres in the Southern Netherlands, tracing the direct links and influences through to the English tin-glazed tile industry and five specific London pothouses (Aldgate, Montague Close, Pickleherring, Rotherhithe and Still Stairs). The chapter concludes with a survey of the evidence for the location and decorative use of Spanish, Flemish, Dutch, English and London tin-glazed tiles found in London. Chapter 4 covers the later tin-glazed tiles dating from 1666 to 1930 found in London. The evidence is reviewed for each of the 11 known London pothouses in production during this period (Bear Garden, Copthall, Glasshouse Street, Gravel Lane, Hermitage, Lambeth High Street, Montague Close, Mortlake, Norfolk House, Pickleherring and Vauxhall). The evidence for Liverpool and Dutch tiles found in London is also presented and the influence of their trade upon London tin-glazed tile production is discussed. The chapter concludes with a survey of the evidence of the location and decorative use of predominantly Dutch, but also English, tiles during this period in London. Chapter 5 presents the results of scientific analysis by neutron activation and inductively coupled plasma spectrometry to determine the place of production of ten tin-glazed tiles found on sites in London dating early–late 16th century. A gazetteer providing further details for some of the sites and buildings with tin-glazed tiles discussed in Chapters 3 and 4 is provided in Chapter 6; buildings within the City of London and immediate hinterland are discussed first, followed by those in the Greater London area. Chapter 7 presents the fully illustrated design catalogue for all the tiles covered in this volume. The early tile designs dating 1500–1666 are arranged in approximate chronological order, grouping similar design types together. The later tile designs dating 1666–1930 are grouped by subject matter and chronology (with the exception of the biblical tiles). The catalogue includes 21 Spanish and 502 English and Low Countries tile design entries, detailing location, provenance, date, brief description including colour and tile size, archive and publication references (see p 87 note).

TEXTUAL CONVENTIONS USED IN THIS VOLUME

The basic units of cross-reference in the Museum of London Archaeology (MOLA) (prior to 2009 known as the Museum of London Archaeology Service (MoLAS)) research archive are the site code and context number. The latter is a unique number given to each archaeological context. In addition, each decorated tile is given an accession number to allow reference to the individual object. Most London sites have a two or three figure site code, although these have not been allocated to tiles found before the mid 20th century. In this case, a tile is referred to by the individual Museum of London (MOL, formerly known as MoL) accession number (eg 15647 from All Hallows, Lombard Street).

In this volume, MOL context numbers are always in square brackets [100]; [+] denotes unstratified. Accession find numbers appear in angled brackets ‹200›. The tile design letter (for Spanish tiles) or number (for English and Low Countries tiles) appears in **bold**. Thus a decorated Spanish tile (**C**) from context 107 with accessioned find number 57 found at 30–35 Botolph Lane (MOL site code BPL95) would appear as: BPL95 [107] ‹57›. A small number of tiles have only context numbers as they are yet to be accessioned. Site codes prefixed HADAS denotes excavations undertaken by Hendon and District Archaeological Society and PCA those by Pre-Construct Archaeology Ltd. Tile reference numbers prefixed EH denote tiles belonging to English Heritage. All tile designs are catalogued and illustrated in Chapter 7; cross-references to Chapter 7 have been omitted.

Measures are sometimes quoted in the text in the units used before metrication in the late 20th century. A foot (comprising 12 inches) is equivalent to 0.3m. Before decimalisation in 1971 the UK monetary system consisted of pounds, which were subdivided into 20 shillings, each of which was further subdivided into 12 pennies or pence. Sums of money are quoted in the text as cited in £, s and d, since modern equivalents would be misleading. Historic county names are given in brackets where differing from the names of modern counties or London modern boroughs. This volume uses the term 'Flemish' to refer to tiles which were made in areas which are part of modern Belgium and the Southern Netherlands (Smith 2002).

RESEARCH ARCHIVES

For Museum of London sites the research archive normally comprises original finds, samples, notes, drawings and digital records, scientific analysis data and full site data. It may be consulted by appointment at the MOL's London Archaeological Archive and Research Centre (LAARC), Mortimer Wheeler House, 46 Eagle Wharf Road, N1 7ED. Online catalogues are also available. The LAARC online catalogue with site information can be accessed at http://www.museumoflondon.org.uk/laarc/catalogue. Note that the site address covers the area(s) of excavation and may differ from the specific properties cited in this volume for the same site code. Museum of London accessioned ceramic tiles can be accessed at http://www.museumoflondon.org.uk/ceramics. Information about sites archived in the LAARC is also available in printed gazetteers (Schofield 1998; Shepherd 1998; Thompson et al 1998).

2 THE MANUFACTURE OF TIN-GLAZED TILES

The basic ingredients for the manufacture of tin-glazed tiles are clay, water, sand and the tin glaze itself. In addition, a ready supply of fuel, normally wood although fragments of coal were found in one tin-glaze ware dump at the Pickleherring pothouse in Southwark (Tyler et al 2008, 18), is needed for the kilns which fired the tiles. Excavations on the production sites in the London area have provided a wealth of information concerning the way in which such tiles were made during the 17th and 18th centuries.

The most important basic ingredient is clay; a special calcareous clay was used for manufacture of tin-glazed tiles. Initially London tilemakers used clay from the Norwich area which was shipped down from Yarmouth, both in Norfolk, until 1680 (Britton 1987, 12). From 1639 until 1725, and again from 1744 to 1785, clay from Boyton, Suffolk, helped meet London requirements (Tyler et al 2008, 17). The need to import clay must have greatly increased the cost of manufacture.

To reduce the amount of clay needed (and therefore the cost of manufacture) imported clays were often mixed with local clays, although this seems to have been a somewhat haphazard process. Clay mixing had the added advantage of reducing shrinkage and warping in the drying process, which made possible the manufacture of thinner tiles (Schaap 1984, 25). London tiles made before the late 17th century frequently show signs of inadequate mixing, with local material standing out as prominent red bands against the normally white, cream or pale pink body of the imported clay. Not all early tin-glazed tiles have evidence of clay mixing: at Rotherhithe, Southwark, around a third of tiles from the waster dumps do not have any bands of local red clay (Tyler et al 2008, 66). They are also absent from the majority of thinner wall tiles made in London from the later 17th century onwards.

Experiments to reduce costs still further seem to have been undertaken at the Aldgate pothouse in the City of London, during the late 16th century. These involved making tiles with local red-firing clay and then adding a thin layer of calcareous clay above (Chapter 3, English tiles). The results proved unsatisfactory, so the more usual practice of clay mixing was adopted.

With the shift from floor tiles to wall tiles during the second half of the 17th century it was no longer necessary for tiles to withstand heavy pressure. Continued improvements in clay preparation allowed the manufacture of even thinner tiles (10–12mm thick), which could be used only for walling. These thinner wall tiles first arrived in London from the Netherlands, since English manufacturers were experiencing difficulty in making tiles thinner than 12mm. In 1677 Dr William Johnson was unable to purchase London-made wall tiles as the pothouses at 'Lambeth and Vauxhall … were yet at a loss in the mixture of their clay and way of burning' (Ray 1973, 35; Chapter 4, London tiles). Johnson went instead to a Mr Sybley to purchase 'Holland tile' (ibid) – almost certainly Dutch blue on white wall tiles.

Dutch tiles could be made thinner because of a process called 'washing the clay' which was introduced into tile manufacture before 1650 (Schaap 1984, 25). This involved wetting the clay before mixing it, resulting in a much more homogeneous mixture. For this reason, these thinner wall tiles do not have the banded texture seen in the thicker English tiles of the same period.

The earliest English wall tiles made using this wet clay process were probably those made by Jan Ariens van Hamme from Delft, who was granted a warrant in 1676 to 'exercise his trade and calling of making Tiles and Porcelain ... after the way practised in Holland' at his pothouse in Vauxhall (Ray 1973, 35). The beginning of English wall tile manufacture also coincided with the exploitation of clay from the banks of the River Medway at Aylesford in Kent from 1681: this was nearer London than previous sources, which would have reduced the cost of transporting the raw clay (Britton 1987, 13; Tyler et al 2008, 17).

At the pothouse the clay mixing (kneading) was initially carried out by a man walking barefoot on the clay body, but by the early 18th century horse-operated pug mills were used for tilemaking in the Netherlands (T P Smith, pers comm). The horse drove a rotating metal blade which churned up and mixed the clay. The actual manufacturing process involved the placing of an appropriate amount of clay into a wooden or possibly metal frame. The clay was then flattened by an implement similar to a rolling pin used for pastry-making into the approximate shape and thickness required. Sand was used at the bottom of the moulding frame to prevent the clay sticking to the workbench below. Both the frame and the circular roller used to flatten the clay are visible in an unusual tile picture dated 1735 showing Dutch tile and pottery manufacture (Ray 1973, 25; Schaap 1984, 39, fig 11).

The tile was then removed from the mould and left to partly dry before being trimmed to shape. This involved placing a square-shaped wooden block on top of the tile. The tilemaker then cut round the block with a sharp knife removing any superfluous clay. This cutting was done at a slight angle to produce a bevelled edge, which allowed the tiles to be laid more closely together with the gap between them filled with mortar to give a more secure attachment.

To hold the wooden block firmly in place while the tilemaker cut round the outside, nails protruded from the block into the clay below. When the block was removed these nails left small holes in the top surface of the clay, near the tile corners.

A detailed study of nail-hole patterns on tiles made at Rotherhithe pothouse has revealed that tiles have either two holes, in diagonally opposite corners, or three holes placed one in each of three corners (Tyler et al 2008, 70–1). The nails used seem to have been either square or round, although the hole shape is often distorted when the wooden block is removed from the clay. Occasionally twin sets of holes are present, showing that the wooden block had to be placed on the clay twice before the tile could be trimmed to shape. These holes are usually visible even after glazing, although they are not prominent as most are partly obscured by glaze.

After being cut out, the tiles are left to dry for a second time before firing in the kiln. This first (biscuit-) firing was undertaken before the glaze was added. It is these unglazed, once-fired biscuit tiles (sometimes known as tile blanks) which are frequently found on London pothouse sites. Presumably they represent faulty or broken blanks which were discarded before they reached the next stage in the manufacturing process, the application of glaze. Tin glaze was made by adding tin oxide (an opacifier) to a lead glaze which turned the glaze white and the whole mixture was suspended in water. The upper surface of the tile was dipped into this white glaze mixture which dried quickly as the earthenware biscuit tile was porous. The tiles to be decorated were then taken to the tile-painters, of whom there were probably a number working at any one time. The pattern was added by covering the tile with paper pricked through with the pattern and sprinkling (pouncing) it with powdered charcoal, which passed through the holes on to the surface. When the paper was removed the outline of the pattern was left on the tile surface to serve as a template for the painter.

It is apparent that the design on an individual tile may not all be the work of the same painter. This is most noticeable on a tile from Brooke House, Hackney, where the central flower has been painted with considerable skill whilst the crude corner decoration has been painted by another, presumably an apprentice (Chapter 6, Greater London; **153**). A feature of later tiles is subtle differences in what is essentially the same design. This is seen most clearly in the purple on white landscape tiles from 38–46 Albert Embankment, Southwark (MOL site code 38ALB89). One tile shows a figure walking across a landscape with a church to his right (**242**); the same scene on another tile has the same building but no spire (**243**). In addition, the same scene could be painted the other way round by reversing the transfer (**245**, **246**). This technique could be used to produce matching, but opposite designs at either side of a fireplace, as can been seen in a fireplace surround of *c* 1770 illustrated by Ray (1973, 28, fig 8).

Occasionally, tile fragments are found which seem to have been used as trial or practice pieces. Among the waste material from the Norfolk House pothouse, Lambeth, were found two biscuit-fired tiles with flower design outlines in what appears to be red ink, possibly painters' practice pieces (**484**, **485**).

Once painting was complete, the tiles were ready for firing a second time. Sometimes on the earlier tin-glazed tiles a second coat of clear lead glaze (coperta) was added to obtain extra gloss and depth of colour (H van Lemmen, pers comm). Both unfired blanks and glazed tiles were fired together. This accounts for the small splashes of tin glaze often seen on discarded tile blanks. The kilns in which the firing took place appear to have been rectangular in shape in London until *c* 1700 after which a bottle shape was adopted (Tyler 1999, 145).

Stacking the tiles in the kiln ready for firing must have been a slow and laborious process. Glazed tiles were stacked vertically, each row separated by a horizontal layer of capping tiles known as kiln shelving or bats. The glazed tiles, set back to back, face to face, were kept separate by long strips of clay running along the top and bottom of each tile. These clay strips, known as setters, have been found attached to a number of tiles found on production sites in London. A decorated tile from Pickleherring pothouse (**95**), has the remains of such a strip on its top surface. Pluis illustrates identical clay strips dated 1640 from a pothouse at Deventer in the Netherlands (Pluis 1997, 94, fig 87). The biscuit-fired floor tiles could be stacked either vertically, in the same way as the glazed tiles, or horizontally, with small fragments of broken tile keeping them apart.

The kiln shelving used between the vertical stacks of tiles could be constructed from flat, rectangular slabs of fired clay, rejected biscuit tiles, or even, in rare cases such as the Pickleherring tile mentioned above, rejected decorated tiles. The flat clay tiles, which were made from distinctive sandy red clay, seem to have been specially made by London potters to serve as kiln shelving. At both the Pickleherring and Rotherhithe pothouses there is also clear evidence of the occasional use of roofing tile (Tyler et al 2008, 36, 65). These were presumably used when the supply of purpose-made clay tiles was insufficient.

Unfired clay tiles were stacked in the base of the kiln, where the temperature was highest, while glazed tiles were stacked in the upper part of the kiln, where temperatures were slightly lower. Firing took around 35 hours, and a further three days were needed for the kiln to cool before any tiles could be removed.

Emptying a kiln was known as 'drawing the kiln'. The failure rate was fairly high; only about a quarter of the tiles would be of the highest quality, while many others were blemished in some way and sold at a lower price. 'Seconds' and even 'thirds' were sold, as a list of wares drawn up in 1696 for tax purposes makes clear (Table 1).

As for the tiles which were badly fired or broken, they could be used only as hardcore or dumped in waste heaps near the pothouse. It is the tiles from these waste heaps which have provided so much vital information on the designs and manufacturing techniques employed by London's tin glaze tilemakers.

Table 1 List of 'fine painted tyles and white tyles' drawn up in 1696 (Ray 1973, 37)

Description	Cost	Unit
Large, the foot being 4 tyles	at 16d	pr. foot
Fine painted small	7d	pr. foot
Ditto [small] –a 2 sort of painted	4d	pr. foot
Ditto [small] –y worst painted	2d	pr. foot
Large. Fine white tyles	8d	pr. foot
Ditto [fine white tyles]. Small. The best	4d	pr. foot
Ditto [fine white tyles, small]. Ordinary white	2d	pr. foot

3 EARLY TIN-GLAZED TILES (*c* 1500–1666)

Tin-glazed tiles were used to decorate the interior of London buildings for over 400 years, but the use of elaborately designed tiles for flooring is part of a much older tradition dating back a further five centuries. These earlier tiles differed in having a lead rather than tin glaze, but their purpose was the same, to create visually impressive floor surfaces reflecting the wealth and prestige of the buildings' owners.

Some of the last decorated lead-glazed floor tiles were used at Sutton House, Hackney, a brick-built manor house dating from 1535 (Chapter 6, Greater London). By this time more fashionable tiles made with a tin glaze were already beginning to be installed in the floors of some of London's finer buildings.[1] These new tin-glazed tiles with their bright and lively multicoloured designs must have looked spectacular compared with those of 15th-century and earlier date.

The earliest tiles decorated with tin glaze were imported into London from the Valencia region and Seville in Spain and Antwerp in Flanders, present-day Belgium, as English tilemakers lacked the necessary skills to produce such tiles (Chapter 2).

SPANISH TILES (SEVILLE)

Anthony Ray

At the time these Spanish tiles were made the traditional tilemaking industry in England, though dying, was far from dead, as many 16th-century examples show, notably the excellent tiles made for Hailes Abbey, Gloucestershire, between 1509 and 1527. There was, therefore, no specific need to import floor tiles from elsewhere, and this in turn suggests that any such tiles were imported by individuals rather than traded commercially. The tiles in the Mayor's Chapel in Bristol, Gloucestershire, where so much of the original pavement has survived, were evidently obtained in this way, and the relative scarcity of examples found in London and elsewhere in England seems to confirm the suggestion.[2] Sir Francis Poyntz (d 1528), who paid for the decoration of the Mayor's Chapel, had been in Spain in 1527 and, though he did not visit Seville, may well have had these tiles sent directly to Bristol from Spain. Equally, anyone whose business took him to the Netherlands could have bought examples there.[3] Tiles are hardly ever mentioned in the published documents, and this too might confirm that they were not a commercial commodity.[4]

The preference for English or imported tiles was doubtless a matter of taste. The English tilemakers clung to their medieval traditions: theirs was a lingering Gothic world at a time when some enlightened individuals were beginning to look to something more modern.[5] There was also the question of decorative effect. English floor tiles, however well made, were subdued in colour whereas the Seville tiles were brighter and above all they were a

[1] Some of these tin-glazed tiles copied the designs found on lead-glazed floor tiles. A Dutch version of tin glaze designs **68** and **69**, together with a lead-glazed tile of the same design, are illustrated by van Dam (1991, 14–15, figs 5, 6).

[2] Williams (1995, 336) mentions that *arista* tiles have been found on 30 sites in Britain. Since then a typical example has been found in Tenby, Pembrokeshire, Wales.

[3] Presumably the 32 tiles similar to **I** in The Vyne, Hampshire, came from Flanders (Blanchett 2000, 21).

[4] The Southampton port books of 1509 record the import of 500 paving tiles valued at 5s, but we have no idea where they came from or what kind of tiles they were (James 1995, 42).

[5] The line-impressed tiles with Renaissance heads illustrated by Eames (1992, 28, no. 29) show that English tilers responded to the challenge.

novelty. Yet they cannot have remained in fashion for long as they were immediately in competition with the painted tiles made in Antwerp by the immigrant Italian potter Guido di Savino who settled there by 1508 (below, 3, Flemish tiles). These Spanish tiles, therefore, are a kind of parenthesis between Gothic and Renaissance, the fashion that after a hesitant start developed so rapidly in the second half of the 16th century both in Spain and England.

In fact it seems that even in Spain *arista* tiles were a novelty. In the 14th and 15th centuries the Spanish tile industry was dominated by Valencia where the potters made huge quantities of tin-glazed tiles painted mainly in monochrome blue, with a great variety of designs, both Moorish and Gothic. Few of these seem to have been brought to England.[6] These were luxury goods made, often on commission, for royalty, the nobility, the church and the guilds, and they were costly, not only because they took time to decorate but also because tin was expensive. When the demand for tiles increased at the end of the 15th century, *cuerda seca* and *arista* tiles, which create colourful and complex designs rapidly without recourse to the hand of a painter and used cheaper materials, were soon being made by skilled artisans to supply the ever-expanding market and continued to do so for several decades.[7] Both types of tile achieve the same kind of effect as *cloisonné* enamels, but do so by different means.

Cuerda seca means 'dry cord' but this is misleading since it implies a raised physical barrier. There is indeed a clear separation of the colours, but this is achieved by means of a 'resist' consisting of a dark pigment, probably manganese, mixed with grease which burns away in the kiln leaving a hollow between the areas of colour. Using this mixture the outlines of a design could be painted over a transferred outline on the surface of the tile – the so-called *cuerda seca plana*. Heraldic and other designs could easily be realised by this means.[8] Alternatively, a raised mould was pressed into the tile to create a slightly sunken pattern which could then be filled with the grease. This technique – known as *cuerda seca hendida* – had been in use in Seville from the 13th century onwards to make tiles with intricate interlace patterns (Ray 2000, 325–7), and it was particularly suitable for lettering as well.

Arista means a ridge, and for the making of these tiles a mould was used to create a raised outline enclosing the compartments. There is no documentary evidence to prove when or where this technique originated. *Arista* tiles were made in huge quantities both in Toledo and Seville perhaps from the end of the 15th to the third quarter of the 16th centuries.[9] The earliest known reference may well record the despatch of such tiles from Seville to Coimbra Cathedral in Portugal in 1503.[10] Among the later installations, pride of place must go to the Casa de Pilatos in Seville, completely tiled by the Pulido brothers in 1536–8 (Sancho 1953), and it is worth mentioning the *arista* copies of 14th-century lustre tiles made by Juan Pulido in 1542–4 for the Alhambra, Granada (Ray 2000, 367, nos 905–908).

The repertoire of designs is considerable, and small variations are commonly detectable in the detail of what is ostensibly the same design. This must indicate that the moulds were duplicated, either to facilitate mass production or to replace ones that were worn or broken, and became modified in the process. Nor can we talk about a standard colour scheme for any particular design. The five colours available to fill the compartments – honey-brown, blue, purple, green (lead glazes) and white (tin glaze)[11] – could be combined in many different ways, though naturally a particular setting would require a uniform colour scheme.

[6] For the recorded examples see Betts (2008b).

[7] In older books the tiles are described as *de cuenca o arista* (ie with hollows or ridges). Today they are usually referred to simply as *de arista*. The *arista* tile did not immediately replace the *cuerda seca* as is sometimes stated – for example the altar frontal of the chapel in the Casa de Pilatos in Seville, Spain (1536–8), has *cuerda seca* tiles with an interlace pattern – but there was probably a decline in their popularity in the second quarter of the century.

[8] For typical examples see Ray (2000, 359, nos 872–874) and splendid armorial panels such as that on the tomb of León Enríquez in Santa Paula, Seville (Martínez 1991, fig 307), of *c* 1505–10 or the panel dated 1503 in the Museo de Artes Populares in Seville (Pleguezuelo 1989, 79, no. 16).

[9] For typical Toledo tiles, which have a redder body, see Ray (2000, 328–51). A corpus of Toledo *arista* tiles by José Aguado Villalba (in prep) is nearing completion and is due for publication. There is no Seville equivalent.

[10] Gestoso 1995, 263ff. The document of 31 October 1503, calls them *azulejos de labores*. The term could apply to both *cuerda seca* or *arista* tiles, but they are more likely to be the latter.

[11] The presence of tin has been confirmed by scientific analysis undertaken by Michael Hughes at the British Museum Department of Scientific Research. The technique of x-ray fluorescence analysis was used to test for the presence of tin in the white area of two Spanish tiles (**A**, **B**) and in one Antwerp tile (**19**) (M Hughes, pers comm).

In Seville, tiles were used extensively in wainscots and so needed large-scale patterns involving the alternation of a central motif and a corner motif. Such patterns are established by four tiles (**C–H**), nine tiles, or 16 tiles (**I**, **J** and ?**K**) (Fig 1). These wainscots were usually framed by narrow bands of green or blue tiles within a border of rectangular tiles and surmounted by a row of cresting tiles, but no corresponding examples have been found in London. This, and the obvious wear on many of the tiles in the Museum of London, suggests that these were once set in a floor, like those in the Mayor's Chapel, Bristol. In 16th-century Seville, floors were quite different. Using plain red floor tiles of rectangular, octagonal or hexagonal shape it was possible to create a wide variety of patterns leaving square spaces that could be filled with small *arista* tiles known as *olambrillas* (**M**, **N**, **O**). For ceilings a special kind of rectangular tile was made, with an unglazed strip at either end which rested on the rafters. Usually these tiles have only half a design, for which reason they are known as *de dos por tabla* (ie one of a pair for use on a ceiling). Design **R** is a typical, though late example.

Fig 1 Reconstruction of the central portion of a 16-tile Spanish design (employing **J** from All Hallows church, Lombard Street, City of London); tiles of this type were made by Niculoso Francisco in Seville around 1510–30 (scale *c* 1:4)

In the second half of the 15th century the most important tilemaker in Seville was Fernán Martínez Guijarro who is specifically called in a document of 1479 as *muy grand maestro de azulejos que no lo hay otro tal en este reino* (a great master of tiles like no other in this kingdom). He supplied the tiles mentioned in the document of 1503, and it is very likely that he was the man who developed the *arista* tile in the last decades of the 15th century. He died in 1509 and it now seems that his place was taken by Niculoso Francisco called 'Pisano', that is to say 'the Italian',[12] who is first recorded in Seville in 1498, where he died in 1529. His importance in the history of ceramics has long been recognised, above all as the inventor of the painted tile picture spread over a large number of tiles. Until recently it was not possible to say much about his involvement in the manufacture of other kinds of tile, though all authorities published the contract of 1518 by which Niculoso agreed to make *arista* tiles (called *de labores*) of four different patterns for the church of San Pablo, Spain.[13] The evidence gathered from what is almost certainly his pothouse in the Calle Pureza, Triana in Seville, discovered by chance in 1987,[14] suggests that he played a crucial part in the tile industry generally. The wasters and fragments found there include many *arista* tiles of various kinds and in various states, some of which not only correspond with examples found in sites associated with Niculoso but also with tiles found in Portugal, Italy and England, including some published here. Although the documentary proof is presently lacking, it would be reasonable to suggest that he was not only the designer of many of these tiles, especially those in Italian style, but also that he in some way supervised their manufacture, supplying the moulds to other workshops as required, and co-ordinated their export.[15]

After his death his sons briefly continued his work as a tile-painter, but it seems that it was the Pulido brothers who then became the principal makers of *arista* tiles. It is interesting to note that 14 of the designs found in the Casa de Pilatos are adaptations of designs associated with Niculoso. It may be that his widow, who did not die until 1548, entered into some kind of agreement with the Pulidos, but the evidence is lacking.

DATING

Unless there is clear documentary or other evidence it is naturally extremely difficult to date these tiles with any precision. If it is agreed that the demand for *cuerda seca* tiles

[12] Earlier writers called him Francisco Niculoso, but he always called himself Niculoso in the many documents relating to him and added, indifferently, 'Italiano', 'Florentino' or 'Pisano': 'Pisano' has the sense of 'Italian' rather than indicating that he was a native of Pisa (see Ray 1991).

[13] Gestoso 1995, 176ff. One of the designs may well be that found on tiles in the Mayor's Chapel, Bristol (cf Ray 2000, 368, no. 912).

[14] See Lorenzo 1987; Pleguezuelo 1992. Very few painted sherds were found, though Niculoso's workshop made many painted pattern tiles, probably on commission. The complete absence of fragments of *cuerda seca* tiles may be fortuitous: there is no reason why Niculoso should not have supplied such tiles.

[15] Gestoso (1995, 388–450) listed hundreds of documents containing the names of potters. Between 1503 and 1519 there are references to tiles made by members of Guijarro's family, but thereafter, apart from Niculoso and the Pulidos, not one potter is specifically called a tilemaker; when described they are mainly called *olleros* (earthenware potters).

VALENCIA REGION TILES

Since the report on Spanish tiles was completed by Anthony Ray, tiles from the Valencia region have been identified by Timothy Wilson and one of the authors (IB) (**12**, **14**, **15**). These were identified just prior to publication so it has not been possible to amend the catalogue order. The tiles have the general term 'Valencia region' as they were made in other places, most notably Manises and Paterna, as well as in Valencia itself (Ray 2000, 41, 314).

Valencia region tiles are already known from sites in Kent and Surrey, and Betts (2008b, 54) has already speculated that they were brought into London by ship for redistribution elsewhere. Their presence in London therefore would be expected.

The London tiles are of elongated hexagonal type and would have been laid with square tiles in a mosaic pavement (Ray 2000, 316–17, pl 70). Later imported Antwerp tiles of the 1520s and 1530s are of similar shape. Valencia region tiles found outside London, where only square tiles are known, are of mid–late 15th-century date. The London tiles are probably contemporary. One London tile was almost certainly from a tiled pavement in Greenwich Palace, Greenwich, whilst another was found during restoration work on Temple church, City of London, in the 1840s (Brown 2005, 82).

declined after *c* 1525 it would be reasonable to suggest a global dating of 1500–30, but for both types of tiles there is the problem that a mould and its replacements could be used over a great many years. The material collected from the Calle Pureza certainly has a 'family resemblance' and the date proposed here for the associable examples found in London (1510–30) only indicates that the designs originated in Niculoso's period of activity from the death of Guijarro in 1509 to his own death in 1529. Design **H**, however, has the thicker glaze surface which is more typical of the tiles made by the Pulidos.

VICTORIAN COPIES

Ian M Betts

One oblong ceiling tile found at All Hallows church, Lombard Street, City of London (**R**; Fig 4, no. 11) is almost certainly a Victorian copy made in either London or Seville. Another Victorian copy, confirmed by inductively coupled plasma atomic emission spectrometry (ICP-AES) and inductively coupled plasma mass spectrometry (ICP-MS; both forms referred to below as ICP analysis), was found at Vine Lane, Southwark (MOL site code VIN88; **Q**; Hughes 2005a). These may be the work of Frederick Garrard who made copies of Spanish *arista* tiles at his factory in Millwall, Tower Hamlets (Middlesex), in the 1870s and 1880s (Brown and Brown 1993, 10; Pearson 2005, 458). Other Victorian manufacturers, such as Maw & Co and Minton, were also involved in their manufacture (Brown and Brown 1992, 9–10).

FLEMISH TILES

The manufacture of tin-glazed pottery and tiles was established in Antwerp in Flanders, then part of the Spanish Netherlands, in the early years of the 16th century probably by Guido di Savino, who was resident and running a workshop by 1508 (Wilson 1999, 9). Guido, who changed his surname to Andries whilst in Antwerp, came from Castel Durante (since 1623 called Urbania) near the city of Urbino in Italy, a well-known centre of tin-glazed pottery production. The use of tin glaze had become established in north-central Italy from about 1440. By the end of the 15th century there were a number of other manufacturing centres such as Venice, Florence and Faenza (Britton 1987, 18).

Since their manufacture had been established by an Italian craftsman, it is not surprising that Antwerp tiles, particularly those of earlier date, have decorative motifs which are characteristic of Italian tin-glazed ware. The shapes of these early floor tiles, which are either square or hexagonal, copy those used in earlier Italian mosaic pavements: the square tiles were surrounded on four sides by interlocking hexagonal, or more accurately, elongated hexagonal tiles (**1–15**). Small triangular tiles were needed where the pavement met the wall (**17–19**).

There are two well-known mosaic tile pavements made using square and hexagonal tiles which are believed to represent products from Antwerp. The first is that relaid in the chapel of The Vyne, near Basingstoke, Hampshire, where three different combinations of hexagonal and square tiles are present. Although they are not in their original position, there is no reason to believe that they were not originally purchased for the manor house. Hurst (1999b, 97) believes they were installed *c* 1522 by Sir William Sandy, who acquired The Vyne on the death of his father in 1496. The actual date of manufacture is slightly less certain. Blanchett (2000, 24) has suggested that each size group may be of different date or alternatively that they were made at different workshops.

The second pavement, dated 1532–3, covered the floor of Herkenrode Abbey, near Liége in modern Belgium.[16] More recently another pavement has been found *in situ* at Hemiksem Abbey, Antwerp (Dumortier 1999, 108, pl 1).

Similar tiled floors must have existed in London since square and hexagonal tiles of this style have been found at a number of sites. One tile (**5**), from 90–94 Old Broad Street, City of London (MOL site code BRO90), is almost identical to a tile from The Vyne and is presumably of similar date (Rackham 1926, 28, pl 12).

A number of square and hexagonal tiles were found in the fill of the basement of Broad Arrow Tower in the Tower of London, Tower Hamlets (Fig 4, no. 5), having previously been used in a tiled pavement somewhere in the building (Gaimster and Hughes 1999, 175–6, pl 13). These tiles are almost certainly Antwerp products, probably manufactured some time during the period 1520–40. Two sizes of hexagonal tile are present, the square tiles fitting with the wider hexagonal tiles. The hexagonal tiles are both polychrome and blue on white, whilst the square tiles are all polychrome. The blue on white design is almost identical to that on a hexagonal tile from Carew Manor, Beddington, Sutton (Surrey) (J Phillips, pers comm). Both polychrome and blue on white hexagonal tiles were also used together in The Vyne and Herkenrode pavements.

Tiles from another mosaic pavement were found at Whitehall Palace, Westminster, in 1964, in a garderobe pit containing demolition rubble from Wolsey's 1520s lodgings at York Place or from Henry VIII's rebuilding of 1532 (Hurst 1999a; Fig 4, no. 15). They comprised a hexagonal tile (**11**) and two square tiles, one with an unusual geometric design (**7**) and another, very worn, with a female bust. Two triangular corner tiles and a small square tile recovered from the same site are probably of similar date (**17**, **18**, **20**). Hurst and Le Patourel (1999, 181) believe the tiles are most likely to have been installed during the rebuilding of 1532 as there are close design parallels with the Herkenrode pavement of 1532–3. However, a more recent find from Whitehall, Horse Guards Avenue, Westminster (MOL site code WIH01) hints at the existence of an earlier pavement. This comprises a tile showing a duck in a landscape (**3**) which is closely paralleled on a tile at The Vyne dating from the 1520s (Blanchett 2000, 13, n).

Later in date from Whitehall Palace is a tile from part of a tile picture (Le Patourel 1999, 147–8).[17] The design, although rather worn, has a characteristically French appearance (**40**), although an origin in the Low Countries cannot be ruled out. Tin glaze tilemaking began at Lyons, Rhône, France, in 1512, spreading to other areas of the country over the following two centuries (Berendsen 1967, 91).[18] The tile picture could have been installed at any date between Henry VIII's rebuilding of 1532 and the destruction of much of the palace by fire in 1698.

Later Antwerp tiles brought over to London during the mid 16th century are all square in shape. They are decorated with a variety of designs such as the heads of figures, flowers and various geometric, circular patterns.

Antwerp is also well known for the production of large tile pictures, painted over a number of separate tiles. The Museum of London has a border of one of these tile pictures, painted in typical Antwerp style, from an unknown site in London (**39**), whilst part of another such border was found during excavations in 1966 near the Old Bailey,

[16] Now in the Royal Museum of Art and History, Brussels, Belgium.

[17] The tile has the Roman numerals XVIII in blue on the back to mark its location in the tile picture.

[18] There are medieval tin-glazed floor tiles in France and the Low Countries dating from the 1290s to the beginning of the 15th century (Norton 1984). There is no apparent link between the medieval tin-glazed tile industry and the reappearance of tin-glazed tile manufacture in Flanders and France during the early 16th century.

Warwick Square, City of London (MOL site code GM133; **37**). The latter may have formed part of a tile picture decorating Warwick Inn, a great medieval house which is believed to have stood on or near the excavation site (Fig 4, no. 17). A second Antwerp tile from the site has a fleur-de-lis painted in the same distinctive style (**26**). Assuming these two Old Bailey tiles did indeed come from Warwick Inn, they were presumably installed after the house passed into the possession of the crown during the reign of Henry VII, but before it was sold, probably by 1559, shortly after which the house was divided up into tenements (Marsden 1969, 10). The remains of a tile pavement, with tiles painted in the same fleur-de-lis design, was found on the site of a manor house at Place Farm, Bletchingley, Surrey (Gaimster and Nenk 1997).

The period of greatest artistic activity at Antwerp lasted from *c* 1520 to 1570, by which time the manufacture of tin-glazed tiles had begun in London itself. Whether Antwerp tiles continued to be brought into England after tin-glazed tiles began to be made in London is uncertain. Even if such tiles continued to be imported it would be extremely difficult to distinguish Antwerp products from those made by immigrants from the Low Countries working in London without recourse to the type of scientific analysis discussed in Chapter 5.

ENGLISH TILES

The spread of tin-glazed tile and pottery manufacture from Flanders northwards into the Netherlands and westwards to England has its origins in the political and religious turmoil which disrupted the Low Countries during the second half of the 16th century. During this period craftsmen from all trades began to flee Antwerp to escape from religious persecution. Suppression of the new religious ideas of the Protestants led to vast population movements from the Southern Netherlands, still in Spanish Catholic hands, to the Northern Netherlands which were held by the Protestants. This migration included many Flemish tilemakers, who established new production centres further north (Schaap 1984, 16–17; Britton 1987, 18–19). The Antwerp tile industry suffered a further blow with the Spanish destruction of the city in November 1576 during which thousands of its inhabitants were murdered and its buildings left in ruins. Antwerp was never again to be northern Europe's most important centre for tin-glazed tile manufacture.

It was during this period of religious persecution and political unrest that Jasper Andries, the son of Guido Andries, the Italian who is believed to have established the first Antwerp pothouse, escaped to England together with his brother George (Joris) and a colleague, Jacob Jansen. In 1567 they settled in Norwich, where they followed their trade of making 'Galley Paving Tiles and Vessels for Apothecaries' (Britton 1987, 20) until 1571 when Jansen went to Duke's Place, Aldgate, City of London, and Jasper Andries to Colchester, Essex, in the same year (Archer 1997, 39). Production at Colchester, however, was short lived as Jasper Andries appears to have moved to Lambeth in 1576.

The 'galley paving tiles' are clearly a reference to tin-glazed floor tiles, although no floor tiles made during the period 1567–70 can be positively identified. It is possible that the floor tiles found at Gorhambury, near St Albans, Hertfordshire, a mansion built between 1563 and 1568, may have been made at Norwich (Archer 1997, 428, N8).[19]

[19] The possible Norwich tiles from Limpsfield New Hall, Surrey, discussed by Archer (1997, 39) have now been analysed by Hughes (2002) and shown to be of Antwerp origin.

ALDGATE, CITY OF LONDON (*c* 1571–*c* 1615 or *c* 1620)

In 1570 Jacob Jansen and Jasper Andries petitioned Queen Elizabeth I to be granted a 20-year patent for sole rights to produce floor tiles and apothecaries' jars, together with a London waterside location for their pothouse. This patent was not granted and their request for a waterside site was also turned down; Jacob Jansen had to be content with a rather cramped site at Duke's Place, Aldgate, some 0.85km north of the Thames (Fig 2).

Jansen is listed at Aldgate in 1571 together with six fellow Flemish potters. One, Martin Taye, recorded as a 'painter of pottes' (Britton 1987, 27), may have decorated some of the early Aldgate floor tiles. The pothouse was situated within what had been Holy Trinity Priory, which on the Dissolution had been granted to Thomas Audley, eventually passing to the Duke of Norfolk (Schofield and Lea 2005). From the 1540s parts of the former priory precinct were let out to others; these must have included buildings suitable for pottery and tile manufacture.

Fig 2 Location of tin glaze production sites in London referred to in the text superimposed on the John Rocque map of 1746 (scale 1:25,000, inset 1:500,000)

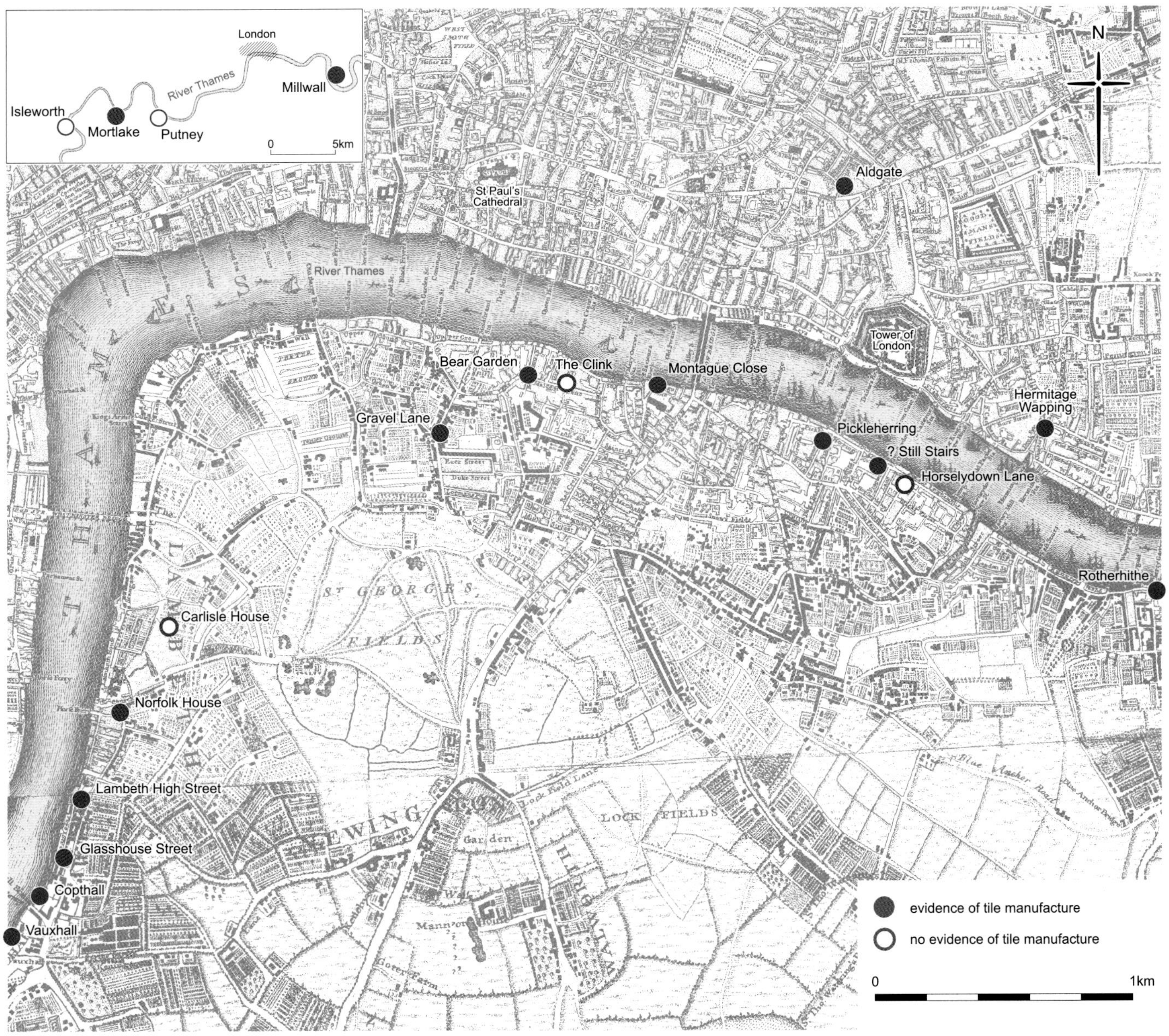

Waste from tin-glazed tile manufacture was excavated from a pit within the western claustral range of Holy Trinity Priory (MOL site code HTP79) in 1979. Included in the pit along with pottery waste were biscuit-fired floor tile blanks and flat tile used as kiln shelving (Betts 2005, 223–4).[20] Small numbers of floor tile blanks have been found at other sites in the Aldgate area, but there are none of the large dumps of waste tiles which have been found associated with later tin glaze manufacture in Southwark.

There are less than a handful of probable decorated waster tiles from the Aldgate area so it is extremely difficult to determine the range of designs painted on tiles made at the pothouse. Based on the evidence from Pickleherring pothouse in Southwark it seems certain that many would have been close copies of contemporary Dutch designs.

Two probable wasters are floor tiles with so-called medallion decoration. Both tiles are extremely unusual in having been made using red-firing local clay for the main tile body with only a very thin coating of the calcareous white-, cream- and pink-firing clay normally used for the manufacture of tin-glazed tiles. On one tile, found at 118 Minories near Aldgate, City of London (MOL site code MIO86), the red clay body was disguised by a thin layer of cream slip (**52**), whilst the other tile, found at Mitre Square, City of London (MOL site code CQU04), has a 1–2mm covering of white-firing clay (**53**). The latter is unique in London in having deep holes set midway along each side, presumably in an attempt to ensure more even firing.

These tiles seem to represent experiments by the Aldgate tilemakers to lower costs by reducing the quantity of calcareous clay needed for each tile, which during this period had to be brought in from either Norfolk or Surrey (Chapter 2). Both experiments ended in failure: in the case of the Minories tile the cream slip soaked into the clay leaving a rough surface on which to paint the finished design, whilst on the Mitre Square tile the thin white clay layer partly detached from the red clay body during firing, which would have rendered it totally unsuitable for flooring. The Aldgate tilemakers were left with no option but to stick to the established practice of using local clay deposits mixed with imported clay to produce cream-, yellow- and white-coloured tiles.

The Minories tile has a multi-circular blue and purple border, as have a number of other medallion-style tiles found in the Aldgate area (**42**, **43**). This has led Betts (1999, 173) to suggest that these border colours may be a distinguishing feature of Aldgate-made tiles, as later medallion-style tiles made at Pickleherring have yellow, brown and brownish-orange in their circular borders (Tyler et al 2008, 56, fig 76, D14, D15; **56–59**, **63–65**).

The Mitre Square tile provides further supporting evidence for this view as this was found with pottery and kiln waste from the Aldgate pothouse and this too has a multi-circular border in purple and blue. The Mitre Square tile is incomplete but appears to show part of a rabbit. Other, probably Aldgate, medallion tiles commonly depict various kinds of animals, such as bears and camels, or have chequerboard or figurative designs set within the multi-circular border. Some examples may have paved part of a mansion, formerly the Duke's Hall, which by 1586 occupied what had been the prior's range, part of the church and the western half of the precinct of Holy Trinity Priory (Schofield 1995, 155–6; Schofield and Lea 2005).

A third discarded waster tile, found at Aldgate in 1974, has a flower decoration blurred by the glaze running during firing (**114**). It was found with another tile with a similar, but not quite identical, flower design (**113**) perhaps the work of a different tile-painter. If these tiles were indeed made at Aldgate it must represent one of the final tile designs

[20] No complete biscuit-fired tiles were found; the fragments have a thickness of 13–19mm.

made at the pottery, since Dutch tiles with this design do not appear until *c* 1610 (Pluis 1997, 226, A.01.05.70). Other polychrome floor tiles found on the same site, which may have been made at Aldgate, have various geometric designs (cf **83**, **94** and what may be the reverse of **89**), and include one tile (**99**) with an unusual semicircular corner decoration of a type not seen on other London tiles.

There is also a single blue on white tile with a Tudor rose design from 62–64 Aldgate High Street (MOL site code AL74; Betts 1999, pl 11; cf **111**). This has one quarter of a rose petal design, so a set of four tiles is required to produce a complete flower. Tiles with this design were made at later London pothouses, but the Aldgate High Street tile is distinctly thicker, suggesting that it was made at Aldgate.[21]

The Aldgate pothouse continued in production until *c* 1615 or *c* 1620. Around the same time tile and pottery manufacture began on new, no doubt more spacious, locations south of the River Thames in Southwark which at this time had begun to develop as an industrial suburb, particularly for the more unpleasant and dirty industries. Black smoke belching out of pottery kilns would not have made an attractive neighbour.

MONTAGUE CLOSE, SOUTHWARK (*c* 1613–*c* 1755)

Pottery production at Montague Close in Southwark (Fig 2) probably began in 1613 for in that year Edmund Bradshawe and Hugh Cressey were granted a patent for making 'Earthenware in the manner of Fiansa', a reference to Faenza in Italy, a well-known centre of tin-glazed pottery manufacture. Presumably, it was intended to manufacture tin-glazed floor tiles, as 'pavinge tyles' are specifically mentioned in the 1613 patent. However, excavations at the site of the pottery (MOL site code HIB79; Dawson and Edwards 1974, 56–61; Britton 1987, 42–5; Tyler et al 2008, 20–5) have produced little tile waste, so it would seem that tiles formed a very small part of the pottery's output. Moreover the tilemaking waste which has been found relates to later wall tile manufacture (Chapter 4, London tiles). Perhaps tiles were made only for a limited period during the long life of the pottery, which closed *c* 1755 (Dawson 1971, 230–1; Dawson and Edwards 1974).

PICKLEHERRING, SOUTHWARK (*c* 1618–1723)

In contrast to Aldgate and Montague Close pothouses, we have a considerable amount of evidence for the designs painted on tin-glazed tiles made at Pickleherring, Southwark (Fig 2), the pothouse established by a Dutchman named Christian Wilhelm in *c* 1618. In 1965 and 1973 large quantities of waster material from both pottery and tile production were found in Potters' Fields, an area of open ground to the east of the pothouse (Tyler et al 2008, 26). Included in this waste material was an unglazed biscuit-fired medallion tile with a camel design, which would have been similar in appearance to **42**. Other medallion tiles feature a leaping fox, a running dog and a jester. Numerous geometric designs were also found (Dawson 1966).

Pickleherring continued in operation until 1723 (Edwards 1974, 69; Tyler et al 2008, 30), but there is evidence to suggest that the manufacture of tin-glazed tiles was limited principally to the first half of the 17th century – a large waster dump dated 1620–50 contained both tiles and pottery, but there was no evidence for tile manufacture in later dumps dated 1660–80 (Britton 1987, 35–6). The reason for the apparent abandonment of tilemaking by 1660 was a switch in fashion away from tiles which could be used for

[21] The Aldgate tile with the Tudor rose design measures 132–134mm square by 19–20mm in thickness. Later London-made tiles with this design are only 12–17mm thick.

flooring or walling to thinner tiles which could be used only as walling. The majority of these thinner mid to late 17th-century wall tiles had to be imported from the Netherlands, as English manufacturers were having difficulties making their tiles sufficiently thin (Ray 1973, 35; Chapter 2).

Further large pottery and tile waster dumps were uncovered in the Pickleherring area during the 1980s and early 1990s. They contained numerous fragments of decorated floor tile some of which are obvious wasters. A total of 17 polychrome and six blue on white designs were found during excavations around the pothouse site between 1987 and 1992 (MOL site codes MOR87, BFS88, BFN88, BTH88, MOR88, VIN88, ABO92). The following tiles from the pothouse site are in the design catalogue: **59**, **63**, **82**, **87**, **95**, **109**, **135**, **137**, **143**, **146**, **175** and **180**. Others are illustrated in Tyler et al (2008, 52–9).[22] Other tiles from the vicinity of the pothouse have been published by Noël Hume which include medallion tiles with pictures of a bird, bear and a camel, as well as various geometric and floral patterns (1977, 54–9, figs I–II).[23] As at Aldgate, many designs used by the tile-painters at Pickleherring are close copies of contemporary Dutch designs.

Both polychrome and blue on white decorative designs are present, although many of the latter are simply blue versions of the polychrome designs made at the pothouse.[24] In the Netherlands blue on white became increasingly fashionable after 1620, partly as a result of the importation of Chinese porcelain, which was much imitated. The fretwork corner motif used on certain Pickleherring medallion tiles (**63**) is similar to that used on porcelain made during the reign of the Emperor Wan Li (1573–1619; Pluis 1997, 536). Dutch tiles brought into London during the mid to late 17th century, for example **188–190**, have similar Chinese-style decorative corner motifs.

It is apparent from the tiles recovered from the waster dumps that certain designs made at Pickleherring were more popular than others; this is also reflected in the designs found on tiles discarded at various sites in London. The medallion-type tiles with animal and bird decoration seem to have been particularly popular. Of the other designs, by far the most common is the Tudor rose, comprising one quarter of the rose petal pattern (**108–111**), four tiles being laid together to form the full flower. Other designs popular with Londoners were the so-called star (**129–132**) and star and tulip patterns (**113–116**).

ROTHERHITHE, SOUTHWARK (*c* 1638–84)

The tin glaze pothouse situated in Rotherhithe started *c* 1638 (Fig 2), but there is uncertainty as to how long production continued. Frank Britton believed that production continued until the owner William Fry moved to the Still Stairs site in Southwark (discussed below) to start a new pothouse in *c* 1663 (Britton 1987, 39), but documentary evidence suggests the owner after 1663 was John Townsend who ran the Rotherhithe pothouse until his death in 1684 (Edwards 1974, 110–11; Tyler et al 2008, 62). Whatever the exact date there is no firm evidence for tile production beyond *c* 1660.

The actual kilns at Rotherhithe have not been located but an extensive series of waster dumps were excavated between 1986 and 1991 (MOL site codes PW86, PW89, PW90, PW91). In these dumps were considerable quantities of pottery, biscuit-fired tile blanks and no fewer than 79 decorated tiles.[25]

Certain Rotherhithe designs are clearly copies of contemporary Dutch designs, but for the first time in London we have clear signs of tile-painters developing their own

[22] The other Pickleherring designs are **81**, **83**, **92**, **104**, **111**, **116**, **120**, **123**, **125**, **129**, **132** and **162**.

[23] The Pickleherring tile designs illustrated by Noël Hume are **42** (with 'tan' and blue circular border), **58**, **83**, **94**, **108**, **111**, **116**, **125**, **130** and **137**, together with a medallion tile with a bird (1977, 55, fig II nos 1–3, 57, fig II nos 1–7, 9).

[24] All but one of the biscuit-fired tiles made at Pickleherring measure 130–135mm square by 12–16mm thick, which is roughly comparable with the decorated tiles which measure 129–140mm square by 13–21mm thick. The only exception is a solitary biscuit-fired tile measuring ? x 123 x 13mm.

[25] The size of the tiles is 125–135mm square by 10–17mm in thickness, but most are 130–135mm square by 12–15mm thick.

individual painting styles. Many of the individual flower and flower vase patterns tend to be painted in a freer, less formal style than their Dutch equivalents. Indeed, some of the Rotherhithe flower tiles are actually quite crudely painted, but this gives them a warmth and spontaneity lacking in more technically perfect Dutch tiles.

Fifteen polychrome and 13 blue on white tile designs have been recovered from near the presumed site of the pothouse, of which 14 are in the design catalogue (77, **126–128**, **132**, **138**, **139**, **142**, **160**, **161**, **178**, **182**, **185** and **194**). The remainder are illustrated in Tyler et al (2008, 84–92).[26] Flowers seem to have been the most popular choice of motif for tin-glazed tiles made in London during the mid 17th century. Many of the Rotherhithe tiles are decorated with tulips and other types of flowers. There are various repeating geometric designs but it is unlikely that production of these multicoloured geometric tiles, by now rather old fashioned, extended much beyond the 1640s.[27] Blue on white tiles were becoming increasingly popular, a reflection of the growing fashion for Chinese-style blue on white decorative ornamentation. Such tiles comprise almost half of all tile designs identified as Rotherhithe products, compared with just a quarter of those made slightly earlier at Pickleherring.

Examination of the tiles discarded by the Rotherhithe pothouse shows that the Tudor rose design in both polychrome and blue and white (**108–111**) continued to enjoy widespread popularity. This was one of the nine designs painted on tiles made at both the Rotherhithe and Pickleherring pothouses[28] which were in direct competition during the mid 17th century.

Slight differences can occur between individual tiles made at the same pothouse. In the case of the polychrome Tudor rose tiles it seems that individual tile-painters used different colours when adding the strapwork corner motif diagonally opposite the rose petals. Such variation had the advantage of allowing the tiles made by each painter to be identified: presumably payment was based on the number of tiles decorated each day. This was the practice at Delft in 1611 when Jan Jansz Vullens was contracted to decorate tiles with flowerpot and marigold designs (Schaap 1984, 22).

The influence of Dutch tile design is still clearly visible even towards the end of tile manufacture at Rotherhithe. A landscape tile with a sailing boat (**194**), probably dating *c* 1650–60, has a spider head corner motif, more commonly a feature of Dutch rather than of English tiles. The Rotherhithe tile-painters may well have been copying thinner (*c* 10–12mm) blue on white Dutch wall tiles with similar boats which were starting to arrive in London during the mid 17th century (**193**, **343**, **344**).

Two other tiles have the thickness (14–15mm) typical of 17th-century floor tiles but are decorated with designs more characteristic of thinner Dutch wall tiles. One has a small-sized landscape set in a circular border and barred ox-head corners (**178**): a design typical of Dutch wall tiles. The tile fragment was probably found at Rotherhithe and scientific analysis has confirmed that it was made at the pothouse (Hughes 2008, 122–7). The other tile, which was probably also made at Rotherhithe, shows a larger landscape scene with spider head corners (**197**).

STILL STAIRS, SOUTHWARK (*c* 1663–85)

In about 1663 William Fry opened a pothouse near Still Stairs in Southwark in partnership with an Edward Osbaldson. The site must have been a little to the east of the existing

[26] The other Rotherhithe designs are **83**, **92**, **101**, **108**, **111**, **116**, **120–122** (or **123**), **124** (or blue on white version of **120–122**), **129**, **135**, **136**, **140**, **141** and **162**; similar to Dutch design **147**.

[27] According to dating by Pluis (1997), production of Dutch geometric tiles seem to have ceased by *c* 1600.

[28] The other designs in common are **83**, **92**, **111**, **116**, **129**, **132**, **135** and **162**.

pothouse at Pickleherring (Britton 1987, 41; Fig 2). Still Stairs was in production for only a short period between *c* 1663 and 1685 and there is some doubt as to whether tin-glazed tiles were ever manufactured. Excavations at Mark Brown's Wharf in 1973 (joint excavation by the Southwark and Lambeth Archaeological Excavation Committee (SLAEC) and the Institute of Archaeology, University of London; MOL site code MBW73) revealed tin-glazed pottery dumps dating from the period 1680–90, believed to be waste from Still Stairs (Hinton et al 1988, 142–5). A single polychrome floor or wall tile was found in these dumps, whilst a further polychrome tile, associated with pottery of 1680 or a later date, came from another dump (Hinton et al 1988, 334, fig 144, nos 1408, 1412, latter is upside down). Both are known Pickleherring designs (**123**, **143**), which seems the more likely source of these tiles, particularly as there is no evidence that tiles with polychrome decoration were being made in London as late as the 1680s.

DUTCH TILES

The earliest Dutch pothouse to have manufactured tin-glazed ware is probably that established by Joris Andries in Middelburg in 1564 (Pluis 1997, 64). Initially, these were floor tiles, but the fashion for tiles as a decorative wall surface developed in the Low Countries about 1580. It was considerably later before they were used for this purpose in Britain. The earliest documentary reference to the use of Dutch tiles in Britain concerns the traveller Sir William Brereton who in 1634/5 brought home tiles with matching pairs of soldiers and horsemen, together with tiles painted with birds and flowers, to decorate his fireplaces in England (Ray 1973, 59). The tiles decorated with horsemen may have been similar in appearance to those found dumped with Great Fire (1666) destruction debris in the cellars of a large tenement building known as Lombards Place (**200**, **201**) in Botolph Lane, City of London (MOL site code BPL95; Blair and Sankey 2007, 31; Fig 4, no. 19). Wall tiles with similar mounted military figures were found associated with a nearby property owned by Thomas Soane near Billingsgate, City of London. This too was burnt to the ground in the Great Fire (MOL site code BIG82; Schofield and Pearce 2009; Fig 4, no. 19).

Both sets of tiles are significant in having a secure pre-1666 date, thus making them some of the earliest Dutch wall tiles known to have been used in this country. The Botolph Lane tiles can be divided into various groups, blue on white designs with soldiers on horseback (**200**, **201**), warships (**193**) and a water nymph riding a fish (**192**), all with barred ox-head corners dating from the period 1635–*c* 1660. Also present are two blue on white landscape tiles with spider head corners (**195**) and a tile with a white diamond with purple corners. The latter is similar to a diamond-patterned tile from Soane's property near Billingsgate (**208**).

Other London buildings clearly had quite grand wall tile decoration by the mid 17th century, such as the banqueting house of Chiswick Manor, Hounslow, recorded in the parliamentary survey of the estate in 1649:

> The Ancient Manor House of Chiswick consisteth of a Hall, a Parlor, a [?] haveing an open Banqueting House paved and the walls set round with paynted Tyles with other convenient Low Rooms and Lodging Chambers over them, a garden, orchard, etc (Draper 1923, 54).

Presumably these 'paynted Tyles' would have been brought in from the Netherlands and are likely to have been tin-glazed. The arrival of imported Dutch tiles from the mid 17th century coincided with an increasing fashion for thinner tiles which were principally used for walling rather than for flooring. In the Netherlands such tiles were frequently placed either side of the fireplace, where they allowed the fireplace surround to be kept clean, or as wall skirting to close the gaps between the walls and the floor or in kitchen areas where cleanliness was important. As well as being cheerful and easy to clean such tiles also offered protection from rising damp and a solution to the problem of flaking lime plaster on walls: they are a traditional element in Dutch interior decoration to the present day.

As well as the figures on horseback, which appealed to Sir William Brereton, floral patterns with various styles of corner motif were brought into London around this time (**149–153**, **165**). The three-headed tulip design seems to have been particularly popular (**151**, **189**).

Early Dutch tiles used in London typically have a thickness of 10–12mm, whilst London-made tiles of the same period were thicker, normally 12–15mm. Being both lighter and thinner, Dutch tiles were far more suited for use as wall decoration than were their English counterparts. The thinner nature of Dutch tiles was achieved by using a different method of clay preparation (Chapter 2).

London manufacturers were no doubt well aware of the growing popularity of thinner Dutch wall tiles which were being increasingly used in London houses from the mid 17th century. They seem to have responded to this competition by producing blue on white tiles with decorative designs imitating those on Dutch tiles. Mention has already been made of the English tile with a sailing boat painted in Dutch style made at Rotherhithe (above 3, English tiles; **194**). Further tiles which appear to be London copies of early Dutch imports have been found associated with Bermondsey House, Southwark (Fig 4, no. 3), built in the mid 16th century by Sir Thomas Pope in the precincts of Bermondsey Abbey (Abbey Street, Long Walk, SE1, Southwark: MOL site code BA84; Steele et al in prep; **174**, **196**), and from an unknown London site (**197**).

Whilst it was possible for London tilemakers to paint Dutch-style designs on their tiles and even set them in walls, they still could not do anything about their greater thickness. It may have been this failure to produce the more acceptable thinner tiles suitable for wall decoration, coupled with a change in fashion away from their use as flooring (highly decorative tin glaze wears very quickly), that led to a rapid decline in the manufacture of tin-glazed tiles in London during the mid 17th century.

Fig 3 Late 16th-century Dutch tiles from the floor in the former prior's lodgings of the Dominican priory of Blackfriars (from top FRI88 [80] <3>, <4> and <5>) (scale *c* 1:2)

LOCATION AND DECORATIVE USE

No tin-glazed floor tiles have been found *in situ* in London, so little is known about the decorative layout of these early tile pavements. The remains of a former *in situ* floor were recovered from the former prior's lodgings of the Dominican priory of Blackfriars (10 Friar Street, 69 Carter Lane, City of London: MOL site code FRI88; Schofield 1998, 268–9; Fig 3; Fig 4, no. 7). These were all Dutch flower vase tiles dating 1570–1600. Victorian reproductions of this design (in this case as walling) in the south-west bedroom at Charlton House, Greenwich, gives a good impression of how the floor would have looked when new (Fig 46). Reproduction of other floor tile patterns (again as walling) can be seen in other parts of the house (Chapter 6, Greater London).

The only *in situ* wall tiles which appear to date before the Great Fire of 1666 are a set of blue on white tulip tiles at Ham House, Richmond upon Thames (Surrey), which may have been installed between 1637 and 1639, and a set of blue on white figurative tiles again at Charlton House, possibly installed by Sir William Ducie in 1659 (Chapter 6, Greater London; Fig 5).

From the evidence that is available it is clear that only the wealthiest citizens could afford the luxury of paving their houses with tin-glazed tiles. On the floor of most London houses, as Alessandro Magno, a visiting Italian merchant, noted in 1562, 'they put straw which they change often as a protection against the damp' (Barron et al 1983, 142).

Among the earliest decorated tiles with white tin glaze are Spanish tiles, imported from Seville into London, probably during the period 1510–40. The majority of tiles so far discovered are from All Hallows church, Lombard Street, demolished in 1939–40 (**A**, **B**, **E**, **H**, **J**, **K**, **L**; Fig 4, no. 11). These were laid sometime after 1494, when the church was enlarged, probably in 1520–30 (Schofield 1994, 85). They may have been purchased from

Fig 4 Buildings in the City of London and immediate hinterland with evidence for pre-1666 tin-glazed floor and wall tiles; (numbered 1 to 21) (major religious house (monastic) precincts are indicated in outline) (scale 1:25,000)

1 – Duke's Place, Aldgate, City of London
2 – Newcastle House, Islington
3 – Bermondsey House, Southwark
4 – Charterhouse, Islington
5 – Tower of London, Tower Hamlets
6 – Royal Navy victualling yard (possibly former abbot of St Mary Graces lodgings), Tower Hamlets
7 – former prior's lodgings, Blackfriars Priory, City of London
8 – Principal Tenement, Tower Hamlets
9 – Temple church, City of London
10 – Guildhall and vicarage of St Lawrence Jewry church, City of London
11 – All Hallows church, Lombard Street, City of London
12 – St John the Evangelist church, Watling Street, City of London
13 – Red Lion Inn, Aldersgate Street, City of London
14 – Norfolk House, Lambeth
15 – York Place/Whitehall Palace, Westminster
16 – Fastolf's Place, Southwark
17 – Warwick Inn, City of London
18 – St Matthew's church, Friday Street, City of London
19 – Lombards Place and Thomas Soane's property, Billingsgate, City of London
20 – Southbridge House (site of Rose Theatre), Southwark
21 – St Bartholomew's Hospital, City of London

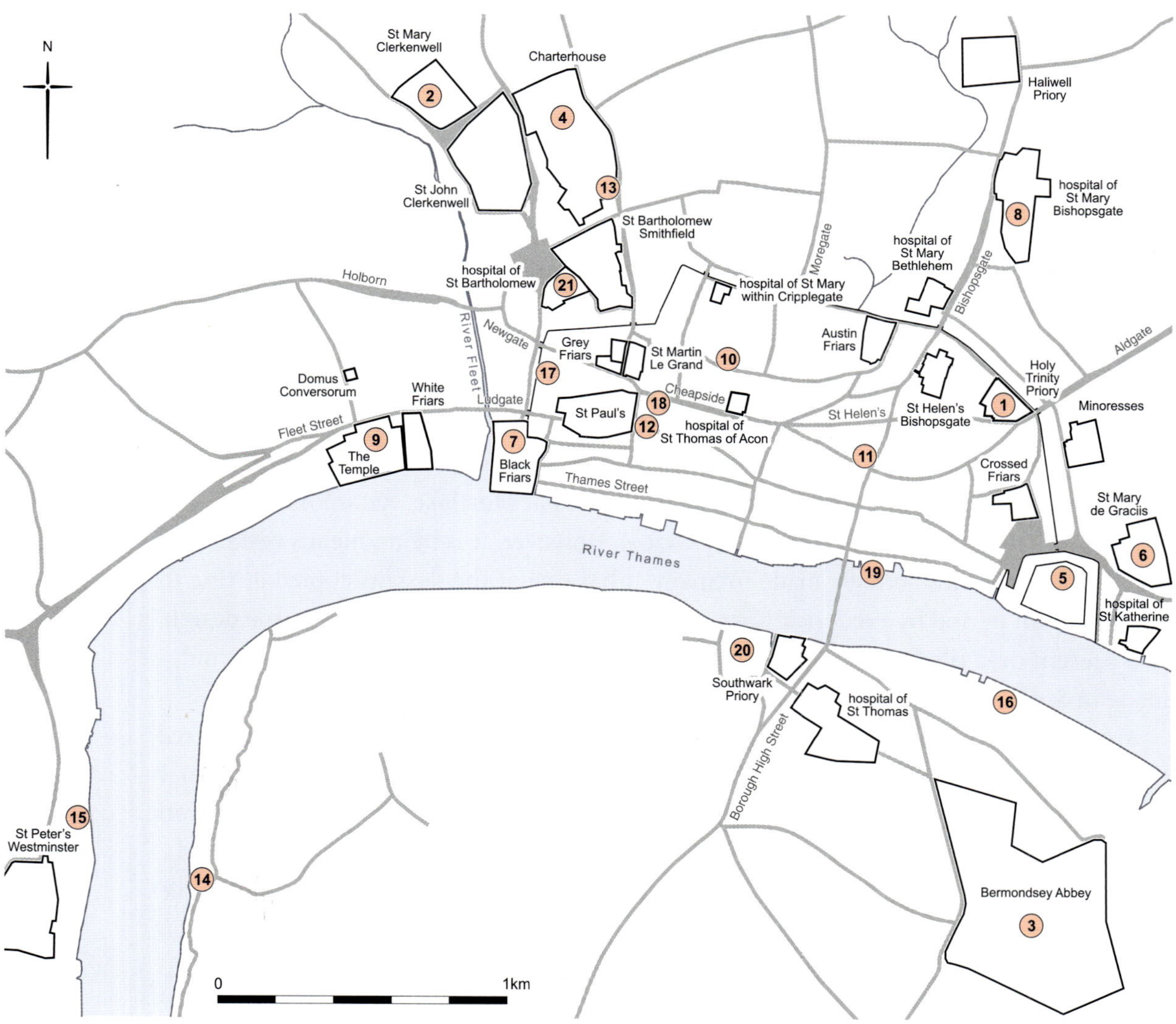

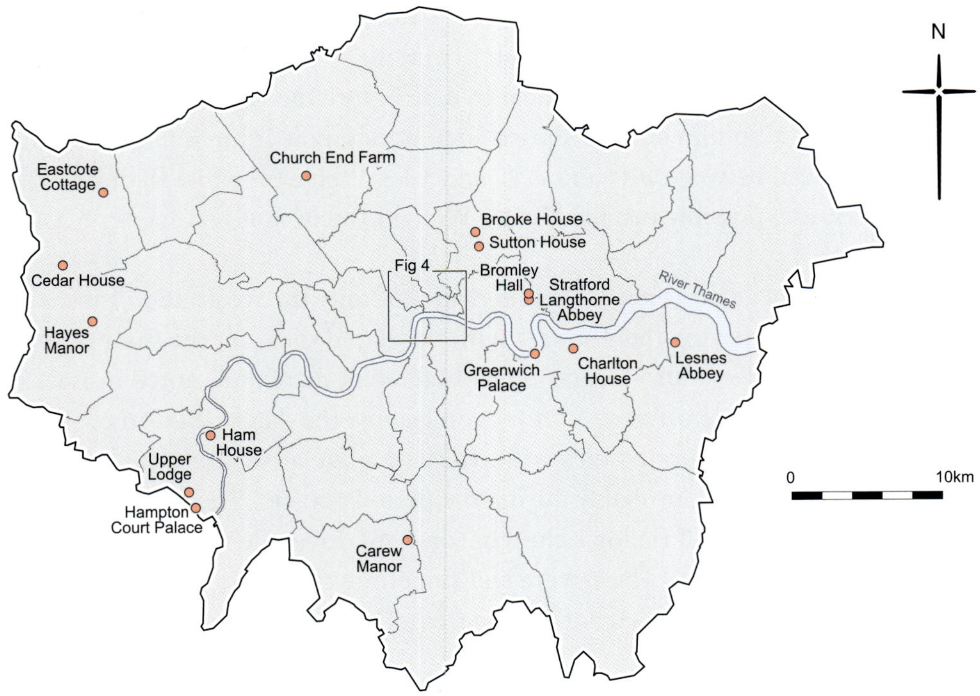

Fig 5 Buildings in the Greater London area with evidence for pre-1666 tin-glazed floor tiles (scale 1:500,000)

Henry Mychele of Southwark who supplied 'syvll' or 'cevell' (ie Seville) tiles at 13s per hundred to the Queen's suite of rooms at Greenwich Palace, Greenwich, in 1533 (Archer 1997, 45; Fig 5). A further important group were recovered from 30–35 Botolph Lane in 1995 (**C**, **F**). These were recovered from demolition debris in the cellars of a large tenement building known as Lombards Place (Fig 4, no. 19).

A number of the Botolph Lane tiles (**F**) have the same design as on some of the All Hallows tiles (**E**), although made with a different stamp. One Botolph Lane tile (MOL site code BPL95 [+] ‹361›) has been subject to ICP analysis which has confirmed that it was made in Seville (Hughes 2005a).

The use of Seville tiles elsewhere in London appears to have been fairly restricted; there are solitary examples from 27–29 Whitechapel High Street, Tower Hamlets (MOL site code WCE01; **I**; Sygrave 2005, 87), 112–116 Lower Thames Street, City of London (MOL site code PEN79; cf **J**) and a single tile has been found at Mortlake, Richmond upon Thames (Surrey) (MOL site code HSL96 [+] ‹30›). However, it is by no means certain that the Mortlake tile was actually made in Spain. It has one of the designs copied during the late Victorian period by Frederick Garrard (Brown and Brown 1992, 9). The same design is also present on a tile from Vine Lane (**Q**) which scientific analysis has shown was not made in Spain (Hughes 2005a; discussed above, 3, Spanish tiles).

Around the time that Spanish tiles arrived in England from Seville, mosaic tin-glazed tiles began to be imported from the Southern Netherlands (most of modern Belgium). In the London area polychrome mosaic tile pavements were installed in royal and aristocratic residences during the 1520s and 1530s. As well as those from the Tower of London and Wolsey's lodgings at York Place (discussed above, 3, Flemish tiles; Fig 4, nos 5, 15), such tiles were also installed at Greenwich Palace (**12**, **16**), a favourite residence of Henry VIII, and at the Manor of the More, Rickmansworth, Hertfordshire, probably during the period of Cardinal Wolsey's occupation between 1522 and 1530 (Rackham 1959, 186–8).

These early mosaic tin-glazed tiles are believed to have been made in Antwerp. A hexagonal tile found between Abbots Lane and Vine Lane, Southwark (Noël Hume 1977, 57, fig II no. 8), has an almost identical design to that found on an Antwerp tile in the Victoria and Albert Museum in London (Lane 1960, pl 31.D). A medallion-style tile with the same chequerboard pattern and multi-circular border as **54** (but with corner motifs of **42–53**) was also found in the same area (Abbots Lane, Southwark: MOL site code ABO92 [668] <2705>). This is probably an Aldgate product of the late 16th–early 17th century. Both may have floored parts of Fastolf's Place, an important moated residence built by Sir John Fastolf in Southwark during the mid 15th century (Blatherwick and Bluer 2009; Fig 4, no. 16).

A solitary piece of hexagonal floor tile has been recovered from Carew Manor Beddington (Fig 5). It probably formed part of a pavement laid down sometime between 1520 and 1539 when the manor was in the ownership of Nicholas Carew (J Phillips, pers comm). Further hexagonal tiles have also been found in waterfront dumps at Trig Lane, Upper Thames Street, City of London (MOL site code TL74; **13**) and Billingsgate Market Lorry Park, Lower Thames Street, City of London (MOL site code BIG82 [1627] <5041>).

A complete hexagonal floor tile was recovered during repair work in the chancel of Temple church, corner of Inner Temple Lane and Church Court, City of London, in 1841 (Brown 2005, 82; Fig 4, no. 9). Although now lost, two further fragments with the same, or a very similar design, are known (**14**, **15**). Recent excavations near the church have produced three further floor tiles, one of which is of similar design to **55**, although with what appears to be a bird (Brown 2005, 83, fig 81). This is a later Dutch design of 1570–1600 (Pluis 1997, 407, A.04.04.01).

It is unlikely that many tin-glazed tile pavements were laid down in monastic buildings before their suppression during the period 1536–9. The best evidence relates to Charterhouse in Smithfield where part of a hexagonal tile was found in 1992 (Charterhouse Mews, Islington: MOL site code PCC92; Betts 2002, 99, fig 95; Fig 4, no. 4; **10**). It may have floored part of Washhouse Court (Barber and Thomas 2002, 38–9), a brick and stone domestic quarters built by the Carthusians in *c* 1500–35 which survives to this day. A small worn square tile was also found at Lesnes Abbey, Bexley (Kent) in October 1962 (Blake 1985, cat no. 1836; Fig 5). It appears to be of early Antwerp type, but its size (87 x 85 x 15mm) is slightly smaller than the square tiles used in the mosaic pavement at The Vyne (Blanchett 2000, 8–19) and in London. Single early Antwerp tiles have also been found on the monastic sites at Sopwell, Hertfordshire, and Titchfield Abbey, Hampshire (Hurst 1999b, 98, Tichfield [*sic*]).

Tin-glazed floor tiles have been found on the sites of various other monastic buildings in the London area (Fig 4), such as St Mary Clerkenwell nunnery, Islington (MOL site codes NEW81, ENG84, CLK86, NEW87, SCT87, SNS87; Sloane in prep), Bermondsey Abbey, Southwark (MOL site code BA84; Steele et al in prep), and the priory and hospital of St Mary Bishopsgate (St Mary Spital), Tower Hamlets (MOL site code SPQ88; Thomas et al 1997), but these seem to date from shortly after the Dissolution when various former monastic buildings were refurbished for secular use (Fig 4). Such buildings, well built in stone or brick, seem to have been a popular choice as London residences for the rich nobility who had the means to install the increasingly fashionable multicoloured tin-glazed floors. The tin-glazed tiles from 36–41 Scotswood Street (**30**, **48**, cf **111**, **131** and an uncertain design in blue on white SCT87 [17] <35>) probably floored Newcastle House, which was largely rebuilt from the ruins of the cloister ranges by William Cavendish, Earl and then Duke of Newcastle, during the second quarter of the 17th century (Sloane in prep; Fig 4, no. 2). The St Mary Spital tiles (**100**, **125**) came from the site of the post-Dissolution 'Principal Tenement', the largest of the former priory buildings used for living accommodation (Thomas et al 1997; Fig 4, no. 8). The building was repaired and adapted by Robert Hare, who occupied it in 1580, but the tiles may have been added during the residency of the Hobart family, who bought the lease in 1606–9 and continued to live there until at least 1650 (Thomas et al 1997, 132, 149). Fifteen early to mid 17th-century floor tiles were found in the vicinity of the gatehouse at Stratford Langthorne Abbey, Essex (Betts 2004; Betts in Barber et al 2004, 127; Fig 5).[29] Five designs are present (cf **56** (with dog), **68**, **102**, **111**, **135**). These were probably added when the gatehouse was extensively renovated after the Dissolution.

On other sites the monastic buildings were demolished to make way for palatial town houses. The tin-glazed tiles found on the site of Bermondsey Abbey probably came from a great mansion built there by Sir Thomas Pope during the 1540s, although the tiles themselves were probably installed a century later (**174**, **196**; Martin 1926, 220).[30] Other large houses built by London's wealthiest citizens may well have contained tin-glazed floor or wall tiles, including the great houses known as Warwick Inn near Warwick Square, City of London, and Norfolk House, Lambeth (Fig 4, nos 14, 17). The construction of Norfolk House is believed to have begun when the title of Duke of Norfolk was conferred on Thomas Howard in 1514 (Jackson 1989). The tin-glazed floor tiles (**33**, cf **68**, **79**) were probably installed when the property was divided towards the end of the 16th century and again in the first half of the 17th century. Excavations between 1988 and 1990 revealed that Norfolk House underwent a considerable amount of modification during this period (MOL site codes NOR88, NOR90; Bloice 1971; Thompson et al 1998, 126; Tyler et al 2008; Chapter 4, London tiles). Residents at this time with sufficient wealth to afford decorated tiled floors included prominent churchmen such as John Whitgift (Archbishop of Canterbury 1583–1604) and his secretary Abraham Hartwell (Jackson 1989).

No fewer than 24 tin-glazed floor tiles have been found on the site of the former abbey of St Mary Graces, Tower Hamlets (MOL site codes MIN84, MIN86; Fig 4), which lay north-east of the Tower of London. Most of the tiles were found scattered around a Royal Navy victualling yard which occupied the abbey site from 1560 (Fig 4, no. 6). The tiles found in the yard are of medallion type (**49**) or have geometric and floral decoration (cf **72**) and are probably late 16th to early 17th century in date,[31] although a medallion tile from Antwerp, which appears to have a flower petal motif, could be somewhat earlier (**8**). Where these tiles were used is not certain, although one possibility is the mansion house, the former abbot's lodgings, which was used as officers' quarters (Grainger and Phillpotts in prep; 2010, 11, 95–6).

Large mansion houses situated in what would then have been open countryside around London (Fig 5), such as Brooke House and Sutton House in Hackney and Ham House in Richmond upon Thames, were also decorated with early tin-glazed tiles. The earliest, from Brooke House, are of polychrome type (**78**, cf **51**, **83**, **84**, **92**) and date from the late 16th–mid 17th centuries. They were probably installed during the ownership of the Grenville family who purchased the property in 1609 (Survey of London 1960, 63).

The earliest tin-glazed tile from Sutton House has part of a figure in a circular frame

[29] In Betts (2004) they are described as coming from the guesthouse/gatekeeper's tenement (Building 3). This building is now known to be the abbey gatehouse (Cowie 2008, 11).

[30] There is one other blue on white tile and four polychrome floor tiles from the abbey site. The designs on three polychrome tiles can be identified: **95**, **102** and **123**.

[31] Other designs present include cf **28**, **45** (dog facing right), **54** (same central design but corners as nos **42–53**), **72** (with two blue bands), **81** (with surviving corner yellow) and **85**. Not all the tin-glazed floor tiles from this site have been examined.

with an oriental-style fretwork corner, popularly known as a Wan Li corner motif, which suggests a date *c* 1620–50 (**66**). The earliest tiles found in Ham House date from the same period. Roughly contemporary are two blue on white tiles found during the excavations in the garden at Ham House in 1993 (Currie 1996, 109, fig 1 nos 5–6). Both are almost certainly London products: one bears a common flower vase design (cf **162**) made at both the Pickleherring and Rotherhithe pothouses, whilst the other has a similar vase decoration.

A number of medallion-type floor tiles (cf **56–58**) showing a figure and various animals within a multi-circular border were found at Upper Lodge, Bushy Park, Richmond upon Thames (Middlesex) (Currie 2003, 119, fig 20; Fig 5). The multi-circular borders are blue and yellow and blue and brown in colour suggesting that they may be Pickleherring products of the early 17th century. Their use can be linked with a probable 16th- to 17th-century brick extension of the original timber lodge built in *c* 1537.

Many churches in London had areas of medieval tiled floor, though tin-glazed tiles seem to have been something of a rarity. Apart from the magnificent, partly tin-glazed, Spanish tiles which graced the interior of the now demolished All Hallows church, Lombard Street, only two other London churches are known to have used tin-glazed tiles. One is St John the Evangelist, Watling Street, City of London, where excavation on the site of the church in 1954 (MOL site code GM160; Schofield 1998, 89; Fig 4, no. 12) revealed a number of tin-glazed polychrome floor tiles (**51**, **101**). The other is the church of St Matthew in Friday Street, City of London (MOL site code GM64; Fig 4, no. 18), which produced an unusually small floor tile with a blue on white chequerboard design (**62**).

Rather unexpectedly, three tin-glazed floor tiles (**73**, **88**, cf **106**) have been recovered from Southbridge House (site of Rose Theatre), 2–10 Southwark Bridge Road, Southwark (MOL site code SBH88; Fig 4, no. 20), although it is not certain where, or if, they were used in the theatre. The Rose Theatre had a relatively short life: constructed in 1587, it underwent rebuilding work in 1592 and was demolished by 1606 (Bowsher 2007, 63).

Further floor tiles, some with unusually complex strapwork floral patterns (**75**, **89**, **90**), were recovered from excavations at Carthusian Street, City of London (MOL site code CTN86). These may have been used in the Red Lion Inn which, according to documentary evidence, was located on the site during the 17th century and fronted Aldersgate Street, 20m to the east (Schofield 1998, 226; Fig 4, no. 13).[32]

Reference has already been made to the pre-Great Fire Dutch wall tiles and earlier Spanish floor tiles found in the destruction debris of a large merchant's house known as Lombards Place (above, 3, Dutch tiles and earlier in this section). It would appear these were not the only tiles used in the property as the same Great Fire debris contained a number of decorated tin-glazed floor tiles. One is an Antwerp tile of the mid 16th century (**24**) and the other 35 are probably London-made tiles of the early–mid 17th century (cf **104**, **108**, **111**, **116**, **118**, **119**, **132**; Betts 2007a, 35–40).

[32] There may be other tin-glazed floor tiles from this site, as not all tiles have been examined.

4 LATER TIN-GLAZED TILES (1666–*c* 1930)

LONDON TILES

It is not certain which type of decoration was applied to early English wall tiles made in London during the late 17th century. As Horne (1989, 17) has already pointed out, they would probably have carried copies of contemporary Dutch tiles.

One set of English tiles which is believed to date from the late 17th century is a series of tiles with blue on white biblical scenes with Dutch-style spider head corners. A number of these tiles have been published by Horne and further examples have been identified amongst the large number of tiles recovered from a tile-lined tank at 2 King Edward Street, City of London (**372**; MOL site code KEW98 [1479] <842>; Betts 2007b; Lyon 2007, 126–7, 130; Fig 6, no. 15).

The spider head corner, although rare, was used on other London-made wall tiles, most notably the purple[1] landscape tiles found at 38–46 Albert Embankment (**239**, **241–247**) and blue on white biblical tiles made at the Norfolk House pothouse (**355**, **371**).

Listed below are the pothouses in the London area known to have made later tin-glazed tiles (along with pottery), beginning with the three pothouses believed to have manufactured wall tiles in the late 17th century (Copthall, Bear Garden and Pickleherring) and following on with, in chronological order, those manufacturing in the 18th, 19th and 20th centuries.

COPTHALL, LAMBETH (*c* 1676–1730)

The first documentary reference to English wall tile manufacture is in 1676 when one Jan Ariens van Hamme (from Delft) was granted the right 'to exercise his trade and calling of makeing Tiles and Porcelain and other earthen wares after the way practised in Holland ... which hath not been practised in this our kingdome' (Ray 1973, 35). Although there is no definite proof, it is believed that van Hamme established the pothouse at Copthall in 1676 on his arrival in England (Fig 2). We do not know the types of tiles he produced, although it is suggested that tiles with narrative-style decoration, such as those depicting the Popish Plot (1679), the supposed conspiracy to murder Charles II and replace him with his Catholic brother (later James II), were made there (Horne 1999, nos 556 A/B; Graves 2002, 100, 4.32).

Tile production, however, may have been short lived as van Hamme died in 1680, although the Copthall pothouse continued, eventually closing in 1730 (Britton 1987, 59). This could account for the rarity of tiles in the Popish Plot series. None have been identified amongst the thousands of wall tiles recovered from excavations in London over the last half century, nor are there any others in the Museum of London collection.

Despite van Hamme's claim to make tiles 'which hath not been practised in this our kingdome', we know from at least one other source that he was not the only potter attempting to make wall tiles at this time. On 3 August 1677, a Dr William Johnson, acting

[1] In some publications the purple colour of decorated wall tiles has been called manganese (Chapter 7, 'Tile colour').

for Viscount Conway, went to pothouses in 'Lambeth and Vauxhall' to buy tiles, but found the potters unable to supply them.

> The day after my coming to the City, according to your commands, I went to Lambeth and Vauxhall to enquire about the tiles, but found them at both places unfurnished, they telling me they were yet at a loss in the mixture of their clay and way of burning them, but was directed by them to Mr Sybley as one best furnished in Holland tile, whom I likewise found so. I have sent down patterns of divers sorts and prices for you to choose from. The way of sale is so much a foot, counting always four tiles to the foot, 10 inches making the Dutch foot. Each tile is covered with a paper and the prices are set on both the tile and the paper (Ray 1973, 35; Edwards 1974, 115).

We may note that a Mr Sybley (a member of the Glass Sellers' Company) appears to be the main supplier in the City, and the difficulty the potters were having to produce the correct sort of clay for tile production. Sybley's connection as a dealer is referred to again below (4, Dutch tiles).

A further point of interest concerning the 1677 account is the mention of two pothouses, one in Lambeth and one in nearby Vauxhall. One of these must have been the pottery established by van Hamme in 1676, but the identity of the other is a puzzle. According to Britton (1987, 50–71) there were no other pothouses in the Vauxhall or Lambeth area until Norfolk House commenced operation in 1680. This leaves just two possibilities: either one of the later pothouses must have started earlier than previously thought or Dr Johnson visited a pothouse for which there is currently no documentary or archaeological evidence.

BEAR GARDEN, SOUTHWARK (*c* 1671–*c* 1705/10)

The earliest archaeological evidence of wall tile manufacture in London is from Bear Garden on Bankside, where a large assemblage of kiln waste was discovered (Benbow House, Bear Gardens, Southwark: MOL site code BAN95; Betts 1998; Mackinder and Blatherwick 2000, 29; Fig 2). This included wall tile blanks 10–12mm thick, typical of the earliest wall tiles, and a partly white glazed (undecorated) tile of the same thickness. The documentary evidence reveals a series of potters connected with the site from 1671 to 1705, the pothouse having gone out of business by 1710 (Mackinder and Blatherwick 2000, 25). There is no indication as to the volume of tiles produced at the Bear Garden pothouse.

PICKLEHERRING, SOUTHWARK (*c* 1618–1723)

Pickleherring provides further evidence for the manufacture of wall tiles in the late 17th century (Chapter 3, English tiles). An inventory of the pothouse following the death of John Robins in 1699 mentions marbled figure tiles, galley tiles and biscuit tiles (Britton 1990, 70, 73, 75, 79), but the quantity present (2266 tiles) represents a small fraction of the pothouse's output (less than 1%). The majority of the inventory lists pottery vessels at various stages of production. There is no indication as to the types of wall tiles made at Pickleherring.

MONTAGUE CLOSE, SOUTHWARK (*c* 1613–1755)

The Montague Close pothouse in Southwark (Fig 2) seems to have concentrated on the production of tin-glazed pottery, although a small percentage of its output in the 18th century did include wall tiles. Among the earlier excavated material described by Dawson and Edwards (1974, 51) were two biscuit-fired wall tiles measuring 129mm square by 8mm in thickness. Further incomplete biscuit-fired tiles measuring 6–8mm in thickness were found during excavation in 1999 (PCA site code MTA99). Only one plain blue tile was found associated with the pothouse. The biscuit-fired tiles were found in post-1730 contexts and in groups associated with the closure of the pothouse in *c* 1755 (C Jarrett, pers comm; Chapter 3, English tiles).

HERMITAGE, WAPPING (*c* 1665–*c* 1773)

Excavations at Hermitage Dock, Wapping, in 1997 (MOL site code HIT96; Tyler 1999, 127–63; Fig 2), on part of the kiln established by John Campion in *c* 1665, revealed a small number of biscuit and decorated wall tiles. The decorated tiles (**486–490**) have previously been published by Smith (1999, 153–5) but are illustrated here in colour for the first time (Chapter 7). Regrettably, they cannot be definitely linked with the pothouse as production ceased in *c* 1773, whilst the decorated tiles were found in deposits dated after 1805. Wall tiles were certainly made at the pottery as four biscuit-fired fragments were found directly associated with kiln 3 dated to the period 1720–*c* 1773.

Two decorated mid 18th-century tiles were sent for ICP analysis (**489**, **490**; Chapter 5) along with six biscuit-fired and three plain glazed tiles. With two exceptions all the tiles analysed were found to have originated from the Hermitage pothouse. The two differing samples were a plain glazed tile which is reasonably close in its chemical composition to tiles made at Pickleherring and a decorated tile (**490**) unlike any from the London production sites so far analysed. The tile does, however, appear to be English (J Horne, pers comm). It may be significant that this tile is painted in a lighter shade of blue than the other decorated examples.

There is also some doubt about the provenance of the two fragments with barred ox-head corners (**486**); regrettably neither was selected for ICP analysis. It is worth noting that the larger piece, at 6mm thick, is thinner than all the biscuit tiles (which measure 7–8mm in thickness). Smith (1999, 155) has already pointed out the close similarity between these tiles and a landscape tile attributed to Liverpool, Lancashire, by Horne (1989, 36, no. 145). The larger piece has dark blue shading with a greyish tinge which is similar to the dark bluish-purple shading on another Liverpool tile in Horne (1989, no. 146).

Significantly, both Horne nos 145 and 146 have almost identical barred ox-head corners to the Hermitage examples which raises the possibility that they were made in Liverpool (below, 4, Liverpool tiles). Both, however, share the same deep blue glaze as the decorated tile confirmed by ICP analysis as being made at the Hermitage pothouse (**489**). This raises a further possibility that they were made at the Hermitage pothouse by tile-painters closely copying Liverpool designs. It is well known that the main production centres at Bristol, Liverpool and London occasionally copied elements of each other's designs (Horne 1989, 9). Delftware production was established in Liverpool in 1710 by London potters (Ray 1973, 41).

NORFOLK HOUSE, LAMBETH (*c* 1680 to *c* 1772–9)

James Barston's pothouse was established at Norfolk House, the former home of the Dukes of Norfolk, near Lambeth Palace, in 1680. During 1967, excavations on the site, located between Pratt Walk and Norfolk Row, revealed two rectangular brick structures and kiln furniture, together with glazed and biscuit sherds of pottery (Bloice 1971). From the proportion of tiles to pottery debris, tile output was relatively modest. Mainstream wares were plates, dishes and bowls, although an astonishing 10,000 tiles were recorded there unsold in 1765 (Britton 1987, 52).

More recent excavations at Norfolk House in 1988 and 1990 (MOL site codes NOR88, NOR90), in pits adjacent to the kiln, have produced several tile wasters and biscuit tiles from the pothouse (Tyler et al 2008, 97–8; Fig 2). The most significant waster is a typical 1725–50 tile showing a blue vase of flowers and carnation corners in a purple border (**422**). The purple appears as a layer of broken bubbles, showing the fugitive nature of this colour (first used by London potters on London mugs of the 1620s; Archer 1997, 18). Flower vase tiles with carnation corners are also believed to have been made at the Lambeth High Street and Vauxhall pothouses (below).

Present with other waste material from Norfolk House are two biscuit-fired tiles with designs painted with what appears to be a red ink-like substance (**484**, **485**). These may be pot or tile-painters' trial pieces or simply 'doodles'. One (**484**) was found associated with a substantial dump of pottery waste dated to 1745–70 (Tyler et al 2008, 97).

A variety of other tiles were found on the site of the Norfolk House pothouse but it is by no means certain that all were made there: some are definitely Dutch. Because of this uncertainty, five decorated along with a similar number of biscuit-fired examples were subject to ICP analysis which confirmed their Norfolk House origin (Hughes 2008, 122–7; Chapter 5).[2] This included the tile waster with the flower vase decoration (**422**) and one (**355**) of two biblical tiles (**371** not analysed) with Dutch-style spider head corner motifs.

Other design types are now known or believed to have been made at Norfolk House:

• Blue on white flower vase tiles with distinctive dotted flower-head corners (**408**, **409**). One tile was analysed by ICP (**408**).

• Blue on white biblical tiles characterised by an unusual variant of the common barred ox-head corner design (**349**, **354**, **365**, **370**). One tile was analysed by ICP (**354**). A biblical tile painted in purple on light blue with a more conventional barred ox-head corner (**348**) was probably also made at Norfolk House.

• Blue on pale blue landscape scenes in circular borders with barred ox-head corners (**256**, **257**). One, showing a fortified house (**257**), is a waster or second and so was selected for analysis by ICP. This confirmed a Norfolk House origin.

• A border tile with Greek key device in blue on white (**452**), formerly attributed to London, 1740–60 (Horne 1989, 399).

VAUXHALL, LAMBETH (*c* 1683–1802)

Very few tiles have been found at Vauxhall (Fig 2), which was in operation between 1683 and 1802, suggesting that they formed only a small proportion of the pothouse's output. Britton (1987, 71, K) illustrates two tiles. One shows a flower vase in polychrome set in a powdered purple border with carnation-head corners, similar to **423** although on this tile the border is in blue. The other tile shows part of a blue on white biblical scene in a circular border. Other known Vauxhall designs are illustrated by Cockell (1974, pl 136), including a blue on purple geometric and floral pattern (cf **438**) and a rectangular border in blue with a flower head and plant stem design (cf **445**). Plain white and dark purple tiles were also present.

[2] The biscuit-fired tiles and the decorated tiles confirmed as Norfolk House products by ICP analysis measure 123–131mm square by 5–8mm.

An unusual feature of the biscuit-fired tiles from Vauxhall is the presence of some tiles with the outline of designs painted on them (Edwards 1984, pl 49). Similar tiles were found associated with the Norfolk House pothouse (**484**, **485**).

GRAVEL LANE, SOUTHWARK (*c* 1694–1748)

Inadequate clay preparation and mixing were a chief cause of the early difficulties in the manufacture of wall tiles. To overcome these problems Nathaniel Oade, owner of the Gravel Lane pothouse (Fig 2), brought over a Dutchman in *c* 1718 on a six-year term in order to improve his own skills (Horne 1989, 117). This must have met with success as an inventory of Oade's goods, taken on his death in 1726, records 12,886 tiles in stock (1775 biscuit fired, 11,111 complete tiles) and a room described as the 'Tiled Parlour', perhaps set up by the Dutch tileman as a showroom where prospective purchasers could inspect designs (Britton 1987, 49, 192). In contrast to the Pickleherring inventory only 27 years previously (where the quantity of tiles represented less that 1% of the pothouse's output), around 10% of the stock was tiles at Gravel Lane. Although a crude indicator of turnover, it does suggest a change in emphasis from the late 17th century to the second decade of the 18th century, from a reliance on imported Dutch tiles to an increasing home industry (R Stephenson, pers comm).

Waster dumps associated with tile and pottery production at Gravel Lane were excavated in 2006 (Great Suffolk Street, Lavington Street, Southwark: MOL site code GLS06). A number of biscuit-fired tile blanks measuring 128–129mm square by 6–9mm thick were recovered, along with decorated tiles and three plain duck-egg blue examples. The latter are unlikely to be from Gravel Lane as ICP analysis of one of the plain tiles revealed a completely different chemical composition from the biscuit-fired tile and pottery found on the site. The decorated tiles, however, closely matched the biscuit-fired material and were almost certainly made at Gravel Lane (Chapter 5).

An interesting range of decorative designs is present: flower vases with powdered purple borders in polychrome (cf **423**; Horne 1989, 62, no. 335) and blue on white (cf **421**, **422**; Horne 1989, 62, cf nos 334, 339, 341); a blue on white flower vase without border flower (cf **408–410**; Horne 1989, cf no. 349); and a landscape tile in blue on white. All these decorated tiles probably date to the period 1730–48.

Excavations at 38–48 Albert Embankment were remarkable for the discovery of 57 purple on white landscape tiles with spider head corners stacked in the 19th-century cellar of a property adjacent to the King's Arms (**238–247**). Showing mortar on their backs, from previous usage, the tiles may be regarded as old stock. Despite their Dutch-style corners, all have typical London landscape scenes, and ICP analysis has shown all but one (**240**) are products of the Gravel Lane pothouse (Chapter 5). It is possible they are the work of the Dutch potter brought over *c* 1718 to assist with the production of wall tiles at Gravel Lane.

Associated with these unusual London-made tiles were portions of three tile pictures: two had five extant blue and white tiles showing birds, foliage and flowers, and were numbered on the back, 10 (letter missing), 16A, 5B, 18B and 21B, to locate each in the picture (**469–473**). These tile pictures resemble a complete panel from Daun and Vallentin's distillery, Lambeth (**464**), and a similar picture illustrated in Horne dated 1720–30 (1989, 114, no. 674) which are thought to have been made at Gravel Lane. The third picture is represented by a single tile showing birds flying by a ship's rigging (blue and white; **463**). These picture tiles have no mortar attached and were apparently never wall-mounted. An edging tile in blue on white (**445**) may have been intended as a border to a picture, used in the same manner as around the Cock and Bottle Inn sign (**461**).

LAMBETH HIGH STREET, LAMBETH (*c* 1732–93)

This pothouse was begun in 1732 by Henry Hodgson and his cousin Henry Forster, and continued production of tin-glazed ware until 1793 (Fig 2). Ray (1973, 98–9, figs 22–7) illustrates the range of tiles found in 1936 by Professor Garner on the site of the Lambeth High Street pothouse and from other sites nearby. Most are landscape and biblical scene tiles with barred ox-head corners similar to that found on **256**. There are also flower vase tiles with dotted flower-head corners, of the type used at Norfolk House (**408**), and a tile with quarter flower-head decoration in each corner (**429**).

The attribution of these designs to Lambeth High Street, however, should be treated with caution as not all the tiles illustrated by Ray were made at the pothouse. A landscape tile with an octagonal white and powdered border (cf **309–311**) is clearly Dutch whilst two tiles with spider head corners are either English, pre-dating Lambeth High Street pothouse, or also Dutch.

Further material from the pothouse was found during excavations in 1973 (129 Lambeth Road, Lambeth: MOL site code L129/73; Thompson et al 1998, 129) and in 1997 (PCA site code LMD97; C Jarrett, pers comm), including numerous biscuit-fired tiles measuring 127mm in breadth by 5–8mm in thickness. The decorated material includes further flower vase tiles and a number of powdered purple landscape tiles with blue quarter rosette corners and landscape scenes set in a plain circular border.

GLASSHOUSE STREET, LAMBETH (*c* 1743–1846)

In 1980 and 1989 excavations were undertaken at 38–46 Albert Embankment (MOL site codes LAM54/80, LAM611, 38ALB89; Thompson et al 1998, 124; Tyler et al 2008), the site of the pothouse shown on John Rocque's 1746 survey (Fig 2). This pothouse, on the north of Glasshouse Street, was operating from at least 1743, manufacturing tin-glazed earthenware, stoneware and porcelain until its closure in 1846. The excavations provided evidence of tiles made in the 'Tyle Kiln' recorded there on John Sanders's insurance policy on 29 September 1743 (Britton 1987, 61–3).

There were two phases of tin-glazed ware production at Glasshouse Street: the first from *c* 1743 to 1784, and the second from 1823 to 1846. From the first phase of production are a number of biscuit-fired tiles found together with plain tiles of various shades of duck-egg blue.[3] The only known decorated tiles likely to have been made at the Glasshouse Street pothouse are a very unusual interlace Chinese-style design in blue on a white background (**430**) and a landscape tile (**213**) painted in similar style to a London-made tile, illustrated in Horne and dated to 1740–60 (1989, 37, no. 148).

A number of biscuit and plain glazed tiles were analysed by ICP (Hughes 2008, 126–8, fig 171). This found a slight chemical difference between the biscuit-fired and glazed tiles, suggesting the use of slightly different clays. There is no reason to believe that the plain glazed tiles were not made at Glasshouse Street. At Gravel Lane the chemical composition of the glazed pottery also differed slightly from the biscuit-fired pottery and tile

[3] The biscuit-fired and plain glazed tiles measure 124–130mm square by 7–9mm in thickness. The probable decorated examples have the same fabric, thickness and distinctive flat backs of the biscuit-fired and plain glazed tiles.

(Hughes 2007b).

More unusual are two biscuit tiles made with the same distinctive white-firing clay used for the manufacture of stoneware pottery vessels. These may relate to the tenure of Henry Bingham and the Moss brothers, who are believed to have made brown-glazed stoneware at the pothouse between 1784 and 1823 (Britton 1987, 61–2). The lack of other stoneware tin-glazed tiles from elsewhere suggests that this was a short-lived experiment which failed, presumably because such tiles would have been much harder to cut and trim to the required size compared with those made from traditional clay.

An even more remarkable find were 84 small mosaic tiles, many covered in the same light blue glaze as the Glasshouse Street tiles mentioned earlier. Others have darker blue, black, light and darker green and yellow glaze (**480**). These were presumably intended to be set into walls where they would have formed intricate mosaic decoration. These tiles, none of which show any evidence of use, were presumably made at Glasshouse Street during the second period of tin-glazed ware production from 1823 to 1846. In 1839 Alfred Singer, the pothouse manager, and his assistant Henry Pether were awarded the patent for a method of manufacture of mosaic tesserae (Edwards 1981, 134).

MORTLAKE, RICHMOND UPON THAMES (SURREY) (*c* 1745–1823)

There is clear evidence for the production of pottery at two sites in Mortlake (Fig 2, inset): at 107 Mortlake High Street the base of a kiln was located and at 61–69 and 71–75 Mortlake High Street the base of a further kiln and the remains of another were found (Stephenson 2003, 69). Both sites produced waste from the manufacture of tin-glazed ware, but evidence for tile manufacture was limited to 61–69 and 71–75 Mortlake High Street (MOL site codes MOT97, HSL96; Sloane and Hoad 2003). Here were found biscuit-fired tiles, together with plain white and decorated examples.[4] Evidence for tile production was not included in the published report on the Mortlake pothouse (Sloane and Hoad 2003, 43–79), so is reported here for the first time.

The earliest documentary evidence of a pothouse at 61–69 and 71–75 Mortlake High Street dates from 1745, but the decorated tiles found on the site were made considerably later (**491–496**). The landscape tiles without borders, which belong to the same group as a number of complete tiles illustrated by Horne (1989, 38, nos 155–166), are dated to the period 1780–1800. The provenance of the tiles in Horne described as 'London' may now be identified as Mortlake. It is also very likely that these tiles and the ones found at 61–69 and 71–75 Mortlake High Street were made prior to 1794 as, at this date, it is known that stoneware became the mainstay of production until a return to tin-glazed ware under William Wagstaff in 1804 (Stephenson 2003, 69).

All but one of the tiles found at 71–75 Mortlake High Street, which are painted a deep blue, are in the same style. They show a maid holding a basket on her head (a waster with two tiles fused together; **491**), a ship and a house (**495**) and landscapes with fence and bushes with the typical Mortlake motif, a 'palm frond'-like bush (**492–494**). The other tile design found at Mortlake shows a landscape scene painted in intense blue set within an elaborate Louis XV floral border with diaper corners (**496**). Although very reminiscent of Liverpool tiles, Ray has already suggested that the neater, tighter designs with smaller figures could be a London variant (Ray 1973, 152). The evidence from the Mortlake pothouse indicates that this is indeed the case.

[4] The biscuit-fired tiles measure 127mm square by 6–7mm thick.

OTHER LONDON POTHOUSES

There is currently (April 2010) no evidence for tin-glazed tile production at the following London pothouses: Horselydown Lane (*c* 1714–72) and The Clink (*c* 1730–62) in Southwark; Carlisle House in Lambeth (*c* 1680–1736); Isleworth, Hounslow (Middlesex) (*c* 1757–1831); and Putney in Wandsworth (*c* 1680–1736) (Fig 2).

LIVERPOOL TILES

The earliest documentary reference to tin-glazed tiles being made in Liverpool dates from 1710, but it was not until the mid 18th century that Liverpool tiles were exported to London. It is not clear why tiles were brought in from northern England when there were a number of London pothouses making tiles during this period. They were also shipped down to Bristol during the same period, despite the presence of tin glaze pothouses in the city itself (Ray 1973, 40).

One explanation for the presence of Liverpool tiles may be the rich variety of decorative schemes employed. Some, such as the polychrome oriental scene and the stylised blue on white flower vase decoration from 2 King Edward Street, City of London (**415**, **416**), and the polychrome flower tiles at 33 Kensington Square, Kensington and Chelsea (Chapter 6, City; Fig 6, nos 13, 15), are unique to Liverpool. Such tiles, therefore, may have been seen as something of a status symbol.

The majority of Liverpool tiles are hand painted, but it is the production of printed tiles for which the city is most famous. The first printed tiles, which date from 1756–7, used wood blocks, as shown on the examples from 2 King Edward Street, City of London (**481**), and Mill Road, Merton High Street, Merton (Surrey) (MOL site code MIS92; **482**). These were quickly superseded by the use of copper plates, which produced a more detailed and clearer picture, as can be seen on a tile from an unknown site in London (**483**). Details of both manufacturing methods can be found in Horne (1989, 124–5) and Ray (1994, 1–15).

The rarity of printed tiles in London suggests that their popularity was limited. Their production ceased *c* 1790, although hand-painted Liverpool tiles may have continued in production for a little longer (Horne 1989, 6).

DUTCH TILES

By the first half of the 17th century there were a great number of Dutch pothouses active, but attributing tiles to particular production centres is often very difficult, except when certain distinctive designs can be linked with a specific pothouse (Pluis 1997, 75).

Many of the Dutch tiles found in London cannot be linked with known production sites, but there are exceptions. The landscape tiles with large octagonal borders from the Fleet Valley, Albert Embankment and elsewhere in London (**269–274**) were made in Rotterdam, the military tiles in the Steam Engine public house, Cosser Street, Lambeth (Chapter 6, City; Fig 6, no. 19), are from Utrecht whilst a series of ship tiles in Charlton House, Greenwich (Chapter 6, Greater London; Fig 7), were made in Harlingen.

It is clear from surviving documentary sources that consumer demand ensured that Dutch tiles were widely available throughout the second half of the 17th and into the 18th century. This was in spite of continued opposition from London tilemakers and a ban on 'painted earthenware' imports from the Low Countries in 1672 and its reinforcement in 1676 (Archer 1997, 41).

The reason the import ban was ignored was that London potters were still finding it difficult to supply the quantity and quality of tiles required as a broadsheet of 1695 explains, although presenting the case of the Glass Sellers' Company who imported Dutch tiles, rather than the London potters who were trying to keep them banned, in their own interests:

> The Company of Glass-sellers have given all the encouragement possible to the *English* Potmakers, having formerly agreed with them to import none from Holland, if they could furnish them with such wares as their trade required at Accommodated Prices: but as a great part of the trade consists in selling white and Painted tiles for Chimnies and the Finest sort of Painted Earthenware for Ornament and Fancy: they could never yet be supplied with any Quantity of either of these sorts that would please People and keep up the vent, so that they have lost many customers for want of such Wares. They were forc'd to send again for *Dutch* or must have lost the chief Part of their Trades; so that if a total Prohibition of their Wares should be attain'd, many hundreds of Families will be depriv'd of their Livelihood, that now subsist by trading therein (Ray 1973, 36).

Two publications – one in 1703 by Richard Neve, the other in 1748 by the architect Batty Langley – give particulars of Dutch tiles, with Langley indicating the shortcomings of London (Lambeth) tiles, particularly their hardness of fabric which made them difficult to 'gage and set'. In his *City and County Purchaser* (1703), Neve (quoted in Ray 1973, 37) describes the types of Dutch tile available:

> xii. Dutch. Of these I shall give
>
> 1 *Their Description* Of these there are 2 kinds, which I shall distinguish by the Apellation of *Ancient* and *Modern*; the *Ancient Dutch Tyles* were us'd for *Chimney-foot paces*: They were Painted with some Antick Figures, and sometimes with the Postures of Soldiers, etc And sometimes with Compartments, and in them some irregular Flourishes; but in general they are nothing so well done, (nor with so lively Colours) as the Modern ones. The *Modern Dutch Tyles* are commonly us'd instead of *Chimney-Corner-Stones* (being plaster'd up in the Jambs) These Tyles seem to be better glaz'd, and those that are Painted (for some are only white) are done with more curious Figures and more lively Colours than the ancient ones: But both these sorts seem to be made of the same whitish Clay as our white glazed Earthen Ware. The *Modern* ones commonly Painted with *Birds, Flowers* etc and sometimes with *Histories* out of the New Testament.
>
> 2 *Their Dimensions* Those which I call *Ancient Dutch Tyles* are 5 1/4 Inches square and about 3/4 of an inch thick. The *Modern Dutch Tyles* are 6 1/2 Inches square and 3/4 of an Inch thick.

Ray (1973, 37) comments, that the 'Antick Figures' and 'Postures of Soldiers' were 'doubtless early tiles, of about 1550–1620', but the reference to soldiers and lack of colour suggests it is more likely that Neve was referring to blue on white Dutch wall tiles of mid 17th-century date. Neve distinguishes these, which appear to have been used in the floor of the fireplace (as seen at 33 Kensington Square, Kensington and Chelsea, and 21 Highgate High Street, Highgate, Haringey (Middlesex); Chapter 6; Fig 6, no. 13; Fig 7), from the 'modern' Dutch tiles depicting birds and flowers in polychrome and biblical scenes in blue or purple which could be 'plaster'd up in the jambs', that is used as wall tiles around the sides of the fireplace.

The reference to 'Modern Dutch Tyles' measuring 6 ½ inches (165mm) is puzzling. Almost all Dutch and English tiles made by the early 18th century are much smaller, generally around 5–5 ¼ inches square (127–133mm) and considerably thinner – around a ¼ inch (7mm). Horne does illustrate a wall tile measuring almost 6 ½ inches square (162mm), one of only two known in England, but this is a London product of 1730–50 (Horne 1989, 27, no. 75).

Batty Langley (quoted in Ray 1973, 38) gives useful information, including prices of Dutch tiles in his *London Prices of Bricklayer's Materials and Works*, published in 1748. The marbled tiles mentioned below would have been similar in appearance to **439–441**.

> CHIMNEY TILES, commonly call'd *Gally Tiles*, for to set the *Coved Sides of Chimnies*, were first brought here from *Holland*, and yet are so continued, as being made of a free kind of Earth, that will not rub on stone: which those made by the *English Potters* at *Lambeth*, etc. will not so freely do, and are therefore troublesome to gage and set.
>
> THERE are diverse kinds of these *Dutch Tiles*, viz. entirely *White, Marbled* and *Painted* with divers Devices, as *Landscapes*, etc. in blue and white colours.
>
> THE *White Sort* is sold by the large Dealers in *Earth Wares*, at *2d per Tile*, the *Marbled Kind* at 3d, at 3 ½d, and at *4d per Tile*, according to their Goodness of Work.
>
> EVERY four *Tiles* is call'd a square Foot, and so paid for: tho' in Fact they measure, when gaged and set, *not more* than 100 square Inches (*each Tile being but 5 Inches square*) whereas *a square Foot contains 144* square Inches: so that *4 Tiles* are very little more than 2 third Parts of a square Foot, which is 96 square Inches.
>
> N.B. THESE sorts of *Tiles* are made by the *White Potters* at Lambeth, and by Mr OADES at his Pot-House in *New-Gravel-Lane* in *Southwark*, where there is a very great Choice. But I think not any of them can be rubb'd and gaged with that neatness as can be with *Dutch Tiles*, unless they have very lately made that Improvement by moderately *opening the Body of their Clay with* Woolwich *Sand*, which I think is no difficult Matter to do.

Nathaniel Oade's efforts to improve his tile manufacture by bringing over a Dutch potter appear to have had only partial success. Dutch imports continued to saturate the market, where they were seen as superior in quality to London-made products. Langley (quoted in Ray 1973, 39) providing advice on tiling fireplaces states:

> *Note also* When Bricklayers, etc. undertake to find the Tiles, if 'tis agreed

that they are to be *Dutch* made, beware that they are not mixed with *English* made Tiles, which is often done, and especially those that are entirely white, as being cheaper.

Customers intending to buy Dutch tiles would have inspected them at a dealer's warehouse or shop: Dr Johnson, went to Mr Sybley, the glass seller in 1677. There were some 50 specialist glass and earthenware shops owned by members of the Glass Sellers' Company (who also had the right to sell tiles) in the City in 1689, as a list of that date makes clear (Table 2). The list includes well-known glass sellers such as John Greene and James Sybley, the latter with his warehouse at London Bridge, Southwark, while Greene supplied Dutch tiles to Ham House, Richmond upon Thames, in the 1670s. Less well known, although evidently wealthy, was Richard Barnes, who is described as assessor, that is he appraised London householders for tax purposes. Barnes is noted as a citizen and member of the Glass Sellers' Company in his inventory of 1690 in the Court of Orphans' records (acting as a 'chinaman') (LMA, CLA/002 inventory no. 2141). The contents of his shop included 'Tyles and Mufflers and apparel … 5 cash of blew pots' (perhaps *bleu persan* – blue with white decoration) and a huge stock of assorted glassware, all appraised and valued by James Sybley.

Ten of the names are marked with an asterisk in Table 2 (the present author's (RW) notation) as being debtors in 1699 of John Robins, late manager of the Pickleherring pothouse (accounting for 58% of the value of his estate), showing where they were purchasing stock (Britton 1990, 81–2). One debtor, Joseph Woodland, was actually a partner in the pothouse and running a shop in the City, as the list shows.

By the 18th century many more glass sellers and chinamen are recorded throughout the capital, offering a greater variety of wares to an ever increasing public demand (Toppin 1937). Part of a delftware shop sign advertising such wares survives (**477**), along with tiles from a similar panel found at 2 King Edward Street with the letters R and L (or E) (**478**, **479**; Fig 6, no. 15). Tiles from a further panel, one with the letters 'OF' and the number '8' on the reverse and the second with 'SS&' with the number '18' on the back, are in Saffron Walden Museum, Essex (Horne 1989, 119).

The London pothouses themselves sold goods from their own warehouses, for example at Hermitage, Wapping (in Henry Holding's possession), at Norfolk House and at the Vauxhall pottery; 'basket women' or itinerant sellers, also distributed wares from the potteries (Tyler et al 2008, 18). In 1699 'several Basket women' at the Pickleherring pottery were included in the list of debtors there, for a debt of £21 13s 3d – the third largest outstanding debt, in a total of £311 6s 3½ d in the estate of John Robins. Their goods included '56 doz Gally Tyles att £1 2s 0d', '800 Tyles att £1 0s 0d' (Britton 1990, 75, 82). Without overheads their prices were very keen, and they caused the members of the Glass Sellers' Company considerable anxiety. An attempt by the glass sellers to have them banned was unsuccessful (Edwards 1974, 22, note 147).

Glass seller
Mr John Allen, master
Mr James Mandwell, warden
Mr John Frith, warden
Mr Humphrey Killbey
*Mr John Greene
Mr Ed Orsgood
Mr Tho Lewin
Mr Na Adams
*Mr Ja Sibley
Mr Tho Alpthorpe
*Mr Chas Weston
Mr Jn Speacer
Mr Jn Gass
Mr Tho Noakes
Mr Rich Barnes, assessor
Mr Rich Wiseman
Mr Robt Farer
Mrs Claredge
Mrs Gerrard
Mr Jn Withers
Mr Tho Inchwell
Mr Ro Swinbob
Mr Wm Woodward
Mr Ed Yarmouth, commissioner
Mr Wm Baldarick
Mr Robt Channock
*Mr Sam Phillips
Mr Jo Archer
Mr [?] Colewell
Mr Don Wattson
Mr Hen Kniveton
Mr Joshua Sharman
*Mr Jacob Elles
*Mr Jo[seph] Woodland, partner at the Pickleherring pottery
Mr Hen Chardey
*Mr Ben Steward
*Mr Robt Fleetwood
Mr Phil Shepherd
Mr R Withers
Mr Wm Margerum
Mr Tho Blackley
Mr Jo Heeter
Mr Wm Forestreet
Mr Rich Bromley, collector
Mr Sa Wattkinson
Mr [?]Weston jnr
Mr Robt Upp
Mr Rich Strracey
Mr Ed Salmon
Mr Chris Sallisbury
Mrs Jn Freeman
*Mr Jonas Clarke
*Mr Jo Norris
Mr Hen Weibly [?]
Mr Jn Perwin [?]
Mr [?]

* denotes a debtor to Barston's estate, Pickleherring, in 1699

Table 2 List of London glass sellers who dealt in glasses and earthenware, 16 September 1689 (GL, MS 366/3)

LOCATION AND DECORATIVE USE

The manufacture of colourful tiles for hearths and walls from the late 16th century created a revolution in the interior decoration of middle-class homes in the Low Countries. They were employed in a wide range of domestic locations including kitchens, dairies, pantries, lavatories, basements and, most characteristically, around fireplaces.

With the restoration of Charles II in 1660, French and Dutch decorative traditions became fashionable, especially the latter, and sombre wood-panelled English rooms might be enlivened with a chimney breast decorated in softwood carving, tiered shelves with fashionable blue and white delftware pottery and tin-glazed delft tiles lining the sides of the grate.

One of the most important locations of fireplace tiles *in situ* is at Ham House, Richmond upon Thames (Fig 7), where the Duke of Lauderdale employed John Greene, the glass seller, to supply Dutch tiles for the fireplaces there in the 1670s. There are two series of tiles: blue and white figurative and floral schemes and 'white' tiles of various hues – from white to pink and pale blue (Chapter 6, Greater London). In terms of the expenses for furnishing Ham House, the tiles were cheap, as the records show (TM, account nos 436–7):

29 January 1672	'For mending Mr Forbess [Arthur Phorbes] chimney with dutch tyles. Bricklay[er] and Lab[our] half a day 00-01-10'
3 March 1673	'For setting chimneys with Dutch tiles'
28 September 1674	'To John Greene for dutch tyles 003-00'

John Evelyn describes Ham as 'furnished like a great Prince's' in a written description of 1678 (Moore et al 1995, 52). Much of the original sumptuous furnishing survives today.

The fashion for delftware was boosted again at the Glorious Revolution with the accession to the English throne of the Dutch Prince William of Orange and his consort Mary in 1689. Queen Mary's elaborate tile sequence installed in a dairy converted from part of the Old Water Gallery at Hampton Court, Richmond upon Thames (Middlesex), is known only from a few tiles in the Victoria and Albert Museum, London, and in the Rijksmuseum, Amsterdam (van Lemmen 1986, 13; Graves 2002, 86, fig 4.20). When the court favoured delftware they generally purchased the grandest pieces, like Mary's giant flower vases from Delft (Archer 1976) whilst tiles for the fireplaces lay more within the purchasing power of the middle classes.

The paintings of the Dutch masters, in particular Johannes Vermeer and Pieter de Hooch, provide valuable information as to how tiles were used in the houses of Dutch citizens during the mid 17th century. Various paintings clearly show the presence of blue on white decorated tiles set into fireplaces whilst a single line of tiles was used as a type of decorative skirting board (Ruger 2001, 49, pl 41, 58, pl 48, 66–7, pls 54–5). Tiles could also be used in the form of decorative panels such as those seen flanking a doorway in a painting by de Hooch of *c* 1658–60 (Ruger 2001, 50, pl 42).

A more unusual source of information concerning the location of tiling can be gleaned from the kitchens of miniature doll's houses. What is thought to be a Dutch example dating from the 17th century in the Victoria and Albert Museum of Childhood (Bethnal Green, London) shows a tiled area with landscape scenes, animals and cherubs located above a stove (Burton 1986, 23). In the late 1940s Willis (1949, 114–22) noted 'Dutch' (undoubtedly tin-glazed) tiles covering the kitchen walls of a number of large houses in Epsom, Surrey, and there is little doubt that similar tiled kitchens could be found in London properties.

Despite heavy losses due to demolition and alteration it is clear from surviving documentary accounts that the principal use of Dutch, and later English wall tiles, in London was around fireplaces. Indeed, the majority of surviving tiles in London still in their original position are found decorating fireplace surrounds. Reference has already been made to Neve's 1703 description of early Dutch tiles being used for '*chimney-foot paces*' and later '*chimney-Corner-Stones* (being plastered up in the Jambs)' and Langley's 1748 description of 'CHIMNEY TILES, commonly call'd *Gally Tiles*, for to set the *Coved Sides of Chimnies*' (Ray 1973, 37–8). In 1739 a house in Leadenhall Street, City of London, had

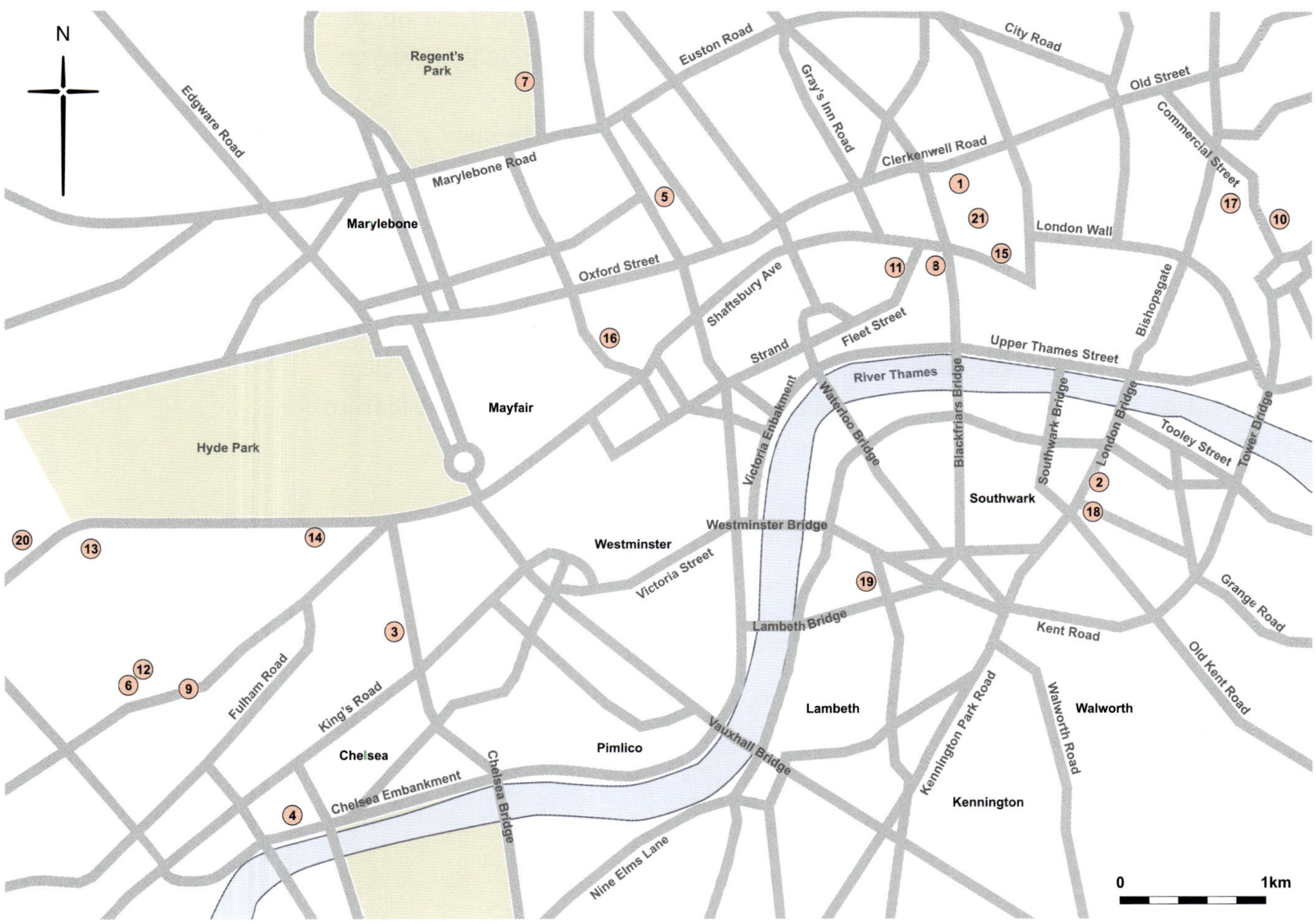

Fig 6 Buildings in the City of London and immediate hinterland with post-1666 tin-glazed wall tiles (scale 1:50,000)

1 – 1–7 Albion Place, Islington
2 – 99 Borough High Street, Southwark
3 – 1 Cadogan Gardens, Kensington and Chelsea
4 – Carlyle's House, 24 Cheyne Row, Kensington and Chelsea
5 – 2 Chenies Street Chambers, Camden
6 – 9 Collingham Gardens, Kensington and Chelsea
7 – 12 Colosseum Terrace, Camden
8 – Court House of St Andrew's, Holborn, City of London
9 – Dora House, 108 Old Brompton Road, Kensington and Chelsea
10 – 3, 12 and 21 Fournier Street, Tower Hamlets
11 – 40–41 Furnival Street, City of London
12 – 39 Harrington Gardens, Kensington and Chelsea
13 – 12 and 33 Kensington Square, Kensington and Chelsea
14 – (Westminster Synagogue) Kent House, Rutland Gardens, Kensington and Chelsea
15 – 2 King Edward Street, City of London
16 – Liberty, 210 Regent Street, Westminster
17 – 30 Spital Square, Tower Hamlets
18 – St George the Martyr church, Borough High Street, Southwark
19 – Steam Engine public house, Cosser Street, Lambeth
20 – Linley Sambourne House, 18 Stafford Terrace, Kensington and Chelsea
21 – St Bartholomew's Hospital, City of London

chimneys 'set with Blew Landskip Galley tiles' in its bedroom chambers, which must have been on the second or higher floors (Metcalf 1984, 99).

Skirting tiles still survive *in situ* in the Great Hall at Ham House where one row of plain white, pink and light blue tiles survives along the south and west walls. Their rarity is not surprising as such tiles could easily be damaged when the floor was being cleaned and are far less likely to have survived later refurbishment and alteration. Further evidence that they were occasionally used in this position is demonstrated by a watercolour view of a housekeeper's room in Whitby Abbey, North Yorkshire (Yorkshire North Riding), dated 1840, which shows a single row of tiles at floor level (Archer 1997, 47).

The rebuilding of London after the Great Fire of 1666 must have given much opportunity to those interested in such decoration. Samuel Pepys had a number of fireplaces 'done with Dutch' tiles in 1666 (Archer 1997, 47), whilst Judge Jeffreys's home in Aldermanbury, near Guildhall, City of London, had six fireplaces 'sett with tiles' in 1679. These tiles, some of which are described as 'painted', are also presumed to be Dutch as Jeffreys purchased '67 ffoote of Dutche tyles' (Melville Balfour 1929, 188–94). Unfortunately there are no recorded survivals.

Dutch tiles were used both at Brooke House and Sutton House, Hackney, at the turn of the century as fireplaces were upgraded, but the most spectacular scheme is that still surviving at Carshalton House water tower, Carshalton, Sutton (Surrey) of 1717–20. Here the walls are covered throughout with Dutch plain white tiles separated by decorative floral borders (Graves 2002, 71, 4.2; Chapter 6; Fig 7; Fig 36).

By the early 18th century London was growing fast and the Georgian houses of Spitalfields, Kensington and Chelsea record the new decorative feature in their neat fireplaces. Tiles helped to prevent damp and to lighten gloomy basements as at 12 Fournier Street, Tower Hamlets (Chapter 6, City; Fig 6, no. 10; Fig 18).

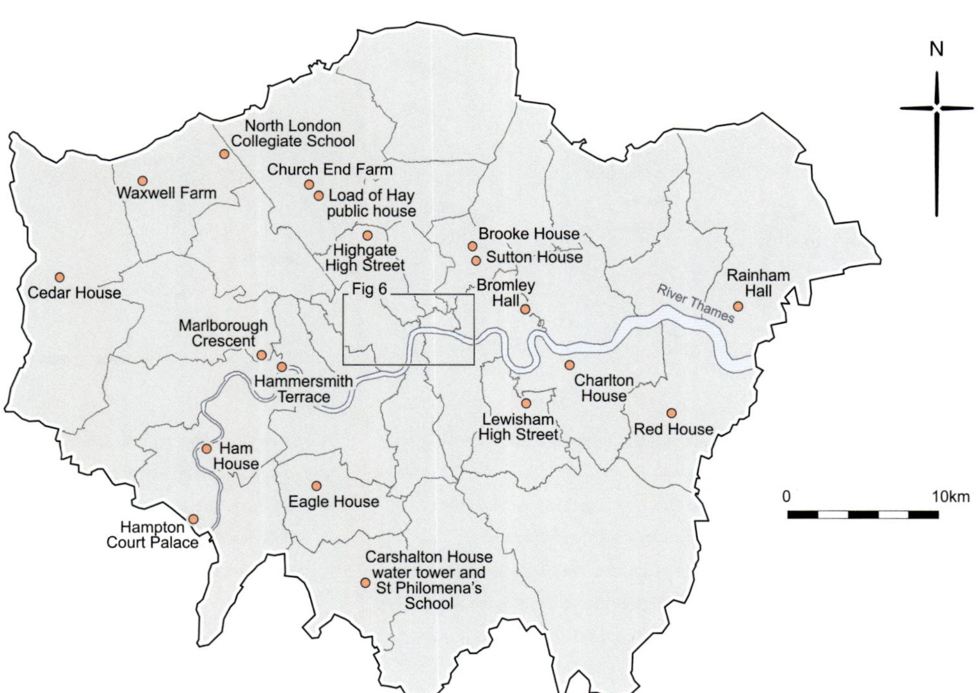

Fig 7 Buildings in the Greater London area with post-1666 tin-glazed wall tiles (scale 1:500,000)

Meanwhile, London tiles were beginning to be more widely used, such as the ship tiles (**339–341**) of the late 17th century from Uxbridge, Hillingdon (Middlesex), and the tiles of bleu persan, one adopting the spider head corner motif, found at Rotherhithe (**313**, **443**). The Uxbridge tiles, excavated from behind a fireplace of the 17th-century property (2–3 Windsor Street, Uxbridge: MOL site code UX83i; Mills 1984), show Dutch merchantmen equipped with guns. Given the trade rivalry at the time, not to mention the Dutch wars of the 1670s, the subject was of great topical interest to Londoners.

By the mid 18th century, London-made tiles were widely available, with landscape and biblical scenes, flower vases and animals, many framed within attractive borders of powdered purple or blue. Polychrome examples of flower vases were especially glamorous. Some, with carnation corners, originated at the Norfolk House and Gravel Lane pothouses. All were best displayed if set as quarries, that is, sets of four matching tiles, which completed the designs of their corner devices. Not all the tiles, however, were set in this fashion, as a surviving tile scheme from Rickard's distillery in Piccadilly, Westminster, shows, where apparently random tiles have been set adjacent to each other (Archer 1997, 433, fig 63). But such random collections, as can be seen at Nonsuch Mansion, Cheam, Sutton (Surrey) (Betts 2008a), may represent material brought together from earlier tiling work.

While the majority of tiles are found as single items and we do not know the type of scheme they were used in, there are a limited number of existing examples of tile picture panels. The dozen tiles (numbered on their backs) composing the two Diana panels are likely to be from a fireplace (**453**, **454**). The neoclassical style of decoration would have interested Londoners well into the 18th century.

The well-known picture panels in the Museum of London collection – the Cock and Bottle from Cannon Street, City of London (**461**), the Dish of Coffee Boy from Baxter's Coffee House, 66 Brick Lane, Tower Hamlets (Britton 1987, 177–8, nos 202–203; Horne 1989, front cover) and the two panels from Daun and Vallentin's distillery in Lambeth (**457**, **464**) – show how attractively day-to-day commercial premises were decorated. In 1710 Daniel Defoe recommended that a pastry cook's shop be lined with 'tiles in panels, finely painted in forest-work and figures' (Defoe 1727, 258–9).

Three other tile panels from Daun and Vallentin's distillery in the Victoria and Albert Museum show a flower vase, landscape and chinoiserie scene (Archer 1997, 421–3, N1–N3). A further chinoiserie panel is illustrated by Horne (1989, 118, no. 676).

Two other tile pictures which Archer believes came from the distillery are a flower vase panel and landscape scene shown in Horne (1989, 114–15, nos 674–675). All the panels, which are dated to 1720–30, have the same glossy glaze and distinctive dark blue colour, suggesting they are the work of a single pothouse. Horne and Archer believe they may be the work of the Dutchmen brought over to work at Gravel Lane in *c* 1718 (above, 4, London tiles).

Tile pictures continued to be made in London into the mid 18th century. Two tile panels from the Old Sun Inn, Saffron Walden, Essex, have definite English allusions: one to Prince Edward, born in 1739 (**456**), and the other to Oliver Cromwell, who stayed there (**455**). The first panel is dated 1739, whilst the other is almost certainly contemporaneous.

The Lambeth High Street pothouse had a fine tile panel as an advertisement adorning its outer wall, as a contemporary watercolour records (Britton 1987, 95, pl T). This tile panel is dated 1751 and bears the proprietor's name 'GRIFFITH', referring to William Griffith, owner from 1747 to 1761.

The survival rate for English tiles left *in situ* is low. The few examples include the 1770s Lambeth tiles in the 'blue loo' at the Commissioners House, Chatham, Kent (van Lemmen 2005, 25; Fig 8). Nearer the capital are the 1740–60 blue and powdered purple tiles in a fireplace at Eagle House, Wimbledon, Merton (Surrey) and the mid 18th-century examples from Rainham Hall, Rainham, Havering, Essex (Chapter 6, Greater London; Fig 7).

Fig 8 Mid 18th-century London-made landscape tiles, Commissioners House, Chatham, Kent (scale *c* 1:4)

The Liverpool pothouses were also providing London with tiles, most notably those found *in situ* in a tiled alcove at 40–41 Furnival Street, City of London (**258–262**, **345**, **346**; Fig 6, no. 11; Fig 22). Here over 16 tiles in blue and white dating to 1750–75 lined part of a brick vault. It is surprising that there are so few of the fine printed tiles from Liverpool which would have been available by this date (**481–483**) but Dutch competition was strong, even into the mid 18th century.

By the late 18th century the London tin glaze industry was succumbing to outside competition, not so much from imported Dutch or Liverpool tiles, as from the cream wares of Staffordshire, and little was made in London after the 1790s. Dutch tin-glazed tiles, still imported into London during the 19th century, captured a small but valuable share of the market even with the advent of mass-produced English Victorian tiles from the 1830s (van Lemmen 2000, 10–11). Thomas Carlyle purchased a set for his fireplace in 24 Cheyne Row, Kensington and Chelsea, in 1853 (Chapter 6, City; Fig 6, no. 4), just as Sir William Brereton had done in Holland in the 1630s (Ray 1973, 59; Chapter 3, Dutch tiles). A variety of blue on white and purple on white landscape tiles were used in two fireplaces at Dora House, 108 Old Brompton Road, Kensington and Chelsea, whilst principally biblical scenes decorated a late 19th- or early 20th-century fireplace at 12 Colosseum Terrace, Albany Street, Camden (Chapter 6, City; Fig 6, nos 7, 9; Figs 14–16). Military figures were favoured on the tiles from Utrecht in the fireplace at the Steam Engine public house in Lambeth, which date to the same period (Chapter 6, City; Fig 6, no. 19; Fig 33;

Fig 34). Polychrome tiles were also brought into London, such as those in Linley Sambourne House (Chapter 6, City; Fig 6, no. 20; Fig 9). More unusual is a series of green on white sailing ships on tiles at Charlton House, made in Harlingen in 1890–1910 (Chapter 6, Greater London; Fig 7).

During this period many tiles were made specifically for the English market. Some of these were of larger size, around 152mm (6 inches) square, such as those used at Charlton House, Linley Sambourne House and 1 Marlborough Crescent, Bedford Park, Ealing (Middlesex) (Chapter 6; Fig 7). A great number of tiles with traditional designs were brought over by the Dutchman Martin van Straaten who, together with Charles Lam, ran a firm called Martin van Straaten & Co based at 28 Newgate Street, City of London, at the beginning of the 20th century. Other London tile importers included Charles Marks, Thomas Elsley and Howard W. Meredith who brought in Dutch tiles from firms like van Hulst in Harlingen, Tichelaar in Makkum and Ravesteijn (renamed Westraven after 1907) in Utrecht in the late 19th and early 20th centuries (van Lemmen 2004).

Fig 9 Late 19th- to early 20th-century Dutch polychrome tiles in the fireplace of the Morning Room, Linley Sambourne House (photo by English School; © Linley Sambourne House, London, UK/The Bridgeman Art Library) (tile size 129–131mm square)

Remarkably, during the late 19th century there was a brief period of renewed tin-glazed tile production in England. In the 1870s and 1880s Frederick Garrard produced a number of highly skilled copies of early blue on white and polychrome tin glaze designs from a factory situated at Millwall, Tower Hamlets. Even more impressive are his close copies of early 16th-century Spanish *arista* tiles produced during the same period (Chapter 3, Spanish tiles, 'Victorian copies'). Garrard tiles can be seen at Charlton House, and possibly in a flat at 2 Chenies Street Chambers, Camden (Fig 6, no. 5), although the latter show similarity to the designs found on contemporary Victorian Dutch tiles. Dutch tiles continued to be brought into London throughout the 19th century and a number of tiles of this date can still be seen in various London buildings (Chapter 6).

When the last tin-glazed tiles were imported into London is uncertain: among the last seem to be those in the Steam Engine public house, discussed above, installed in the late 19th or early 20th century (Chapter 6, City) and those at the North London Collegiate School, Edgware, Barnet (Middlesex) (Chapter 6, Greater London; Fig 7), which were probably added in 1910. Demand for hand-painted Dutch tiles fell quickly during the beginning of the 20th century, in both the Netherlands and Britain (van Lemmen 1986, 28). Dutch production continued but the use of such tiles had fallen out of fashion in England by 1930.

5 SCIENTIFIC ANALYSIS

Michael J Hughes

INTRODUCTION

Provenance studies using chemical analysis depend upon the fact that clay varies in composition from place to place, so ceramics made at different places from locally available clay will have different compositions. Ceramics of known origin are analysed to form a database: ceramics of unknown origin can then be analysed and the results compared to the database to find their place of origin. The results are reported here of two small projects on the chemical analysis of tiles, carried out at different times and using neutron activation analysis and inductively coupled plasma spectrometry.

NEUTRON ACTIVATION ANALYSIS OF ANTWERP-PRODUCED TILES

Ten tin-glazed tiles of early to late 16th-century date, found on sites in London were tested to determine their place of production, which was thought to be the Low Countries (**1**, **2**, **4**, **8**, **21**, **22**, **26**, **34**, **37**, **38**).

A neutron activation analysis (NAA) project was undertaken by the British Museum's Department of Scientific Research (now Conservation, Documentation and Science) on tin-glazed pottery of this period produced in London and the Low Countries (Hughes and Gaimster 1999, 57–89; updated in Hughes and Gaimster 2002, including corrections to the table of analyses). Biscuit wares from Holy Trinity Priory, London, and from Norwich were obtained to represent English production, together with other examples supposed on stylistic grounds to be English. Biscuit wares from production centres in the Low Countries – Antwerp, Amsterdam, Haarlem and Utrecht – were analysed. The results showed that pottery produced in these two major areas could be distinguished by chemical analysis, and that further distinctions could be made between the products of the four centres in the Low Countries. This data forms the reference material against which analyses of the Museum of London (MOL) tiles could be compared. No tiles were analysed in the main project, but previous comparisons between analyses of tin-glazed tiles and pottery made in the same production centre (eg Seville and Siena) have shown that the main difference is usually in slightly lower concentrations of elements in tiles than in pottery, while the relative proportions of the elements are roughly the same. In northern Europe especially, both tin-glazed pottery and tiles had to be made by mixing an iron-rich, calcium-poor red clay with a calcium-rich white-firing clay, so that similar preparation of the clay was required for the two ceramic types.

The early tin-glazed floor tiles selected for analysis were drawn from a number of excavation sites in London, and from the collections of the MOL. Related types of tin-glazed tiles were made at Rouen, Seine-Maritime, in northern France, and it was necessary to analyse a representative group of these to add to the reference database; three Rouen tiles were selected from the British Museum.

NEUTRON ACTIVATION ANALYSIS TECHNIQUE

The technique of neutron activation has had a wide range of applications to analysis of materials (Parry 1991). It was extensively used at the British Museum for over 20 years until 2002 (Hughes 2007a) on a wide range of ceramic provenance projects including a number on medieval and post-medieval pottery. These included Hispano-Moresque and other Spanish tin-glazed pottery (Hughes and Vince 1986; Blake et al 1992) and Italian maiolica (Hughes 1991; Hughes et al 1997). For this work, powder samples were taken from each tile by drilling with a 2mm diameter tungsten carbide drill bit mounted in a low-voltage electric hand drill, and analysed using the normal neutron activation techniques used in the Department of Scientific Research (Hughes et al 1991; Hughes 2007a). The powdered samples were irradiated with thermal neutrons at the Imperial College Ascot reactor, using for calibration six portions of British Museum Standard Pottery in each batch. The samples were returned after irradiation to the British Museum and counted on a gamma spectrometry system for the induced isotope activities. Computer programs were used to process the results and calculate the concentrations of 28 elements in each sample, using the standard pottery calibrations. Portions of a National Bureau of Standards material (NIST 1633A Coal Fly Ash) were regularly included as samples to check the analytical procedure, and no inter-batch bias was encountered. The analytical results are given in Table 3. Concentration below the detection limit commonly occurs for some trace elements (niobium (Nb), nickel (Ni) and zirconium (Zr)) which have relatively high detection limits under these analytical conditions. The loss of this data is not significant. The errors for the majority of the elements range from about 2% to 5%.

RESULTS AND DISCUSSION

Table 3 indicates that, with few exceptions, the pattern of the analyses are all fairly similar, with a relatively narrow spread in concentration values for each element. This would suggest a common origin for all the London tiles. Of the major elements measured, the calcium (Ca) percentages are at a high level (14–17% for most samples) which is typical of post-medieval tin-glazed pottery. From visual inspection of the data on the tiles it was clear that the analyses were unlike those of pottery produced in London but were consistent with production in the Low Countries, specifically Antwerp. The three Rouen tiles differ significantly from all the London tiles in the elements caesium (Cs) and zinc (Zn), and to a lesser degree in thorium (Th). The London tiles, therefore, are not consistent in composition with typical Rouen-type tiles which were analysed.

The main method of interpreting the data, however, was using computer-based multivariate statistical methods, which take the concentrations of all the elements into consideration. The data on the MOL tiles were compared as test samples to that in the database of London and Low Countries tin-glazed pottery making use of the statistical program of discriminant analysis (Orton 1980; Baxter 1994; Shennan 1997).[1] Discriminant analysis found the elements which best distinguish between the pottery produced in

[1] Analysis using the SAS system computer-based data management system with statistical facilities (Hughes et al 1991).

	London										Rouen		
Sample no.:	6972-1-R	6972-2-W	6972-3-Y	6972-4-L	6972-5-N	6972-6-Q	6972-7-T	6972-8-X	6972-9-K	6972-10-W	6972-11-Y	6972-12-L	6972-13-N
Design no.:	**26**	**1**	**4**	**37**	**22**	**8**	**2**	**38**	**34**	**21**			
Accession no.:	MOL 32.9/1	MOL 6927	MOL 11902	MOL GM131 [ER1155] ‹2›	MOL 26122	MOL MIN86 [7514] ‹4122›	MOL A25388	MOL TOL79 [161] ‹59›	MOL BIG82 [721] ‹999›	MOL CQD88 [1015] ‹563›	BM MLA53, 4-1,68	BM MLA53, 4-1,71	BM MLA53, 4-1,73
Element													
Na	0.16	0.24	0.14	0.24	0.15	0.26	0.17	0.29	0.86	0.22	0.28	0.25	0.27
K	1.51	1.08	1.26	1.09	1.46	1.35	1.40	0.97	1.80	1.28	1.52	1.48	1.57
Rb	94	66	83	57	86	102	92	81	138	63	126	107	107
Cs	6.23	3.60	4.14	3.54	5.10	5.40	6.23	5.17	8.66	4.22	14.57	11.77	11.99
Ca	14.6	20.6	16.8	17.0	15.7	14.1	15.1	14.7	16.2	8.4	16.4	14.3	14.7
Sc	9.73	7.11	8.71	6.94	8.37	9.56	8.86	7.83	10.23	8.63	11.58	9.56	9.89
Fe	2.63	1.77	2.22	1.85	2.13	2.87	2.30	1.99	2.80	2.30	3.38	2.71	2.85
Cr	83.3	63.2	75.3	68.6	69.3	105.4	83.8	81.5	87.4	73.9	93.7	72.8	75.1
Co	17.7	9.9	26.0	9.4	13.3	27.3	10.6	11.9	16.9	13.3	28.6	15.2	13.5
La	29.5	26.0	25.7	21.2	23.8	25.9	25.3	24.3	26.5	27.1	30.0	27.8	27.3
Ce	61.3	52.2	50.2	42.0	51.0	53.5	55.3	47.5	63.1	49.6	64.3	58.8	54.8
Nd	27.4	26.3	25.2	20.5	23.4	25.9	24.6	24.5	30.4	25.0	30.1	30.2	27.0
Sm	5.22	4.63	4.35	3.80	4.46	4.45	4.43	4.24	6.11	4.52	5.88	5.26	5.17
Eu	1.15	0.88	1.00	0.95	0.96	0.96	1.01	0.98	1.52	0.90	1.34	1.08	1.10
Yb	2.51	1.99	2.04	1.99	1.96	2.11	2.04	1.80	2.10	2.02	2.10	2.20	2.81
Lu	0.42	0.32	0.31	0.31	0.33	0.37	0.33	0.33	0.33	0.32	0.39	0.36	0.47
Hf	7.99	5.47	7.20	5.75	5.87	7.78	6.58	6.87	4.66	6.24	6.44	7.24	8.49
Th	10.6	7.8	8.5	7.0	8.1	9.5	8.6	8.0	9.2	8.1	11.6	10.5	9.9
U	2.13	1.98	1.85	1.66	1.82	1.79	2.20	1.69	3.14	1.58	2.10	2.16	2.14
Nb	-	-	-	12.6	-	-	-	-	-	12.9	-	14.4	16.9
Ni	-	-	-	-	-	17.2	-	-	-	-	-	-	17.8
Ta	2.54	1.30	3.16	1.47	1.80	2.42	1.54	1.68	1.72	0.59	0.93	0.86	0.83
Tb	0.99	0.77	0.75	0.65	-	-	0.65	0.69	1.06	0.71	0.82	0.84	0.85
Zn	57.7	38.0	45.9	96.3	52.1	65.7	60.2	50.7	65.2	50.3	72.7	70.1	70.2
Zr	250	-	185	-	-	-	-	168	-	-	-	216	188
As	19.6	10.4	11.9	7.8	7.3	32.8	12.2	8.7	10.6	10.2	23.6	18.2	17.7
Sb	1.7	1.9	1.7	1.8	2.1	8.3	1.6	5.3	4.2	3.1	2.3	2.2	3.8

Na sodium; K potassium; Rb rubidium; Cs caesium; Ca calcium; Sc scandium; Fe iron; Cr chromium; Co cobalt; La lanthium; Ce cerium; Nd neodymium; Sm samarium; Eu europium; Yb ytterbium; Lu lutetium; Hf hafnium; Th thorium; U uranium; Nb niobium; Ni nickel; Ta tantalum; Tb terbium; Zn zinc; Zr zirconium; As arsenic; Sb antimony
Results expressed in parts per million
'-' indicates below the detection limit

Table 3 Neutron activation analysis of tin-glazed tiles from London and Rouen

London and the Low Countries; the tiles were then tested and found to be classified on the basis of their chemical composition with Low Countries pottery.

There were also subtler differences in composition between the products of the different centres of production in the Low Countries, and the results showed in detail that the tiles seemed closest to the composition of pottery from Antwerp. Data had been obtained in the main project (Hughes and Gaimster 1999, 60–1) on reference samples from three kilns in the centre of Antwerp: from the National Museum of Navigation (excavated in 1978), where analyses were made of five unglazed wasters of the mid 16th to early 17th century and three fragments of 'Malling' jugs; from Schoytestraat (Dumortier 1999, 108), nine biscuit wares of the late 16th to early 17th century; and from Steenhouwersvest, 12 biscuit wares of 1556 to 1562/72 (Veeckman 1999, 115). The Antwerp pottery and MOL tiles data were combined and this time a principal components analysis was carried out. Principal components analysis is a very useful method for examining the composition pattern without any prior assumptions about grouping the samples. The results can be shown graphically, with each sample indicated as a point on the plot of the first two principal components (PC1, PC2; Fig 10); points which are close to each other indicate samples of similar chemical composition. The ellipses have been added to Fig 10 to aid in the interpretation by indicating specific groups of samples, for example from the same kiln; the tiles are represented by solid circles. Since Antwerp was a major production centre for tin-glazed pottery and the potters did have more varied clay resources to exploit than in other centres such as Utrecht and Haarlem (van Wageningen 1988) we would expect a range of compositions for the pottery, and the slight differences between the products of the three kilns is not surprising. The differences between the kiln products included different inter-element ratios, implying different clay sources or mixtures of red and white clays.

Fig 10 Plot of the first two discriminant scores arising from neutron activation analysis of the reference pottery from sites in London (stars), Haarlem (triangles) and other Low Countries sites (squares), with the Museum of London tiles used as test items (solid circles). The tiles all plot in the region of the graph consistent with production in the Low Countries

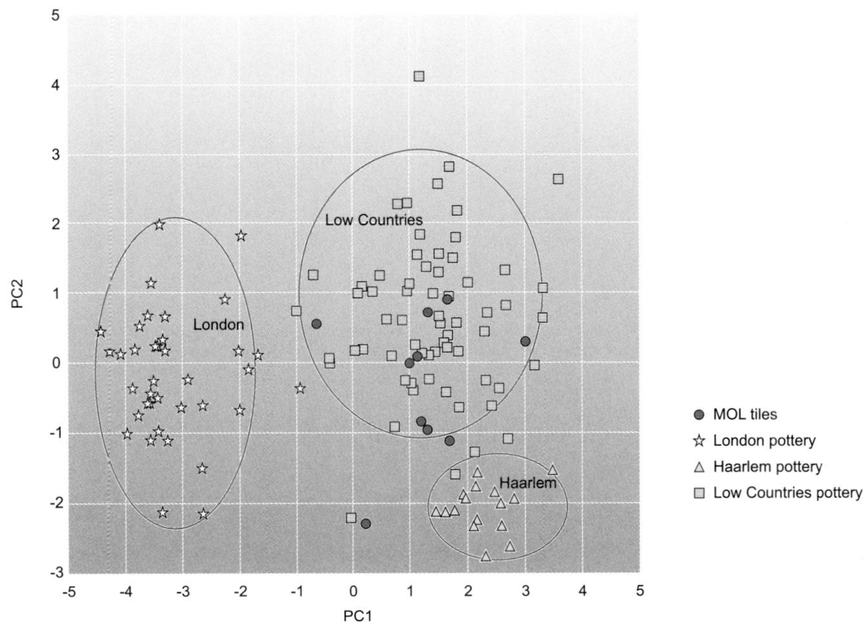

Of the MOL tiles, one (**34**) falls within the composition spread of samples from the kiln at Schoytestraat, and three others (**2**, **8**, **38**) fall within or very close to the samples from the National Museum of Navigation (Fig 11), although more recent analysis shows more of a separation (Gaimster and Hughes 1999, 179, fig 16.3). The rest of the tiles fall into an area of the principal components plot which was generally occupied by Antwerp-produced pottery, including two early 16th-century pieces from the Archbishop's Palace, Antwerp (a flower vase and a large jug; diamonds on Fig 11), two kiln biscuit sherds from the Schoytestraat site which differed from the main group (squares), a 'Malling' jug found in London and another found on the waterfront at Antwerp (open circles). 'Malling' jugs, named after an example found in the church at West Malling, Kent, are globular in shape with a spherical body and a wide parallel neck and mottled coloured glazes inside and out. Art-historical opinion, now confirmed by neutron activation analysis (Hughes and Gaimster 1999, 61–2), views them as produced in the Low Countries, specifically at Antwerp. The association of the MOL tiles with the Antwerp biscuit wares points to production in that city. The main differences between the pottery from the National Museum of Navigation and the tiles and associated Antwerp-produced samples, from the eigenvectors (contributing chemical elements) on the principal components analysis, is that the tiles have lower concentrations of scandium (Sc), iron (Fe), sodium (Na) and rubidium (Rb) and slightly higher concentrations of hafnium (Hf). One of the tiles (**21**) is in a sandier fabric than the others, but is not significantly different in chemical composition.

The only other published neutron activation analyses on Dutch ceramics seem to be

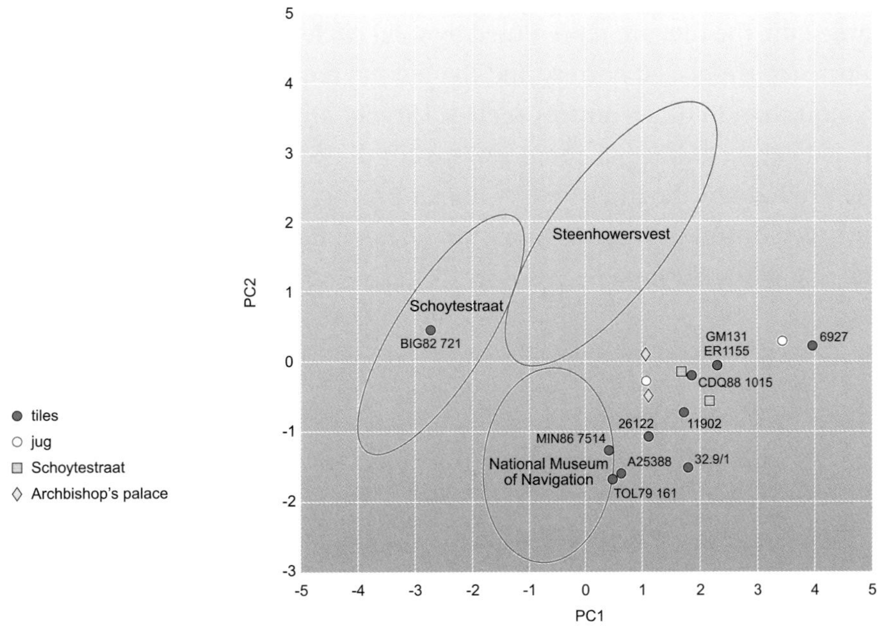

Fig 11 Principal components analysis of the tin-glazed tiles from London and reference pottery produced in Antwerp.[2] The ellipses enclose the samples from the three kilns, while the tiles are shown as solid circles. Two biscuit wares from the Schoytestraat kiln (squares) overlap with some of the tiles, as do two Malling jugs (open circles) and pottery from Antwerp (diamonds)

those of 12 tiles in the Philadelphia Museum of Art (Lins 1984). The analyses are in broad agreement with the general trace element pattern we observe for ceramics from the Low Countries, while detailed examination of their data proves informative. Five different tile designs were analysed, with some duplicate analysis of each design, including polychrome tiles with ornamental fruits in landscapes, which seem nearest in design to the London tiles. Detailed comparison shows that these polychrome tiles (Schaap 1984, 49, nos 11:3-A, 2-B and 2-A) are very similar indeed to the London tiles for the concentration of 14 out of the 19 elements measured in common in both analyses, which indicates closely similar compositions, that is they are probably of the same origin. This is useful independent confirmation of the Low Countries manufacture of the MOL tiles.

In conclusion, neutron activation analyses on all ten tiles are consistent with their production in Antwerp. Almost all have a fairly similar composition, suggesting production over a limited time range or in a limited number of workshops, with consistent use of clay sources.

INDUCTIVELY COUPLED PLASMA ANALYSIS OF LONDON-PRODUCED TILES

Neutron activation analysis continues to be used for analysis of ceramics by a number of laboratories. Analysts, however, have recently turned to inductively coupled plasma technique (abbreviated to ICP) as a viable and more widely available alternative which has been systematically used in Britain for a number of years (Hughes 2005b). Recently a major chemical analysis project has been undertaken using ICP on tin-glazed wares from the five main London pothouses: Aldgate, Glasshouse Street, the Hermitage factory at Wapping, Norfolk House, Pickleherring and Rotherhithe. Biscuit and glazed tiles were included from each pothouse with the exception of Aldgate where only pottery was analysed. Full discussion of the technique used and the results are included in Hughes (2008), so only a brief outline of the ICP results is given here.

[2] The first principal component (PC1) accounts for 26% of the composition variability in the whole dataset, and samples towards the right of the diagram have higher concentrations of thorium, hafnium and the rare earth elements, and lower concentrations of iron, scandium and the alkalis: sodium, rubidium and caesium. The second component (PC2) accounts for a further 19%, and samples towards the top have higher concentrations of scandium, iron, thorium and the rare earths, and lower concentrations of caesium and hafnium.

A total of ten tiles from four pothouses and a further 11 from one other were analysed by ICP. This material included both biscuit-fired and glazed examples – mainly decorated but also including plain glazed tiles from Glasshouse Street and Hermitage, Wapping. The biscuit-fired tiles and, in the case of Glasshouse Street and Hermitage, biscuit-fired pottery vessels, were included in the analysis because it was certain that these represented unfinished products from each pothouse.

A number of decorated tiles selected for analyses are illustrated in the design catalogue: **82** and **95** from Pickleherring; **178** from Rotherhithe; **257**, **354**, **355**, **408**, **422** from Norfolk House; and **489** and **490** from Hermitage. For each pothouse where tiles and vessels were analysed, there are almost always clear chemical differences between the two types (Hughes 2008, fig 171). At Rotherhithe the biscuit and glazed floor tiles are identical to each other but differ from the vessels, and at Glasshouse Street all three groups are different. At Norfolk House the vessels are different from all but one tile and there are slight differences between the biscuit and glazed tiles. In contrast, at Hermitage, Wapping, there are no obvious distinctions between all three groups. However, where they do differ the chemical differences can mainly be accounted for by different proportions of the red and white clays and perhaps sand temper used for the prepared clay.

The other two odd samples found on the site of the Hermitage pothouse differ from the other glazed tiles present and both the biscuit-fired wall tiles and pottery in having significantly lower amounts of the main clay element aluminium (Al). The plain blue glazed tile is reasonably close to the tiles from Pickleherring, which may be its place of manufacture, whilst the other (**490**) is unlike anything else analysed, suggesting it could be from an unidentified English pothouse or is a Dutch import.

Five decorated, five biscuit-fired and one plain tile found at Great Suffolk Street (Gravel Lane) were analysed (Hughes 2007b). The decorated and biscuit-fired tiles showed consistency in clay chemistry indicating they were all made of the same clay. They were also similar chemically to biscuit-fired tin-glazed pottery analysed from the site, indicating the use of the same clays for tiles and pottery. An exception was the plain glazed tile (MOL site code GLS06 [435]) which was significantly different in clay chemistry, with notably high magnesium (Mg) and low levels of many other elements. Its clay was unlike that of London-produced tin-glazed wares and analysis suggests it is probably a Dutch import.

Two tiles from 38–46 Albert Embankment (part of the same group as **238**, **239**, **241–247**), believed to have been made at Gravel Lane, were also analysed as part of the same project (Hughes 2007b). Their analyses proved to be consistent in chemical composition with the decorated and biscuit-fired tiles and tin-glazed wares, indicating that they were made at Gravel Lane. The two are not identical in chemistry so they are not made from the same batch of clay but are closer to each other than the full range of chemical composition seen for the ceramics from the site, suggesting some association with each other.

The most recent ICP analysis involved five tiles in the catalogue (**16**, **41**, **65**, **67**, **210**). The results show that **65** is a London product, probably from the Pickleherring pothouse, whilst the others were probably made in Antwerp (Hughes 2009). A sixth tile from Bishopsgate Goods Yard (East London Line Extension), Bethnal Green Road, Shoreditch High Street, E1, Hackney (Middlesex) (MOL site code BGX05 [522] <1498>), with the same design as **117–119** was also analysed and was found to be another London product, again probably from Pickleherring.

6 GAZETTEER OF TIN-GLAZED TILES IN LONDON BUILDINGS

Tin-glazed tiles can still be found in a number of buildings in the City of London, its immediate hinterland and the Greater London area. Other tiles formerly *in situ* have now been removed or, in one case (Load of Hay public house, Hendon, Barnet (Middlesex), below), apparently lost during demolition. Certain other tiles have been found during excavation work, but can be associated with a known building. (A number of buildings listed below are private residences and are not open to the public.)

For each building visited the number of tiles and their location has been noted as well as their colour. Incomplete tiles are counted in the total number present. Most individual design types have not been recorded since such a survey would be worthy of a publication in its own right. An exception has been made where individual designs can be used to determine the origin of the tiles and in certain cases their date of installation in the building.

Other buildings known to have tin-glazed tiles, but not visited, are also noted. There are undoubtedly other London buildings that contain tin-glazed tiles, such as Westminster Abbey, Westminster (V Simeoni, pers comm), which do not appear here. Research for this gazetteer was completed in 2002 and the range of evidence covered reflects the authors' experience working within the study area. It is hoped this survey provides an indication as to what may be found elsewhere in London and beyond. The properties are listed in alphabetical order, grouped within the City of London and immediate hinterland (6, City) and in the Greater London area (6, Greater London).

CITY OF LONDON AND IMMEDIATE HINTERLAND BUILDINGS

1–7 ALBION PLACE, EC1, ISLINGTON

Twenty-seven tiles found *in situ* at Albion Place (MOL site code JAN90; Fig 6, no. 1) were removed to the Museum of London. The building (now demolished) in which they were found was probably 19th century (G Malcolm, pers comm), although the tiles themselves are clearly earlier. Presumably they originally decorated one of the four earlier 18th-century tenement buildings which stood on the same site (Thompson et al 1998, 106).

A plan of 19 of the *in situ* tiles, drawn before removal, shows six horizontal rows of tiles which would have originally been at least five tiles wide. Somewhat unusually each horizontal tile course was offset half a tile length to the rows above and below. All the tiles are decorated except one row of two plain white, one plain pink and one decorated tile. At least one further plain white tile is attached to the right but is not marked on the plan.

The decorated tiles are mainly biblical scenes in blue on white and purple with barred ox-head corners. The corner decoration indicates that most are Dutch. For details see right.

99 BOROUGH HIGH STREET, SE1, SOUTHWARK

A purple wall tile (EH 1534.3) is from a now demolished building in Borough High Street (Fig 6, no. 2). The landscape tile has spider head corners and is very similar in appearance to **238**, **239**, **241–247** which may have been made at the Gravel Lane pothouse in London *c* 1700–30. Size: 127 x 127 x 6–7mm.

1 CADOGAN GARDENS, SW3, KENSINGTON AND CHELSEA

Cadogan Gardens is a development of the 1890s between King's Road and Sloane Square (Weinreb and Hibbert 1993, 115; Fig 6, no. 3). It is currently in private ownership. The porch of 1 Cadogan Gardens is covered with an elaborate collection of Spanish tiles, mainly of *arista* type from Toledo and Seville, dating to the late 15th–16th century (Fig 12). The tiles remain *in situ* and have still to be studied in detail, but include rectangular ceiling tiles (Fig 13, centre; Ray 2000, 363–4, nos 886, 890), square tiles (including **E**, **G**; Ray 2000, 337, 349, nos 769, 845, 846) and small *olambrillas* (including a variant of **N**). Of earlier date are four worn *cuerda seca* tiles with a complex interlace pattern (Fig 13, bottom; similar to Ray 2000, 326, no. 708) which were probably made in Seville during the 15th century. Also present are a smaller number of painted tin-glazed tiles, presumably Spanish, and two large painted tile plaques with the monograms of the Spanish kings. The plaques, made in Seville around 1700, were originally fixed to a property belonging to the city's Royal Hospital (Pearson 2005, 222). Berendsen (1967, 69) illustrates an almost identical tile plaque. Further tiles are set into the porch floor. Size: 206–207mm square (*cuerda seca* tiles); 369 x 140mm, 132–135mm square, 121–122mm square (*arista* tiles); 68–75mm square (*olambrillas*).

1–7 ALBION PLACE

BLUE ON WHITE

- Biblical tiles in circular borders with barred ox-head corners, one of which is illustrated in the catalogue (**358**). Most of the corners are damaged but are closely paralleled on Dutch tiles dating *c* 1660–1750 (for similar corners see van Dam 1991, 91, no. 124; Pluis 1997, 552, C.07.00.24–25 and 27). The tile thickness suggests a date after 1680. Size: 129–130mm square x 7–8mm thick.
- Two English blue on white biblical tiles are also present, one is again illustrated (**374**). These are slightly smaller than the Dutch examples. Size: 125–127mm square x 8mm thick.
- Blue on white landscape scenes showing a shepherd playing a flute. It is almost certainly English; Horne (1989, 29) says this subject is repeated time and again on London-made tiles dated 1740–60. Size: ? x 127 x 7mm.
- Landscape scene without borders showing a waterside warehouse and boat. Dutch, 18th century. Size: ? x 129 x 7mm.
- Landscape scene with classical building and two figures talking. Horne (1989, 26, no. 67) shows an almost identical scene on a London tile dated to 1730–50. Size: 125 x 126 x 7mm.
- Figurative landscape scene with two-line octagonal border and quarter flower corners. The corner motif is Dutch and is dated by Pluis (1997, 559, C.12.00.10) to 1750–70. See **278** for similar garden scene with a stone balustrade. Size: 130 x 130 x 7mm.
- Two cherubs in a scallop chariot pulled by a dolphin, small barred ox-head corners. Dutch, Harlingen, the same design is shown on a tile in van Dam (1991, 81, no. 93, bottom right) dated 1650–80 although this is thicker and therefore possibly earlier. The Albion Place example probably dates to *c* 1670–1700. Size: 126 x 127 x 8mm.

PURPLE ON WHITE

- Dutch biblical tiles in circular borders with barred ox-head corners. Tiles with similar corners are illustrated in Schaap dated to 1740–1850 (1984, 119–20, nos 147–148). Size: 128 x 128 x 7–8mm.
- English biblical tile. The barred ox-head corners and the circular border are distorted, the result of glaze movement during firing. The corners are similar to those present on various London-made biblical tiles dated *c* 1720–60 (Horne 1989, 77–109). Size: 127 x 127 x 9mm.
- Combed slip tile in purple, similar to Pluis (1997, 579) D.08.00.03. Dutch, *c* 1700–1800. Size: ? x 128 x 7mm.

BLUE, PURPLE ON WHITE

Blue on white landscape scene with windmill in powdered purple border with quarter rosette corners. A virtually identical tile is illustrated in Ray (1973, no. 228) dated 1725–50. Ray gives the provenance of this design as Bristol, but the Albion Place tile is almost certainly a London product of the same date (for London tile of this type see Horne 1989, 21, no. 31). Size: 126 x 128 x 7mm.

Fig 12 Early 16th-century Spanish *arista* tiles, porch, 1 Cadogan Gardens (scale *c* 1:4; complete tiles range in size 121–140mm square)

Fig 13 Fifteenth-century *cuerda seca* and early 16th-century Spanish *arista* tiles, porch, 1 Cadogan Gardens (complete *arista* tile size (centre) 369 x 140mm)

CARLYLE'S HOUSE, 24 CHEYNE ROW, SW3, KENSINGTON AND CHELSEA

Carlyle's House is part of a terrace of red brick houses built in 1708 (Fig 6, no. 4). It is currently under the guardianship of The National Trust. Thomas Carlyle lived in the building from June 1834 until his death in 1881 (Weinreb and Hibbert 1993, 127–8). The front parlour fireplace has 24 tiles in total: 12 tiles on each side of the grate. All are purple on white landscape tiles, some with figures, others without, set in Louis XV borders with diaper corners. The fireplace and the tiles were installed in 1853. The National Trust guidebook (Campbell 1992, 18) describes the tiles as coming from Holland where landscape tiles with the same elaborate border decoration were produced from 1740 to 1920 (Pluis 1997, 529, B.12.00.04). Size: *c* 132–135mm square.

2 CHENIES STREET CHAMBERS, 9 CHENIES STREET, WC1, CAMDEN

The flats were built by Ladies Residential Chambers Ltd and opened in 1889 (Fig 6, no. 5). They are currently in private ownership. Photographs supplied by Lynn Pearson show a tiled fireplace surround and tiled lower walled area. The polychrome tiles have all the same design, which has similarities to 19th-century tiles made in the Netherlands. Chris Blanchett, however, believes the pale green areas suggest the work of Frederick Garrard, a London tin glaze tilemaker working in the 1870s and 1880s (Chapter 4, Location and decorative use; below, 6, Greater London, 'Charlton House').

9 COLLINGHAM GARDENS, SW5, KENSINGTON AND CHELSEA

Collingham Gardens was constructed in 1883–8 (Cherry and Pevsner 1991, 547; Fig 6, no. 6). It is currently in private ownership. There is a tin-glazed tile fireplace at this property (L Pearson, pers comm).

12 COLOSSEUM TERRACE, ALBANY STREET, NW1, CAMDEN

Extending north–south to the east of Regent Park, Albany Street was progressively laid out during the 1820s (Weinreb and Hibbert 1993, 10; Fig 6, no. 7). A number of tiles were rescued in 1994 from an already badly damaged tiled fireplace in a front downstairs room and are now part of the MOL collections (MOL site code CTA94; Betts 1994). The fireplace originally comprised 24 tiles at either side of the fire, mainly biblical scenes, with a panel of 20 landscape tiles above. The dating of the individual designs suggests that the fireplace was added some time during the late 19th or early 20th century but incorporated earlier Dutch and English tiles.

The horizontal tiled area comprised Dutch landscape tiles set within an elaborate square border (**285**). Size: 130–131mm square.

For details of the tiles set either side of the fireplace see right.

12 COLOSSEUM TERRACE

BLUE ON WHITE

- Dutch biblical tiles with distinctive corner motifs dated to the period 1890–1920 (Pluis 1997, 553, C.07.00.36). Size: 129–132mm square.
- Dutch tile dating *c* 1650–1700 showing a soldier and with spider head corner motifs (**338**). Size: 125mm square.
- Landscape scene with spider head corners (**233**). The same design is shown on two early 18th-century Dutch tiles in van Sabben and Hollem (1987, 118, no. 386). Size: 129mm square.

PURPLE ON WHITE

- Biblical scene showing The Entombment (John 19 v. 41). This is presumably English as Ray (1973, 128) stated that this is not a Dutch design. The same design is depicted on English tiles in Ray (1973, 129, no. 93) and Horne (1989, 106, no. 641). The latter, although clearly the work of a different painter, is found on a London-made tile of 1740–60. Other London biblical tiles in purple on white with the same style of barred ox-head corner are dated by Horne to 1730–60. Size: 130 x 131mm square.

COURT HOUSE OF ST ANDREW'S, 5 ST ANDREW STREET, HOLBORN, EC4, CITY OF LONDON

The Court House was one of a number of buildings designed by Samuel Sanders Tuelon and completed in 1871 (Fig 6, no. 8). It is currently in private ownership. Its most striking feature is a great mantelpiece dating to the early 17th century at the earliest. Around the fireplace is a single row of 29 alternating purple on white and blue on white biblical tiles believed to have been added when the mantelpiece was installed in its present position in the early 1870s (Sharp 2004, 194, fig 1). The tiles are very similar to a Dutch biblical tile made at Makkum in 1860–70 illustrated by Pluis (1997, 389, A.03.08.11). Size: 129–133mm square.

DORA HOUSE, 108 OLD BROMPTON ROAD, SW7, KENSINGTON AND CHELSEA

The housing in the Clareville Grove area, of which Old Brompton Road forms the southern boundary, was constructed after May 1820, the date when Catherine Lee agreed to let the open ground to the builder and bricklayer William Blake. This property was one of the first houses constructed, the house being first leased to Harriet Lloyd in September 1822. The front of the building was refaced in 1885–6 when the house, along with 110 Old Brompton Road, was adapted as a studio for a firm of photographers (Survey of London 1975, 19–25). Dora House is currently in private ownership (Fig 6, no. 9).

Hall

Tile fireplace with 70 Dutch tiles (Fig 14; Fig 15). These are all blue on white and include landscape scenes with carnation-head corners similar to Pluis (1997, 368, 377) designs A.03.01.28 and A.03.02.05. The carnation-head corners are also similar to those used on Pluis (1997, 567) designs C.17.00.03–05. These tiles can be broadly dated to 1750–1930. Size: 131–132mm square.

Fig 14 Tiled fireplace, hall, Dora House (tile size 131–132mm square)

Reception

A fireplace with a collection of 70 Dutch tiles with blue on white landscape scenes set within purple Louis XV borders with diaper corners (Fig 16). This is another long-lived design which was in use between 1740 and 1920 (Pluis 1997, 372, 529, A.03.01.46, B.12.00.04). Size: 128mm square.

Due to the wide date range of the tiles in both fireplaces it is not certain whether they are original to the 1820s house or were added when the house was remodelled in the 1880s. The Survey of London believes the late Victorian front elevation was Dutch-inspired. If so, it is possible that the Dutch theme was extended to the installation of the two Dutch-tiled fireplaces at the same date.

Fig 15 Detail of 19th-century Dutch landscape tiles, hall, Dora House (scale *c* 1:4)

Fig 16 Detail of 19th-century Dutch landscape tiles, reception room, Dora House (scale *c* 1:4)

3 FOURNIER STREET, E1, TOWER HAMLETS

This house, together with 1 Fournier Street, was built by Joseph Drew probably in 1755 (Survey of London 1957, 216–17; Fig 6, no. 10). It is currently in private ownership. A back first floor room has a fireplace of purple on white Dutch tiles, although some are now missing. Originally there were 32 tiles at each side of the fireplace but only 25 now survive at each side. All but one show biblical scenes with spider head and barred ox-head corners (Fig 17). The other shows a landscape scene with barred ox-head corners. They probably date to the construction of the building in the mid 18th century. Size: 124–127mm square.

Fig 17 Mid 18th-century Dutch biblical tiles in first floor fireplace, 3 Fournier Street (scale *c* 1:4)

12 FOURNIER STREET, E1, TOWER HAMLETS

The house was built in 1726 by the carpenter William Tayler (Cherry et al 2005, 416; Fig 6, no. 10). Decorated tiles cover two sides of a basement light well at the back of the building. The tiling scheme is not intact as many of the tiles from the upper part of the wall are no longer present, but 159 tiles survive *in situ*. The property is currently in private ownership.

The decorative scene comprises a single continuous line of flower vase tiles in blue with octagonal powdered purple borders and carnation corners. Above, in the southern wall opposite the window, is a central diamond pattern created by a line of purple on white landscape and biblical tiles with spider head and barred ox-head corners (Fig 18). Inside the diamond is a series of blue on white tiles, all but one with barred ox-head corners. They comprise Dutch biblical tiles and Dutch and English landscape tiles. The latter include an early blue on white English landscape tile (1700–30) (Fig 19) with an

Fig 18 Tiled southern wall of light well at the back of 12 Fournier Street (tile size 125–129mm square)

identical design to that on a purple tile found at 38–46 Albert Embankment (**245**), a Liverpool landscape tile (1750–75) (Fig 20) and a later blue on pale blue London tile (*c* 1760–90) (cf **256**, **257**; Horne 1989, 30, nos 89–92).

The wall area to either side of the diamond pattern is covered by (1700–50) Dutch tiles with landscape scenes, boats, a swan and a moth or butterfly, all with spider head corners (cf **234**, **235**). The same tiles cover most of the western side wall above the line of the flower vase tiles (Fig 21). There is also a single row of landscape tiles without borders or corners. These are difficult to date but are presumably 18th century. Size: 125–129mm square.

Fig 19 Detail of early 18th-century English landscape tile with spider head corners, southern wall, 12 Fournier Street (scale *c* 1:2)

Fig 21 Early–mid 18th-century Dutch landscape tiles on the western wall of the light well, 12 Fournier Street (tile size 125–129mm square)

Fig 20 Detail of 18th-century Dutch (purple on white) and English, Liverpool (blue on white) landscape tiles, southern wall, 12 Fournier Street (scale *c* 1:2)

21 FOURNIER STREET, E1, TOWER HAMLETS

Another house constructed by William Tayler, 21 Fournier Street was built under a lease of 1725 (Fig 6, no. 10; Survey of London 1957, 218). It is currently in private ownership. The basement light well has tin-glazed tiles covering all three sides. The *in situ* tiles have not been examined in detail but have been briefly examined at pavement level.

Most of the tiles are plain white, but there are a number of purple tiles with marble decoration and purple on white landscape and biblical tiles. Other tiles are blue on white and blue with octagonal powdered purple borders. Size: unknown.

40–41 FURNIVAL STREET, EC4, CITY OF LONDON

The tiles (now removed) were found set in an alcove at the northern end in the eastern side of a brick-lined vault beneath 40–41 Furnival Street, a late 17th-century L-shaped building (MOL site code FUR87; Schofield 1998, 248; Fig 6, no. 11). The back of the alcove was lined with 16 blue on white square tiles in a panel four tiles wide by four tiles high which is bordered to the right by four border tiles (Fig 22). There were further tiles on the left side of the alcove, but these are obscured by a metal pipe so it is unclear how many were present. The majority of tiles are now in the Museum of London.

The square tiles show landscape scenes, boats and isolated solitary figures, all with barred ox-head corners (**258–262**, **345**, **346**). According to Horne (1989, 39), these are typical of the many thousands of similar tiles made in Liverpool in 1750–75. One tile shows a slightly different style of barred ox-head corner but probably belongs to the same group. Size: 124–130mm square x 6–7mm thick.

The origin of the border tiles is less certain. Two types are present, one decorated in blue on white (**444**) and the other in white with a powdered blue background (**450**). The blue on white tile has a similar pattern to that found on a London border tile of 1750–70 illustrated by Horne (1989, 70, no. 398), although he notes that tiles of similar design are

Fig 22 Eighteenth-century English, Liverpool tiles lining the alcove in a brick-lined vault, 40–41 Furnival Street (tile size 124–130mm square; 0.1m scale)

also known on Dutch tiles. The floral edging tile with the powdered blue ground is particularly unusual in London, although the same design is present on a border tile from The Mitre Hotel, Hampton Court Bridge, East Molesey, Richmond upon Thames (Surrey) (MOL site code MHL92 [+] <18>). The bluish background and slightly indistinct pattern suggests this is also English (H van Lemmen, pers comm), although it is not certain if it is from London or Liverpool. Size: 125–127 x 62–67 x 7mm.

Among the fragmentary blue on white tiles from the left side of the alcove is a black on white tile with an unusual imitation marble design (**441**).

39 HARRINGTON GARDENS, SW7, KENSINGTON AND CHELSEA

The house, built in the 1880s, is reported as having a 'large fireplace with delft tiles' (L Pearson, pers comm.; Fig 6, no. 12). The property is in private ownership.

12 KENSINGTON SQUARE, W8, KENSINGTON AND CHELSEA

The house was built *c* 1702 and is currently in private ownership (Fig 6, no. 13). There is a tiled fireplace in the entrance hall of this building, a black and white photograph of which is illustrated in the Survey of London (1986, pl 11a). The photograph appears to show late 18th- or early 19th-century landscape tiles (almost certainly blue on white), similar to those used at 33 Kensington Square (below). These are surrounded by a decorative border of rectangular tiles in a similar manner to a fireplace at Rainham Hall (below, 6, Greater London).

33 KENSINGTON SQUARE, W8, KENSINGTON AND CHELSEA

This building has five fireplaces, probably installed when the house was constructed in the early 1730s for music publisher and instrument-maker John Walsh the elder (Survey of London 1986, 39; Fig 6, no. 13). The property is under guardianship of The National Trust and is leased as a private residence. All tiles, which total 364, are in blue on white except for those on the third floor. Size: 125–130mm square.

The fireplaces on the ground and first floor comprise figurative landscape tiles with spider head corner, small barred ox-head corner or no corner motifs. These alternate with isolated figures and either spider head corner or no corner motifs. It is apparent that the tiles with the isolated figures are painted in a different style to the landscape tiles. This indicates that they are either from different delftware factories or are the work of separate tile-painters from the same factory.

Many of the tiles with isolated figures show children engaged in a wide variety of activities. Among the delightful scenes are children on stilts, skipping, playing on swings, doing handstands, playing piggy-back and playing with spinning tops: all everyday scenes in early 18th-century Dutch life. Others show cherubs, musicians, horse-riders, fishermen or people simply talking.

Ground floor (46 tiles)
Blue on white, 12 tiles set vertically either side of the fireplace with 22 tiles set in the floor in front. Interestingly, the tiles used as flooring do not have the alternating pattern discussed above but comprise mainly isolated figures with random landscape tiles.

First floor, east side (120 tiles)
Completely tiled fireplace with 96 vertical tiles and 24 horizontal examples set in the alternative pattern described earlier (Figs 23–5). Some of the figurative landscape tiles have biblical scenes. Most of the other tiles show landscape scenes (cf **234**, **235**) but there are tiles with an insect, a bird and what appears to be a fish. All have spider head corners.

Fig 23 Tiled fireplace, first floor east side, 33 Kensington Square (© National Trust)

Fig 24 Detail of 1730s Dutch tiles, first floor east side, 33 Kensington Square (© National Trust) (tile size 125–130mm square)

Fig 25 Detail of 1730s Dutch tiles, first floor east side, 33 Kensington Square (© National Trust) (tile size 125–130mm square)

First floor, west side (88 tiles)
Very similar to the east fireplace with 68 vertical tiles and 20 horizontal tiles set in the fireplace front. These are set in the same alternate pattern.

Second floor (69 tiles)
Twenty-four tiles set vertically either side of the fireplace with 21 tiles set horizontally in front (Fig 26). The tiles are less elaborate than those on the first floor as most show only isolated figures with no corner motifs. The only exceptions are five possible early–mid 18th-century Dutch landscape tiles with spider head corners; these may represent later repairs (Fig 27). Two are situated directly in front of the fire where any burning logs or coal falling from the fire would have done most damage.

Fig 26 Tiled fireplace, second floor, 33 Kensington Square (© National Trust)

Fig 27 Tiled fireplace frontage showing detail of 1730s Dutch tiles with two possible early–mid 18th-century replacements, second floor, 33 Kensington Square (© National Trust) (tile size 125–130mm square)

Fig 28 Tiled fireplace with 18th-century Dutch and English tiles, third floor, 33 Kensington Square (© National Trust)

Fig 29 Tiled fireplace frontage with 1730s Dutch tiles, third floor, 33 Kensington Square (© National Trust) (tile size 125–130mm square)

Third floor (41 tiles)

A smaller fireplace, possibly a later replacement, with a varied assortment of 20 vertical tiles with 21 tiles laid horizontally in front (Fig 28). The latter are mostly Dutch landscape tiles of early–mid 18th-century date with spider head corners which, from their battered and cracked appearance, would seem to be original (Fig 29).

The vertical tiles are a mixture of Dutch tiles, probably contemporary with those in the rest of the house, and later Dutch and English tiles. The latter include two with polychrome flower designs and a landscape tile with an octagonal border, all made in Liverpool in 1750–75 (for similar tiles see Horne 1989, 53, nos 275–277, 25, nos 61–63 respectively). Also present is a blue landscape tile with a circular powdered purple border with blue cherub-head corners, probably made in London *c* 1725–50. Two similar tiles are illustrated in Horne (1989, 19, nos 17–18).

2 KING EDWARD STREET, EC1, CITY OF LONDON

A large number of mid 17th- to 18th-century tiles were found lining a water cistern associated with a building rebuilt after the Great Fire of 1666 (Merrill Lynch Financial Centre, formerly known as King Edward Buildings (GPO site), MOL site codes KEB92, KEW98; Lyon 2007, 126–7, 130; Fig 6, no. 15). They are a diverse mixture of Dutch and English designs with both Liverpool and London types represented. Particularly rare in London are two woodblock-printed tiles made in Liverpool by John Sadler between 1756 and 1757 and copperplate designs made by Sadler's successor Guy Green, and probably Sadler's apprentice Richard Abbey, between 1770 and *c* 1780.

Illustrations of each of the main design types can be found in Betts (2007b, 150–63), and many of the more important designs are also illustrated in the design catalogue (**210–212, 214, 230, 234, 236, 254, 255, 263, 266, 275, 277–279, 284, 288, 291–293, 302, 305, 321, 327, 342, 353, 372, 373, 382, 388, 390, 395, 402, 404, 406, 411, 415, 416, 419, 424–427, 429, 434–436, 438, 447, 459, 462, 474, 475, 478, 479, 481**).

LIBERTY, 210 REGENT STREET, W1, WESTMINSTER

Two tiled fireplaces are in the Tudor house, a black and white fantasy building on the south site of Great Marlborough Street built in 1922–3 to the design of architects E T and E S Hall (Survey of London 1963, 307; Fig 6, no. 16). The building is currently in private ownership.

Third floor

Fireplace with a bizarre mixture of blue on white, purple on white, blue and purple on white and polychrome tiles. There are 64 tiles set in a totally random pattern. Present are landscapes (33 tiles), ships (13 tiles), flowers or ornaments (8 tiles), biblical scenes (5 tiles), figures (2 tiles), soldiers (2 tiles) and an animal (1 tile). They display a variety of borders and corner motifs.

The fireplace decoration comprises principally a mixture of reused 17th-century Dutch tiles with late 18th-/early 19th-century tiles from the same country. The former include two tiles with design **189** and another with a dog set in the same border as **183**. The later tiles include two blue and purple landscape tiles of similar design to those at Dora House (above; Fig 16), a two-colour lattice and floral pattern dated 1860–1900 (Pluis 1997, 111, 139, no. 63) and a blue on white copy of a Valencian tile design dated *c* 1860–1910 (Pluis 1997, 334, A.01.70.21). The latter are also present in Linley Sambourne House (below). Size: 126–132mm square.

Fourth floor

Large fireplace with 270 Dutch tiles, although 34 are largely hidden from view (Fig 30). The majority of tiles, most of which appear to be of 17th-century date, show isolated figures with no corner decoration. They are bordered by tiles with a wide variety of border and corner motifs which are mainly decorated with flowers, landscape scenes and mythical figures. One tile is upside down, whilst two others are placed sideways (similar tile placement was noted at Rainham Hall; below, 6, Greater London). All the tiles are

Fig 30 Nineteenth-century tiled fireplace with 17th-century Dutch tiles, fourth floor, Liberty

LIBERTY – FOURTH FLOOR

- Three-headed tulip design in barbed circular border with Wan Li corner motifs (cf **189**) dated 1620–60 (van Dam 1991, 53, no. 54; Pluis 1997, 417, A.05.04.04).
- Flower vase design. Tiles with similar corner motifs dated by Pluis to 1625–50 (1997, 551, C.07.00.15).
- Flowers set within a lozenge-shaped border with spider head corners. Tiles with this design were made from 1630 until the 20th century (Pluis 1997, 527, B.10.00.08), but the example in the fireplace would appear to be 17th century.
- Flower vase within similar lozenge border but with fleur-de-lis corners; similar tiles are dated to 1640–70 (van Dam 1991 69, no. 76; Pluis 1997, 527, B.10.00.05).
- Rabbit set in circular border with same corner decoration as seen on **167–171**. Tiles with the same corner and border arrangement are dated 1630–50 by Pluis (1997, 551, C.07.00.18).

blue on white, but a small number have certain decorative elements painted in purple. Size: 126–132mm square; 126–128mm square (with isolated figures).

The tiles with the isolated figures (cf **314**) are difficult to date precisely, but were probably made *c* 1680–1750. Further design types can be dated (see left).

LINLEY SAMBOURNE HOUSE, 18 STAFFORD TERRACE, W8, KENSINGTON AND CHELSEA

Construction of Stafford Terrace began in 1868 and 18 was one of the last to be occupied, having been leased to a Mrs Elizabeth Bentley in May 1871 (Fig 6, no. 20). The house passed into the possession of Linley and Marion Sambourne in 1875 (Robbins et al 2003, 12, 16) and is currently in the ownership of the Royal Borough of Kensington and Chelsea.

Fig 31 Tiled fireplace, Principal Bedroom, Linley Sambourne House (photo by English School; © Linley Sambourne House, London, UK/The Bridgeman Art Library) (tile size 130–131mm square)

Morning Room (32 tiles)

Sixteen polychrome Dutch tiles set either side of the fireplace (Fig 9). These are all polychrome flower vase tiles with diamond borders dating to 1880–1930 (Pluis 1997, 141, top, 422, A.05.08.05). A very similar tile from Brooke House is illustrated in Fig 35. Size: 129–131mm square.

Roy's Bedroom (12 tiles)

Six blue on white Dutch tiles set either side of the fireplace, all showing mounted soldiers in a circular border with ox-head corners. These are of large type (148–150mm square) made specifically for the British market (van Lemmen 2005, 39). Most were made by Ravesteijn (renamed Westraven after 1907) in Utrecht during the late 19th–early 20th century.

Principal Bedroom (40 tiles)

Fireplace covered by 40 unusual blue on white Dutch tiles (Pluis 1997, 334, A.01.70.21; Fig 31). They are dated by Pluis to 1890–1910, but the start date would appear to be too late as the design can be found in a short piece on art tiles in *The Furniture Gazette* of 22 April 1876 (Anon 1876; H van Lemmen, pers comm). The design is copied from a mid 15th-century Valencian tile design which is known on tiles from Woking Palace, Surrey (Betts 2008b, 65, fig 3). Size: 130–131mm square.

ST BARTHOLOMEW'S HOSPITAL, WEST SMITHFIELD, EC1, CITY OF LONDON

St Bartholomew's Hospital is the oldest hospital in London, being founded in 1123 (Fig 4, no. 21; Fig 6, no. 21). Most of the tiles were installed during a major rebuilding of the hospital in the mid 18th century. There are 153 tiles in the museum archives at the hospital, all but one of which are wall tiles.

The single floor tile was found below the surface of the courtyard adjacent to the King George V block opened in 1937. It is a polychrome tile of similar design to **104–107**. London; early–mid 17th century. Size: ? x 139 x 19mm.

South wing

These wall tiles (see below) are believed to have been installed in bathrooms in the south wing of the hospital which was completed in 1739 and demolished in 1935 to make way for the King George V block. It is also possible some tiles could have come from the north wing (1738), west wing (1752) or east wing (1768) (St Bartholomew's Hospital, pers comm). If the tiles are from the south wing, then they may be slightly earlier than some of the published dates given below, as may some of the tiles installed in the north wing.

North wing (James Gibb's house)

A number of tiles were recovered from the north wing constructed in 1738 (see right).

Location uncertain (possibly south wing)

As the tiles believed to be from the south wing are all English and these (see far right) come from a separate box marked 'Dutch', it is possible that the Dutch and English tiles from the south wing were separated at some stage.

ST BARTHOLOMEW'S HOSPITAL – SOUTH WING

BLUE ON WHITE

- Landscape tiles painted in similar style to **211**, **212** and Horne (1989, 39–40) nos 167–181. Liverpool; 1750–75. Size: 127mm square x 7mm.
- Landscape in circular border, barred ox-head corners. Similar to Horne (1989, 29) nos 80–88. Two tiles show almost identical scenes to that on Horne nos 71 and 88. London; 1740–60. Size: 127–129mm square x 7–8mm.
- Classical ruin in barbed medallion border with quarter flower-head corners (**499**). A landscape tile with this very rare corner/border arrangement is in Ray (1973, 169, no. 278). Liverpool; 1750–75. Size: 126–127mm square x 6mm.
- Landscape in very unusual spotted circular border with Michaelmas daisy corners (**500**). The same design is in Archer (1997, 454, N138) where it is described as Bristol or possibly Liverpool, 1750–75. Size: 125mm square x 6mm.
- Landscape in Louis XV border with diaper corners. Similar landscape tiles are shown in **288**, **289** and by Horne (1989, 45), nos 209–217. One scene, showing a milkmaid with a churn, is shown in Ray (1973, 155, 210). Liverpool; 1750–80. Size: 127mm square x 7mm.
- Flower vase with circular border and unusual flower-head corners. Similar flower vases are illustrated by Horne (1989, 62–3, nos 341, 346, 349, 351). London; 1730–60. Size: 126mm square x 7–8mm.
- Flower vase design with dotted flower-head corners. The flower vases and corner decoration show similarities to six tiles in Horne (1989, 60, nos 320–325). London; 1720–40. Size: 126mm square x 8–9mm.
- A similar flower vase design but painted in paler blue on a slightly bluish-white background. Similar corner decoration to Horne (1989, 61), no. 332 (cf **408**, **409**). London; 1740–70. Size: 126mm square x 6mm.
- Crude flower vases. One has a very similar vase to that shown on a tile in Horne (1989, 66, no. 369). Liverpool; 1750–75. Size: 124–127mm square x 8mm.
- Flowers in barbed medallion border with quarter flower-head corners. A similar tile is illustrated by Horne (1989, 64), no. 358. Liverpool; 1750–70. Size: 126mm square x 7mm.
- Flowers with unusual flower corners. A similar tile is illustrated by Horne (1989, 67), no. 380. Liverpool; 1780–1800. Size: 127mm square x 6mm.
- Flowers set in extremely rare jagged border (**501**). Liverpool; *c* 1760–80. Size: 123–125 square x 7mm.
- Stylised flower design. As Horne (1989, 71) no. 408, but without corner decoration. Liverpool; 1760–90. Size: 125–127mm square x 8mm.
- Tiles showing goats and sheep which derived from a book of etchings by Nicolaes Berchem (**504**). Similar tiles can be found at Nonsuch, Surrey (Betts 2008a, 15). Liverpool; 1750–75. Size: 126mm square x 7mm.
- A Tamarisk tree (**502**). The same design is in Ray (1973, 209, no. 470) and Archer (1997, 474, N225). Liverpool; 1750–75. Size: 125–126mm square x 7mm.
- Very rare biblical tile showing Samson pushing down the philistine temple (Judges 16 v. 29) (**503**). London; 1740–60. Size: 130mm square x 7mm.

BLUE ON WHITE WITH PURPLE BORDER

- Blue on white landscape scenes set in octagonal powdered purple border with blue on white ragged flower corners. One tile, showing a harbour scene, is very similar to two tiles illustrated by Archer (1997, 457, N149–N150). Liverpool; 1750–75. Size: 124mm square x 6mm.
- Blue on white landscape scene in scalloped circular powdered purple border with blue on white quarter rosette corners (cf **303**, **304**). Horne (1989, 20–21, nos 22–30) illustrates one Liverpool and seven Bristol tiles in the same decorative style. ?Liverpool; 1725–50. Size: 122–124mm square x 8mm.

ST BARTHOLOMEW'S HOSPITAL – NORTH WING

BLUE ON WHITE

- Landscape in circular border, barred ox-head corners. One scene, showing a man carrying a basket, is found on London tiles in Ray (1973, 139, no. 138) and Horne (1989, 30, no. 94), whilst another showing a tower is on another London tile in Ray (1973, 163, no. 250). London; 1740–60. Size: 127–129mm square x 7–8mm.
- Landscape in circular border, barred ox-head corners. One tile has a similar scene to that shown on a tile in Ray (1973, 175, no. 306). Liverpool; 1740–75. Size: ? x 127 x 6–7mm.
- Biblical scene in circular border, barred ox-head corners. The barred ox-head corners are similar to London biblical tiles illustrated in Horne dated to 1730–60 (Horne 1989, 79, no. 463, 80, no. 466, 85, no. 502). Among the scenes represented are: Cain slaying Abel (Genesis 4 v. 4), Jephthah setting out against the children of Ammon (Judges 11 v. 32), Jonah and the whale (Jonah 2 v. 10), the Annunciation (Luke 1 v. 28), the dutiful servant (Luke 17 vv. 7–10), and the Crucifixion (John 19 v. 26). London; 1730–60. Size: 129mm square x 8–9mm.

PLAIN

- Pale blue. Probably London; 1700–1800. Size: 125mm square x 6mm.

ST BARTHOLOMEW'S HOSPITAL – LOCATION UNCERTAIN

- Landscape scene covering whole tile. **224** shows a similar scene, but with buildings above the boat on the right. Dutch; 1700–1800. Size: 128mm square x 7–8mm.
- A more crudely painted landscape scene covering whole tile. A similar boat is present on a Liverpool tile in Ray (1973, 175, no. 303). Liverpool; 1740–75. Size: 126mm square x 7mm.
- Landscape with spider head corner (cf **226–230**). Dutch; 1700–50 (one may be 1700–1800). Size: 129–130mm square x 7–8mm.
- Landscape in circular border, barred ox-head corners. Dutch; 1700–1800. Size: ? x 128 x 9mm.
- Landscape in circular border, spider head corners. Dutch; 1700–1800. Size: 128mm square x 7mm.
- Landscape in octagonal border with quarter flower-head corners. Similar to **271–274**. Dutch, Rotterdam; 1740–80. Size: 128mm square x 6mm.
- Biblical scene in circular border, barred ox-head corners. Scenes include the return of the prodigal son (Luke 15 v. 20) and the last supper (Matthew 26 vv. 20–25). The latter is not an English design. Dutch; 1700–1800. Size: *c* 130mm square x 7mm.
- Landscape with birds, spider head corners. One, showing a swan, is almost identical to a tile illustrated by van Sabben and Hollem (1987, 129, no. 398). Dutch; 1700–50. Size: 129mm square x 7–8mm.
- Flower vase, barred ox-head corners. Same design as **402**. Dutch; 1670–1700. Size: 125mm square x 9mm.
- Flower vase, with same fleur-de-lis corners as **405**, **406**. Dutch; 1700–1800. Size: 127 x 128 x 7mm.
- Three-headed tulip in wavy circular border, Wan Li corners. Same design as **189**. Dutch; 1620–1700. Size: 125mm square x 9mm.

PURPLE ON WHITE

- Landscape, spider head corner. Dutch; 1700–1800, or later. Size: 129 x 128 x 7mm.
- Biblical, circular border, ox-head corners (not barred). Christ at the column (John 19 v. 1). ?Dutch; 1700–1800. Size: 128 x 129 x 7mm.

BLUE ON WHITE WITH PURPLE BORDER

- Landscape set in octagonal, powdered purple border with carnation corners. Horne (1989, 22–4) shows a number of London tiles painted in a similar style. London; 1740–60. Size: 125mm square x 9mm.
- Landscape set in elaborate wavy circular, powdered purple border with fleur-de-lis corners (**505**). A Dutch tile with this design is in Pluis (1997, 519, B.01.00.25). Dutch; 1720–50. Size: 125mm square x 8mm.

ST GEORGE THE MARTYR CHURCH, BOROUGH HIGH STREET, SE1, SOUTHWARK

The present building, a replacement of a medieval church, was constructed in 1734–6 (Cherry and Pevsner 1983, 576; Fig 6, no. 18). It is currently in the ownership of the parish. The vestry fireplace is lined with 84 decorated blue on white Dutch biblical tiles dating from the period 1770–1810 (Fig 32). Identical biblical tiles made at Makkum are illustrated in Pluis (1997, 389, A.03.08.12, 528, B.11.00.07). A total of 56 tiles line the back of the fireplace, whilst a further 14 tiles are located along each side.

The back and the two side panels are framed by a single row of 51 plain white glazed tiles which have been cut to a rectangular shape. These tiles, which measure 153mm in length, are larger than the decorated examples. It is not certain whether they are tin-glazed or later Victorian machine-made products. Size (decorated tile): 129–130mm square.

Fig 32 Detail of late 18th- to early 19th-century Dutch biblical tiles, St George the Martyr (tile size 129–130mm square)

30 SPITAL SQUARE, E1, TOWER HAMLETS

Thirty-six tin-glazed tiles decorated the front of a fireplace in the first floor back room (Fig 6, no. 17). The house was built by William Goswell in about 1739 and demolished in 1922. The fireplace can be seen on two black and white photographs in the Survey of London volume for Spitalfields (1957, 68, figs 30a and c). Unfortunately, the tiles are very indistinct, although they appear to be landscape scenes set in circular borders.

Fig 33 Tiled fireplace, Steam Engine public house (tile size 130mm square)

STEAM ENGINE PUBLIC HOUSE, COSSER STREET, SE1, LAMBETH

The Steam Engine public house is currently in private ownership (Fig 6, no. 19). The fireplace is tiled with 46 decorated blue on white and four very thin rectangular plain white tiles (Fig 33). The decorated tiles have a military theme with foot soldiers and mounted horsemen and have stylised spider head corners (Fig 34). They have been identified by Chris Blanchett as being by Ravesteijn (renamed Westraven after 1907) of Utrecht and date to the late 19th or early 20th century (L Pearson, pers comm). Size: 130mm square.

Fig 34 Detail of late 19th- or early 20th-century Dutch tiles in fireplace, Steam Engine public house (scale *c* 1:4)

WESTMINSTER SYNAGOGUE, KENT HOUSE, RUTLAND GARDENS, SW7, KENSINGTON AND CHELSEA

This house was built in 1872–4 for Lady Ashburton, widow of William Baring Bingham, 2nd Baron Ashburton (Fig 6, no. 14). It is currently in the ownership of Westminster Synagogue. The old library on the first floor had delft tiles located at either side of the fireplace. The arrangement was somewhat unusual in consisting of an alternating pattern of blue on white and purple on white tiles. A colour photograph of the fireplace showing the arrangement is illustrated in the Knightsbridge volume of the Survey of London (2000, 135, pl 118c). The fireplace was removed during renovation work and sold at auction in 2002/3 (P Ashleigh, pers comm). Its current whereabouts is unknown.

GREATER LONDON AREA BUILDINGS

BROMLEY HALL, 43 GILLENDER STREET, BROMLEY-BY-BOW, E14, TOWER HAMLETS (MIDDLESEX)

Bromley Hall is a much altered late 15th-century brick tower house (T P Smith, pers comm). Five tiles were found with other building debris within the building (MOL site code BTI02; Smith 2003; Fig 5; Fig 7).

English, London, probably Aldgate pothouse

Late 16th- to early 17th-century medallion floor tile with central chequerboard design of **54**, but with more usual corner decoration seen on **42–53**. Two other blackened corner fragments may have the same design. Size: 16–17mm thick.

English, London, probably Rotherhithe pothouse

Floor tiles with diamond borders and fleur-de-lis corner motifs dating to 1640–70. One of the latter has unusual light blue shading. There are Dutch tiles with similar border and corner decoration (van Dam 1991, 69, no. 77; **147**) and similar tiles were made in London at Rotherhithe (Tyler et al 2008, 87, fig 141, D12). Size: 11–14mm thick.

English/Dutch

Blue on white wall tile, probably mid–late 17th century, with small-sized barred ox-head corner motif. It is possible that this came from a tiled fireplace known to have been present in the building. A description of the house in 1900 mentions that one fireplace was 'tiled round with interesting old figured tiles' (Survey of London 1900, 17), almost certainly tin-glazed. Size: 10mm thick.

BROOKE HOUSE, JUNCTION OF LEA BRIDGE ROAD AND UPPER CLAPTON ROAD, E5, HACKNEY (MIDDLESEX)

The earliest part of the house was probably built for William Worsley, who owned the estate from 1476 to 1496.

BROOKE HOUSE – FLOOR TILE

- A geometric pattern (cf **92**). Probably made in London some time in the late 16th–mid 17th century as tiles of this design were produced at both Pickleherring and Rotherhithe. EH 1702; size: 138 x 135 x 15–16mm.
- Fleur-de-lis corner of interlocking strapwork design in blue and orange (cf **83**, **84**). English, London, Pickleherring or Rotherhithe, *c* 1618–50; 85.3.195i; size: ? x ? x 14mm.
- Medallion tile with central chequerboard pattern in blue and orange set in multi-circular blue and purple border (cf **51**). English, London, Aldgate or Dutch, late 16th–early 17th century; 85.3.195ii; size: ? x ? x 15–16mm
- Two tiles with strapwork pattern with semicircular corner decoration (**78**). English, London or Dutch, late 16th–early 17th century; 85.3.195iii and iv; size: 134–135 x 134–135 x 15–16mm.

?FLOOR TILE

- Dutch flower design in green, purple and blue with crude blue barred ox-head corner (cf **153**). EH 1700; size: ? x 133 x 14mm.

Fig 35 Selection of 19th- to early 20th-century Dutch tiles recovered from Brooke House (tile size 124–130mm square)

The installation of a delftware tiled floor may relate to the later form of the house, surrounding a double courtyard, dated between 1630 and 1666. Later alterations were made in the early 18th century when the house ceased to be a private residence and was divided up. The wall tiles (Fig 35) seem to date from after 1758, when Brooke House became a lunatic asylum. The house, which was damaged by bombing in the Second World War, was demolished in 1954 (TNA: Tudor Hackney; Survey of London 1960, 67–75; Fig 5; Fig 7).

English Heritage (EH) has 17 tin-glazed tiles from Brooke House comprising floor (see previous page) and wall tiles (see right), with four further floor tiles from Brooke House in the Museum of London.

BROOKE HOUSE – WALL TILE

- Polychrome flower vase design in octagonal powdered blue border with red carnation-head corners (Fig 35, top left). Probably Dutch, flower vase designs with similar corners are dated by Pluis to 1800–1930 (1997, 428, A.05.08.42). EH 1697; size: 124 x 127 x 6mm.
- Polychrome flower vase in diagonal border (Fig 35, top middle); a Dutch tile design dated to 1880–1930. Almost identical tiles are illustrated by Pluis (1997, 141, no. 66, 422, A.05.08.05). EH 1699; size: 129 x 130 x 7mm.
- Polychrome landscape scene with a typical Dutch border design (Fig 35, top right); a similar tile is illustrated in Pluis (1997, 369, A.03.01.33). The bright colours are typical of Dutch landscape tiles of the 19th century (Schaap 1984, 174). Printed tile catalogues show that tiles of this design were made at both Harlingen (van Lemmen 1986, 25) and Utrecht (Pluis 1997, 162, no. 110). The Brook House tiles are probably late 19th or early 20th century in date. EH 1528.1/4/5 (three tiles); size: 129 x 126 x 7mm.
- Polychrome landscape tiles in octagonal Louis XV border with diaper corners (Fig 35, bottom left). This border was used on Dutch tiles from 1740 to 1920 (Pluis 1997, 529, B.12.00.04), but the painting style and colouring indicate a late 19th- or early 20th-century date. Again this design is in the Harlingen and Utrecht tile catalogues illustrated by van Lemmen (1986, 25) and Pluis (1997, 162, no. 110). EH 1530.1; size: 130 x 128 x 7mm.
- Blue version of above (Fig 35, bottom middle), probably from the same Dutch tile factory as the polychrome examples. EH 1533.1/2/3/4/5/6/7 (seven tiles); size: 130 x 129 x 7mm.
- Boy with hoop, very small spider head corners in blue (Fig 35, bottom right). The corners are very similar to a tile in Pluis (1997, 557, C.08.00.16), dated 1800–40. Pluis also shows a late 19th-century tile with fairly similar spider head corners together with a boy playing with a hoop (1997, 383, A.03.06.07). The Brooke House tile is also probably 19th century in date. EH 1531; size: 131 x 130 x 6–7mm.
- Blue floral arrangement with winged cherubs; a Dutch design dated 1740–1850 (**417**). EH 1696; size: 131 x 130 x 6–7mm.

CARSHALTON HOUSE WATER TOWER, WEST STREET, CARSHALTON, SM5, SUTTON (SURREY)

The tiles at Carshalton House water tower (Fig 7) have been the subject of a detailed study (Skelton 1998) so only a brief summary will be given here. According to recent research by Andrew Skelton, who has kindly provided much of the information below, the water tower was probably built 1717–20. It is currently in private ownership. A document dated

Fig 36 Tile-lined bath, Carshalton House water tower, Carshalton (tile size (plain) 125–127mm square, (decorated, complete) 130–131mm square)

to *c* 1722 lists 'a bathing roome lined with galley tyles paved with marble [and] two marble baths' (Skelton in prep). The tile surrounds on the walls are clearly those mentioned in the document, but not those in the bath itself. These must have been installed when the two marble baths were replaced by the present single bath sometime before 1815.

The tiles on the walls, now believed to be Dutch, comprise extensive areas of white tiles divided by bands of decorated tiles (Fig 36). All the decorated tiles have vases of flowers in blue on white set within an octagonal powdered purple border with carnation-head corners (Fig 37).

Fig 37 Detail of early 18th-century Dutch flower vase tiles, Carshalton House water tower (scale *c* 1:4)

The plain tiles surrounding the current single bath have a thick uneven glaze and some have dished depressions in the tile centre. According to Chris Blanchett (pers comm) these features are typical of Dutch-made tiles. They occur in a variety of shades of light blue, cream and pink, and in this respect are very similar to the plain Dutch tiles used at Ham House (below). There is no indication as to date of the plain tiles used in the water tower bath. Size: 125–127mm square (plain); 130–131mm square (decorated, complete); 127–128mm square (decorated, trimmed).

CEDAR HOUSE, VINE LANE, UXBRIDGE, UB10, HILLINGDON (MIDDLESEX)

This is a handsome brick-built house mainly dating to the 17th century, although the more interesting features of the interior rooms seem to be the result of the 'Jacobeanising' efforts of the 19th and 20th centuries (Cherry and Pevsner 1991, 337). It is currently in private ownership (Fig 7).

Ground floor office (84 tiles)

Large fireplace lined with a random mixture of mid 17th- to 18th- or early 19th-century Dutch tiles showing a wide variety of decorative designs (Fig 38). The majority of the tiles are blue on white, although at least two black on white (Fig 39) and blue and purple on white tiles are present (others may be hidden from view behind a filing cabinet). The latter are painted in blue but have the central design outlined in purple, as at Waxwell Farm, Pinner, Harrow (Middlesex) (below). The random position of the tiles suggests that they were added during the 19th or 20th century, but it is possible that the 17th- and 18th-century designs may originally have come from other rooms in the building.

Fig 38 A selection of mid 17th- to early 19th-century Dutch tiles, ground floor fireplace, Cedar House (tile size 125–130mm square)

The decorative designs depicted comprise boats, animals, birds, military figures, sea monsters and fish, landscapes and biblical scenes. The biblical and some of the landscape scenes are set in circular borders. There is also a variety of corner motifs present comprising spider head, barred ox-head and fleur-de-lis corners. A number of the latter have more elaborate borders with semicircular decorative elements on the tile sides (cf **183**, **184**); these tiles can be dated to 1620–50 (Pluis 1997, 531, B.13.00.01). Size: 125–130mm square.

Ground floor toilet (25 tiles)

A small toilet cubical with blue on white landscape tiles set along three sides in a horizontal line at waist height. All are Dutch landscape tiles with barred ox-head corners. The corner decoration is very similar to that on a biblical tile in Pluis, dated to 1890–1920 (1997, 553, C.07.00.36). Size: 130–131mm square.

First floor (48 tiles)

Fireplace with 24 Dutch tiles set either side of the grate (Fig 40). They are in blue on white, although four tiles have the central boat design picked out in purple. They are set in an alternating decorative pattern of animal tiles and ship tiles (Fig 41). The animal tiles have circular borders while the boat tiles are without borders. The middle tile at the base of the left-hand panel should be an animal tile, but this has been replaced at some stage with a tile showing a mythical sea creature.

Some of the animals are set in highly decorative circular borders with a spotted zigzag motif which Pluis dates to 1620–50 (1997, 521, B.02.00.08). Others have less elaborate borders but are dated to around the same period (1630–50). It seems possible that these Cedar House tiles, apart from the later replacement, are part of an original early–mid 17th-century fireplace. Size: 125–127mm square.

Fig 39 Detail of unusual black on white tile, ground floor fireplace, Cedar House (scale *c* 1:2)

Fig 40 Fireplace, first floor, Cedar House (tile size 125–127mm square)

Fig 41 Detail of early–mid 17th-century Dutch tiles, first floor fireplace, Cedar House (scale *c* 1:4)

CHARLTON HOUSE, CHARLTON ROAD, CHARLTON, SE7, GREENWICH (KENT)

Construction of the house by Sir Adam Newton began in *c* 1607 and was practically complete by 1612. Decorative repairs and additions were made by Sir William Ducie in 1659, whilst during the ownership of the Wilson family in the 19th century domestic buildings were added to the south of the house (RCHM(E) 1930, 31; Fig 7). Charlton House is currently in the ownership of Greenwich Council. It is of particular interest in the study of tin-glazed tiles as many of the fireplaces have close copies of earlier Dutch and Spanish floor tile designs. These tiles have been examined by Chris Blanchett, who has kindly provided the following information:

> Many of the tiles are products of Frederick Garrard who was based at West Ferry Road, Millwall, London and produced tiles in imitation of early delftware and Spanish *arista* tiles. They are convincing imitations and their true origin is only apparent on close inspection. The tin glaze that Garrard used on his delftware tiles has a very 'silky' feel and absorbs the green colour which runs slightly into the surrounding white. The yellow he used was based on chromium rather than the arsenic yellow of traditional Dutch tiles. This yellow is better developed and sinks completely into the tin glaze, unlike the old pigment which tends to stand on the surface. The body clay which Garrard used is a deep brick red, unlike the rather pinkish red clay of early Dutch tiles and this is evident sometimes where the tin glaze is slightly thinner. The tiles were probably manufactured in the 1870s or 1880s. Garrard was still designing tiles in the late 1880s but died in 1893 (Pearson 2005, 458).

Fig 42 Late 19th-century reproductions of a 17th-century Dutch and English tile design, Entrance Hall, ground floor, Charlton House (tile size 130mm square)

Ground floor

ENTRANCE HALL (192 TILES)

Fireplace with 96 polychrome tiles with floral decoration on each side of the grate (Fig 42). These are Victorian copies of a 17th-century Dutch and English tile design. For 17th-century examples see **104–107**. Size: 130mm square.

Fig 43 Early–mid 17th-century Dutch tiles, Red Parlour, ground floor, Charlton House (tile size 128–131mm square)

RED PARLOUR (*c* 120 TILES, SOME OBSCURED FROM VIEW BEHIND A STOVE)

Blue on white Dutch tiles dated to 1620–60 line three sides of a fireplace (Fig 43). Some of the tiles are discoloured and cracked, suggesting that they may be in their original position. If this is so, they may have been added during Ducie's refurbishment of the house in 1659. All show either a single military figure, sometimes mounted, or single persons involved in various activities. The corner motifs are of barred ox-head or fleur-de-lis type (Pluis 1997, 361, 543, C.02.00.07 and fairly similar to A.02.13.01), or a more unusual variety (see **203–205**; illustrated by Pluis 1997, 547, C.04.00.02). Size: 128–131mm square.

DELFT CORRIDOR

Not delft tiles but a complete covering of machine-made 19th-century blue on white tiles. A detached tile from the same factory shows seven ridges on the base but no maker's marks. They are all French tiles by Blin Freres, Aubagne, Bouches-du-Rhône (C Blanchett, pers comm). Size: 147mm square.

STUDY (14 DELFT TILES)
Tiled fireplace containing a mixture of delft tiles and the French tiles used in the Delft Corridor. The former comprise 12 decorated blue on white tiles with a flower vase in a circular border with crudely painted Wan Li corner motifs. A similar tile made at Harlingen in the Netherlands in 1870–90 is illustrated by Pluis (1997, 141, no. 66). The remaining two delft tiles show a landscape scene with figures set in a circular border and with small spider head corner motifs. They are very similar to two Dutch tiles in van Dam (1991, 115, no. 140) dated 1760–1810 and a tile in Pluis (1997, 378, A.03.03.04) *c* 1790. Size (delft tiles): 130mm square.

Fig 44 Late 19th- to early 20th-century Dutch tiles with sailing ships, Green Room, first floor, Charlton House, Charlton, Greenwich (tile size 147mm square)

First floor

GREEN ROOM (78 TILES)
Tiled fireplace with distinctive green and blue on white Dutch tiles decorated with boats and ships (Fig 44). Pluis shows a very similar tile dated 1890–1910 from the factory at Harlingen (1997, 143, no. 72, top right). Size: 147mm square.

Second floor

SALOON (108 TILES)
Fireplace with polychrome floral tiles. These are Victorian copies of a 17th-century Dutch and English tile design. For a 17th-century example see **101**. Size: 132mm square.

LONG GALLERY (129 TILES)
Fireplace with back and sides covered with 129 blue on white tiles with Tudor rose and strapwork design (Fig 45). This is a Victorian copy of a well-known tile design made in London during the late 16th–mid 17th century. For a 17th-century example see **111**. Size: 130–131mm square.

Fig 45 Late 19th-century reproductions of a late 16th- to mid 17th-century Dutch and English tile design, Long Gallery, second floor, Charlton House (tile size 130–131mm square)

DUTCH ROOM (120 TILES)
Polychrome tiles with central interlace pattern covering fireplace back and sides. These are Victorian copies of a 17th-century English tile design. For 17th-century examples see **83** and **84**.
Size: 132mm square.

SOUTH-WEST BEDROOM, PRINCE HENRY ROOM (97 TILES)
Fireplace with back and sides decorated with polychrome flower vase tiles (Fig 46). This is a Victorian copy of a late 16th-century Dutch tile design. For a late 16th-century example see **134**. Size: 132–134mm square.

WHITE DRAWING ROOM (104 TILES)
Fireplace covered on the back and sides with polychrome flower design (Fig 47). This is a probable Victorian copy of a late 16th-century Dutch tile design. Size: 129–133mm square.

Fig 46 Late 19th-century reproductions of a late 16th-century Dutch tile design, South-West Bedroom, second floor, Charlton House (scale *c* 1:4)

DRESSING ROOM G (14 TILES)

Fireplace with 12 square and two rectangular Spanish *arista* tiles (Fig 48). Garrard also made copies of Spanish *arista* tiles, so these too are probably late Victorian. Square tiles with the same design were made in Toledo, Spain, in 1550–75 (Ray 2000, 342, no. 798). Toledo also produced similar rectangular-shaped tiles (Ray 2000, 350, nos 852–853). Size: 149mm square; 149 x 49mm (rectangular tiles).

Fig 47 Late 19th-century reproductions of a probable late 16th-century Dutch tile design, White Drawing Room, second floor, Charlton House (scale *c* 1:4)

Fig 48 Probable London-made late 19th-century Spanish *arista* tiles, Dressing Room G, second floor, Charlton House (square tile size 149 x 149mm)

CHURCH END FARM – FLOOR TILE

- Corner of polychrome floral and geometric design (cf **68**), although only the blue on white corner survives (Gapp and Willey 2005, 69, fig 64). London or Dutch, late 16th–mid 17th century. Size: ?x ? x 16mm.
- Small fragment showing animal head in yellow outlined in yellow. No surviving dimensions.
- A further polychrome tile was recovered from Church Terrace, opposite Church End Farm, in 1973–4 (HADAS site code CT73–74, [D3] <20>). This is a so-called medallion tile showing what appears to be a fox with Dutch style of corner decoration (cf **55**). Dutch, 1570–1600. Size: 134 x ? x 17–19mm.

CHURCH END FARM – WALL TILE

- Mounted soldier in purple on white, Dutch, *c* 1680–1750.
- Landscape or biblical scene with barred ox-head corners, English or Dutch late 17th–18th century.
- Landscape scene in blue on white, English or Dutch, 18th century.
- Flower vase with flanking birds, set in octagonal powdered purple border with carnation-head corners (Gapp and Willey 2005, 69, fig 65). A very similar design is shown on London tiles of 1740–60 illustrated by Horne (1989, 62, nos 340–341; cf **421**).

CHURCH END FARM, CHURCH END, HENDON, NW4, BARNET (MIDDLESEX)

The first phase of Church End Farm dates to *c* 1625–66, but most of the tiles recovered were probably added during the second phase dated to 1660–1760 when the farmhouse was extended (Brunning et al in Pearce 2005, 27–30). The farmhouse was damaged during the Second World War and subsequently demolished (Fig 5; Fig 7).

Both tin-glazed wall and floor tiles were recovered during excavations on the site of the farm between 1961 and 1966 (HADAS site code CEF61–66). These are discussed in Gapp and Willey (2005, 69–70), so only a brief summary is presented here (see left). Only certain tiles have been measured. The floor tiles could have come from the first phase of Church End Farm, but there is also the possibility they may derive from Church Farm farmhouse (now Church Farmhouse Museum) or from St Mary's church, both of which lie in close proximity to the site. The wall tiles are more likely to be from Church End Farm.

EAGLE HOUSE, HIGH STREET, WIMBLEDON, SW19, MERTON (SURREY)

The tiles are in a large Jacobean house constructed in 1613, with major additions in *c* 1730 and 1986–7. The property is currently in private ownership (Fig 7).

First floor bedroom, Pitt's Room

Fireplace with 24 tiles either side of the central fire. Rather oddly, one tile in the left-hand panel (top row, third tile from left) has been set upside down, although this is largely hidden from view by the overhanging mantelpiece. All show blue on white figurative landscape scenes set in an octagonal powdered purple border with blue on white carnation-head corners (Fig 49). The corner motif and the decorative style of the central landscape is very similar to a London tile illustrated in Horne (1989, 23, no. 47), whilst another has a figurative landscape very similar to that shown on another London tile (Horne 1989, 29, no. 83). The Eagle House tiles are London products dated to 1740–60. Size: 130mm square.

It is possible that the tiled fireplace was added during the ownership of the Ivatts who, in *c* 1730, added a north wing with an oak-panelled dining room and a fine marble chimneypiece. Alternatively, it could date from after 1766, when the house was sold to George Bond, a member of a wealthy family of London merchants (Milward 2001, 12–14).

Fig 49 Mid 18th-century English, London tiles, Pitt's Room, first floor, Eagle House (scale *c* 1:4)

EASTCOTE COTTAGE, 2 FIELD END ROAD, EASTCOTE, HA5, HARROW (MIDDLESEX)

Eastcote Cottage is currently in private ownership (Fig 5). The first phase of the cottages dates to *c* 1530–80. The tiles are attached to a brick chimney stack installed *c* 1600–50, but were probably added later, when the house was remodelled in the late 19th or early 20th century (Clarke 1999, 23–4). Not seen by the authors, but photographs (now lost) of the tiled fireplace were sent to the Museum of London in 1998. The tiles were identified as 'tin-glazed tiles in Dutch style' which 'probably date from about 1620–50'. It is not known if the tiles are still *in situ*.

HAM HOUSE, HAM STREET, HAM, TW10, RICHMOND UPON THAMES (SURREY)

Ham House is under the guardianship of The National Trust (Fig 5; Fig 7). The well-known plain tiles which adorn many of the fireplaces at Ham House were installed in the 1670s (Chapter 4, Location and decorative use). They are present in a number of rooms including the Great Hall, Yellow Satin Bedroom, North Drawing Room, Duchess's Private Closet and Green Closet.

Less well known are the fireplaces with decorated blue on white tiles and it is these which are discussed in more detail below. All are similar in size to the plain tiles: *c* 124–129mm square. The figurative and landscape tiles are probably contemporary with the plain tiles, suggesting they were installed by the Duke of Lauderdale, but a series of triple-headed tulip tiles are somewhat earlier. They may have been installed by William Murray who remodelled the interior of Ham House between 1637 and 1639 (Moore et al 1995, 5).

Basement

DUCHESS'S BATHROOM (22 TILES)

A single row of blue on white Dutch landscape and figurative tiles set around a fireplace (Fig 50). The fireplace is believed to be a later addition so the tiles were probably moved here from elsewhere in the house. In addition to the landscape scenes there are tiles showing a boat, cattle, dogs, insects, a fruit bowl and a bird. No corner decoration is present which dates them to after *c* 1660 (Pluis 1997, 17). The decorative designs present are similar to a number of tiles, again without corner decoration, illustrated by van Sabben and Hollem (1987, 102, 125, nos 357, 393), dating to the second half of the 17th century.

Fig 50 Fireplace with Dutch tiles, probably 1670s, Duchess's Bathroom, basement, Ham House (© National Trust) (tile size *c* 124–129mm square)

First floor

CLOSET FOR BEDROOM OVER CHAPEL (54 TILES)

A fireplace with 27 tiles set at either side of the grate. All have the same common three-headed tulip design (cf **189**). The border design is dated by Pluis to 1625–50 (1997, 525, B.07.00.01), whilst tiles with the same tulip pattern but with a variety of other borders belong to the period 1620–60 (van Dam 1991, 53, no. 54; Pluis 1997, 417, A.05.04.01–6). The Ham House tiles, therefore, probably date to the second quarter of the 17th century.

Second floor

FLAT 1 BATHROOM (23 TILES)

A fireplace surrounded by a single row of blue on white tiles with the same three-headed tulip design seen on the first floor fireplace (Fig 51). The second floor at Ham House was remodelled in the Victorian/Edwardian period. It is likely, therefore, that the tiles were moved here from elsewhere in the house.

Fig 51 Detail of early–mid 17th-century Dutch tulip tiles showing work of two tile-painters, flat 1 bathroom, second floor, Ham House (© National Trust) (scale *c* 1:2)

FLAT 1 LIVING ROOM (16 TILES)

A single row of eight blue on white tiles set either side of a fireplace (Fig 52). These are contemporary with those found in the basement fireplace, a number of designs being common to both. Present are landscape tiles, a boat, cattle and a bird.

Fig 52 Fireplace with Dutch tiles, probably 1670s, flat 1 living room, second floor, Ham House (© National Trust) (tile size *c* 124–129mm square)

FLAT 1 BEDROOM (23 TILES)

A fireplace surrounded on all three sides by plain tiles. These are mainly various shades of light blue and pink (Fig 53). There is also a white tile and two with a peach colour; the latter two are possibly later replacements. Most of the tiles are very similar in appearance to the plain tiles used extensively elsewhere in the house and are almost certainly contemporary with them. However, some of the tiles used in this second floor fireplace are badly made, with evidence of glaze movement during firing on certain examples. This may be why they were banished to the top floor.

Fig 53 Detail of plain Dutch tiles, probably 1670s, showing colour shades, flat 1 bedroom, second floor, Ham House (© National Trust) (tile size *c* 124–129mm square)

7 HAMMERSMITH TERRACE, W6, HAMMERSMITH AND FULHAM (MIDDLESEX)

This terrace house building of the mid 18th century is currently owned and maintained by the Emery Walker Trust (Fig 7). The dining room has a tile-lined fireplace decorated with blue on white tiles with flowers, ships and soldiers. Some plain white tiles are also present. Not visited by the authors, but the fireplace can be seen in a photograph in Reid (2003, 71, fig 3).

HAMPTON COURT PALACE, HAMPTON COURT ROAD, KT8, RICHMOND UPON THAMES (MIDDLESEX)

Hampton Court Palace is in the private ownership of the Queen on behalf of the nation (Fig 5; Fig 7). A fireplace with seven tiles at each side of a fireplace in the Museum Room has been seen briefly by one of the authors (IB). There are 13 blue on white tiles and an unusual polychrome example featuring a duck. One blue on white tile has a barbed circular border with leaf corners (cf **187**; Pluis 1997, 525, B.07.00.01). This is a Dutch design of 1625–50. The remaining tiles, which have barred ox-head and spider head corners, show biblical scenes, landscapes, a ship, a soldier and a mythical beast. Most are Dutch, but some of the landscape tiles could be English. Size: *c* 120mm square.

HAYES MANOR, CHURCH ROAD, HAYES, UB3, HILLINGDON (MIDDLESEX)

There are no excavation records currently known for this site (MOL site code HY78), but according to Jon Cotton (pers comm) it was a small excavation which revealed a few medieval and later features. The site lies in the vicinity of an early manor house. The delftware tiles were found with a brick wall and other possible walls believed to be part of the Hayes manorial complex (SMR 050514/00/00). By 1398 the site contained a hall, two granges and a cattle shed, and numerous repairs were recorded in the later 15th century. The manor house, now called Hayes Court, was in use until at least 1677 when it was occupied by William Wayland (VCH 1971, 26–9; Fig 5).

Four floor tiles were found on the site; they were probably installed in the first half of the 17th century as all have designs made at both Pickleherring and Rotherhithe in *c* 1618–50. Both polychrome and blue on white tiles are present (cf **108**, **130**, **132**). Size: ? x ? x 13–16mm.

21 HIGHGATE HIGH STREET, HIGHGATE, N6, HARINGEY (MIDDLESEX)

This property is part of a handsome terrace comprising 17–21 Highgate High Street, built in 1733 (Cherry and Pevsner 2002, 407). The property is currently in private ownership (Fig 7).

Fig 54 Detail of 19th-century Dutch tiles, 21 Highgate High Street (tile size *c* 129–130mm square)

The front living room has a fireplace with 54 blue and white Dutch tiles set horizontally in front (Fig 54). They comprise alternating landscape tiles in circular borders with figurative scenes without borders. Both have the same style of spider head corner. The landscape scenes, which include one with a boat, all lack figures, whilst the figurative tiles show a variety of scenes such as skipping, golfing, sledging, catching a ball and playing a game known in one of the author's (IB) Yorkshire childhood as 'finger, thumb or dum', and with variant names in northern and midland England. Opie and Opie (1984, 294–301) note the playing of the game in the Low Countries, hence its appearance on a Dutch tile at Highgate High Street (cf **325**). Size: 129–130mm square x 7mm thick.

These tiles date to the second half of the 19th century and are more likely to be late 19th century in date. Similar tiles can also be seen at the Treasurer's House in York, North Yorkshire, and at Fanhams Hall, Ware, Hertfordshire, where up to 3000 grace the kitchens and corridors (van Lemmen 1990, 25–6, figs 7–9).

Similar Dutch landscape tiles with not too dissimilar corners are dated by van Sabben and Hollem (1987, 126, no. 394) to the early 19th century, whilst van Dam (1991, 116, nos

141–142) illustrates landscape tiles painted in a similar style and other tiles with similar corner motifs dated 1760–1825. The figurative tiles are similar to slightly later tiles from Utrecht dated 1860–90 (van Dam 1991, 119, no. 150). The Highgate tiles, therefore, may have been installed some time during the early–mid 19th century.

LEWISHAM HIGH STREET, LEWISHAM, SE13, LEWISHAM (KENT)

This property is currently in private ownership (exact location withheld). The tiles are in a fireplace in the ground floor room in a building of late 17th-century date, but were probably installed in the late 18th or early 19th century (Fig 7).

There are 40 blue on white tiles arranged around three sides of a fireplace (Fig 55). The top left- and right-hand corner tiles could be from Liverpool or the Netherlands, the rest are certainly Dutch. The Dutch tiles are of landscape type, some with figures present, others without. They are arranged with alternating patterns of circular border and non-border tiles, all of which have spider head corners. Some of the tiles are similar in style to designs illustrated by van Dam (1991, 115, nos 139–140), dated to the period 1760–1820.

The two corner tiles are somewhat different, comprising a flower vase set in a barbed medallion border with quarter flower-head corners (cf **499**, with the same corners and border). The tiles' origin is uncertain: a similar Liverpool tile dated to 1750–70 is shown in Horne (1989, 64, no. 358), whilst Dutch tiles with similar flower vase design were made from *c* 1760 onwards (Pluis 1997, 429, A.05.08.48). Size: 125–128mm square.

Fig 55 Detail of late 18th- to early 19th-century Dutch tiles in a fireplace, Lewisham High Street (scale *c* 1:4)

LOAD OF HAY PUBLIC HOUSE, 9 BRENT STREET, NW4, BARNET (HERTFORDSHIRE)

Part of the building had a single row of blue on white tiles with military figures and stylised spider head corners along the top of the ceiling. Unfortunately, they were not recorded before the building's demolition in 2004, but they were examined by one of the authors (IB) and found to be Dutch tiles of 19th- to early 20th-century date (Fig 7).

1 MARLBOROUGH CRESCENT, BEDFORD PARK, W4, EALING (MIDDLESEX)

A number of late Dutch tiles imported into London by Thomas Elsley were rescued from a house at Bedford Park during demolition (Fig 7). These are now in the South London Gallery, London. Two of the design types present are illustrated by Pluis (1997, 319, 337, A.01.40.04, A.01.70.41), dated to 1885–1920, whilst a third design is illustrated by Macfarlane (2005, 16). Size: 152mm square.

NORTH LONDON COLLEGIATE SCHOOL, CANONS DRIVE, EDGWARE, HA8, BARNET (MIDDLESEX)

The original core of the school is a Georgian house built in the late 1740s by cabinetmaker William Hallett (Weinreb and Hibbert 1993, 569). A tiled fireplace, present in an upper room, probably dates from 1910, when the original building was enlarged, embellished and heightened by C E Mallows for Sir Arthur Du Cros, founder of the Dunlop Rubber Company (Cherry and Pevsner 1991, 298). The building is currently in private ownership (Fig 7).

Fig 56 Detail of Dutch tiles, *c* 1910, North London Collegiate School (scale *c* 1:4)

The fireplace is decorated with blue on white tiles illustrating tradesmen involved with various professions, such as rat-catcher, fisherman and fruit seller. Each tile has an isolated figure with barred ox-head corners (Fig 56). There are 28 tiles set vertically: 20 decorated and eight plain white, and at least six decorated tiles set horizontally in front of the fire. The latter are partially obscured by a firmly attached carpet so the total number of tiles present could not be determined. Size: 129–131mm square.

A Dutch tile in Pluis (1997, 550, C.07.00.11) has the same subject matter (a street vendor) as on one of the tiles and is painted in similar style. This tile dates to 1880–1910, which fits in well with the suggested 1910 date for the Collegiate School tiles.

RAINHAM HALL, THE BROADWAY, RAINHAM, RM13, HAVERING, ESSEX

Rainham Hall is an elegant three storey Georgian house completed in 1729 (Cherry et al 2005, 187; Fig 7). There are six tiled fireplaces together with an area of tile panelling in a basement room. Unfortunately, there is evidence of considerable alteration and replacement. The ground floor fireplaces have pristine tiles directly adjacent to heavily sooted fireplace backs. These are later replacements installed in the 19th or early 20th century, perhaps when the house was restored by Colonel H H Mulliner in *c* 1920. It is currently in the guardianship of The National Trust.

Basement

STILL ROOM (ORIGINALLY 196 TILES)

The basement room seems to have been used as a dairy and the tile panels copy, in a modest way, the ornamental dairy buildings constructed on the great estates during the 18th and 19th centuries. These dairies had a practical function to supply the household with butter, cream, milk and cheese. Tiles were added as a way to keep the dairy cool as well as providing an easily cleaned and decorative wall finish (Graves 2002, 110–11).

The original layout of the tiles comprised five rectangular panels of plain and decorated tiles, comprising 196 tiles. Four panels comprised 35 tiles in each, whilst the fifth (right-hand side) was larger and contained 56 tiles. Somewhat regrettably, the tiles have been slightly reordered to make five panels of 35 tiles each. The discussion below refers to the original layout shown in photographs taken in 1989 (National Trust: J Bethell, neg; F Scoones, neg nos F21, F29, F33, L22).

The majority of decorated tiles show landscape scenes set in thin octagonal powdered purple ground borders with quarter rosette corner decoration. These formed a one-tile-wide border around each of the five panels (105 tiles). The latter figure excludes the top right corner of the large panel where a border tile was replaced at some stage with a blue on white tile with a three-headed tulip pattern (cf centre, **189**). The border and corner decoration date this tile to 1625–50 (Pluis 1997, 525, B.07.00.01). Inside the five panels are 64 plain white, 24 blue on white landscape tiles with no border or corner decoration and, in the centre of two panels, single blue and white tiles with a landscape scene set within a studded octagonal border (cf **277**). The latter is a Dutch design dating to 1730–1920 (Pluis 1997, 530, B12.00.15). However, it is probably 18th century, as are most of the other decorated tiles present, which are also probably Dutch. Size: 126–127mm square.

The use of single rows of octagonal bordered powdered purple tiles around plain white tiles has certain similarities to the decorative scheme used at Carshalton House water tower (above).

Ground floor

DRAWING ROOM (ORIGINALLY 72 TILES)

Twenty tiles are located at either side of the fireplace, but these would appear to be later replacements. Impressions in the mortar above the current areas of tiling show that there were originally 36 tiles at either side, making a total of 72. The current tiles show blue on white landscape scenes with boats and ships set within an octagonal Louis XV border with diaper corner motifs. They are all Dutch and can be dated broadly to 1740–1920 (Pluis 1997, 529, B.12.00.04; cf **286**, **287**). Size: 130mm square x 7mm thick.

DINING ROOM (ORIGINALLY 48 TILES)

Fireplace with 21 blue on white tiles to the left and a further 22 tiles to the right. Mortar impressions show that the fireplace originally had 24 tiles on each side, making a total of 48. All but two tiles of those surviving have landscape scenes, mostly figures and boats set in a circular border with carnation-head corners (Fig 57). The tiles are Dutch and from their corner decoration and design can be dated to *c* 1790–1930. Some of the landscape scenes are identical to those on the Dutch tiles used at Dora House, 108 Old Brompton Road (above, 6, City; Fig 15). Size: 129–131mm square x 7mm thick.

The remaining landscape tiles are also Dutch. One has a studded octagonal border and quarter flower-head corners, similar to Pluis (1997, 561) design C.12.00.24 dated 1730–1920 (cf **277**). The other has a similar square border to Pluis design nos 41 and A.03.01.33 (1997, 133, 369), dated 1780–*c* 1910 (cf **285**).

Fig 57 Detail of late 18th- to early 20th-century Dutch landscape tiles, Dining Room, ground floor, Rainham Hall (© National Trust) (scale *c* 1:4)

First floor

EAST CORNER, BLUE ROOM (ORIGINALLY 54 TILES)

Fireplace with 25 tiles to the left (plus one missing tile) and 28 tiles to the right. Unlike those on the ground floor this fireplace appears to have kept its original tiling. The use of rectangular blue on white border tiles in an internal border is an unusual feature of this fireplace (Fig 58). They are probably London-made as Horne illustrates a border tile with the same design dated 1750–70 (1989, 70, no. 398; cf **445**). Size: 126–129 x 66–67mm.

The associated square tiles display an alternating chequerboard pattern of plain white

Fig 58 Detail of 18th-century English, London and Dutch tiles, Blue Room, first floor, Rainham Hall (© National Trust) (border tile size 126–129 x 66–67mm)

and decorated examples. The latter would seem to be an unusual mixture of London and Dutch tiles. Three Dutch blue on white landscape tiles have a corner motif and studded octagonal border similar to that used on a tile in the dining room. They are similar to Pluis (1997, 530) design B.12.00.15 of 1730–1920. A blue on white landscape tile with an octagonal powdered purple border and blue on white quarter rosette corners is also Dutch.

The London-made tiles include a landscape scene with the same subject matter as a tile in Horne (1989, 27, no. 71) and similar powdered blue octagonal border and carnation corners to tiles of 1740–70 (Horne 1989, 23, 62, nos 44, 342). Another tile with a similar border, but in powdered purple, is also present. This has the distinctive flower vase and two bird design: this is a feature of London tiles dated 1730–50 (Horne 1989, 62, no. 334; cf **421**). Other tiles present may be either Dutch or English. Size: 127–130mm square.

A feature worth noting is the presence of two tiles, one on each side of the fireplace, set sideways. A similar feature was noted on the fireplace at Liberty in Regent Street (above, 6, City).

WEST CORNER, GREEN ROOM (36 TILES)

Eighteen tiles set either side of a fireplace. There is a wide assortment of border designs and border motifs present, most of which, rather oddly, pre-date the construction of the hall by some 80 years.

The earlier Dutch tiles in the fireplace are blue on white or, in the case of one landscape tile, blue on a distinctly pink glaze. They comprise landscapes, flowers and animals together with single tiles showing a military figure, a mythical sea creature and a biblical scene with David and Goliath (1 Samuel 17 v. 48). The corner decorations are mainly a mixture of spider head, barred ox-head and fleur-de-lis types. Two tiles, both with tulips, have more unusual leaf corner motifs. An identical corner is present on a Dutch tulip tile in Pluis (1997, 411, A.05.01.03) dated 1620–50. This is also the date given to tiles with a further unusual border/corner arrangement (cf **183**; Pluis 1997, 531, B.13.00.01).

The eight later tiles in the fireplace comprise six blue on white landscapes set in either a studded octagonal border (cf **277**), as in the dining room, or a plain border, as shown in Pluis (1997, 530, B.12.00.13). The other two blue on white tiles have powdered purple octagonal borders and blue on white corner motifs. One has a landscape scene with quarter rosette corners similar to tiles in van Dam (1991, 103, no. 118; cf **297–301**). The other has carnation-head corners with a similar flower vase to that on an English tile (Horne 1989, 62, no. 334; cf **421**). This tile is probably an English tile of 1730–50, whilst the other later tiles appear to be Dutch tiles of the 18th to early 19th century. Size: 121–129mm square.

NORTH CORNER ROOM (36 TILES)

Nine purple on white and nine plain white tiles set in a chequerboard pattern at either side of a fireplace, making a total of 36 tiles (Fig 59). The bottom four tiles on the left side are recent replacements using spare tiles found at the Hall. However, the two decorated tiles match the others so well that it is not inconceivable that they originally came from this fireplace.

The tiles are all of barred ox-head type; six have landscapes whilst the remainder show scenes of a biblical nature. A number of biblical scenes are similar to those used on London-made tiles illustrated in Horne (1989, 82, 94, 109, nos 483, 484, 557, 657), but the style of the barred ox-head motif indicates that these tiles are Dutch, probably of 18th- to early 19th-century date. Size: 126–128mm square.

SOUTH CORNER ROOM (48 TILES)

Twenty-four tiles set either side of the fireplace. They comprise two vertical lines of eight decorated tiles separated by a vertical line of alternating plain white and decorated examples. Some of the tiles are blurred, a result of the glaze moving during firing. All the tiles are Dutch and are of similar date to the earlier tiles in the Green Room.

Many of the tiles have the well-known Dutch three-headed tulip pattern with either a leaf pattern or Wan Li corner motifs dated to 1620–60 (cf **189**; Pluis 1997, 417, 525, A.05.04.04, B.07.00.01). There are also tulips set in a diamond border with fleur-de-lis corners, the latter similar to Pluis (1997, 542) design C.02.00.05. One flower tile has an oval border similar to **180** and Pluis (1997, 523) B.04.00.04, dated 1620–50. A further flower tile has barred ox-head corners: an identical tile dated 1640–70 is in Pluis (1997, 425, A.05.08.22). Size: 121–129mm square.

Fig 59 Detail of alternating 18th- to early 19th-century plain white and purple Dutch biblical and landscape tiles, north corner room, first floor, Rainham Hall (© National Trust) (scale *c* 1:4)

RED HOUSE, RED HOUSE LANE, BEXLEYHEATH, DA6, BEXLEY (KENT)

This red brick-built house was constructed between 1859 and 1860 for William Morris and his new wife Janey and designed by Philip Webb (Garnett 2003, 7). The house is currently under the guardianship of The National Trust (Fig 7). The blue on white Dutch tiles in the dining room fireplace (erroneously called Staffordshire tiles in Garnett 2003) were probably installed in the 1880s or 1890s (Fig 60). A mixture of designs are present, but most are early and late 19th century. They include landscape scenes in circular borders with carnation-head corners, landscapes set in octagonal borders with quarter flower-head corners, landscapes in square borders (cf **285**) and a landscape set in a circular border with spider head corners. Also present are isolated figures, mounted military figures and ships with spider head and barred ox-head corners. More unusual are tiles with a sunflower and a sunflower leaf which reflect the tastes of the Dutch Arts and Crafts movement of the 1870s and 1880s. Size: 120mm square.

Fig 60 The dining room fireplace, Red House (tile size 120mm square)

ST PHILOMENA'S SCHOOL (FORMERLY CARSHALTON HOUSE), POUND STREET, CARSHALTON, SM5, SUTTON (SURREY)

A group of 23 Dutch tiles were recovered from a toilet block demolished in 2006 (Fig 7). The tiles remain in the private collection of St Philomena's School. They were in part of the school buildings believed to have been rebuilt in 1893–1913. All the tiles, which are of exceptionally fine quality, show flower vases with unusual flower-head corners (**412–414**). Jonathan Horne (pers comm) believes they could be 19th century in date, although the decorative design appears to copy earlier Dutch tiles made in Rotterdam in 1740–80 (Pluis 1997, 429, A.05.08.46). Size: 127–128mm square.

SUTTON HOUSE, 2 AND 4 HOMERTON HIGH STREET, E9, HACKNEY (MIDDLESEX)

A floor tile (**66**) and a number of wall tiles were found during renovation work in 1990, although none were *in situ* (MOL site code SUT90; Thompson et al 1998, 64; Fig 5; Fig 7). The building was constructed in 1534–5 by Sir Ralph Sadleir. Some of the wall tiles may have been installed during extensive alterations undertaken between 1741 and 1743 under the ownership of John Cox (Gray 1997, 20). The tiles are now part of the MOL collections.

The blue on white wall tiles comprise landscapes, military figures (Gray 1997, 17) and a biblical scene. These have barred ox-head and spider head corner motifs and are of 18th- to early 19th-century date. Also present is a later ship tile with barred ox-head corners dating to *c* 1880–1930. These tiles are probably all Dutch. Of possible English origin is a mid 18th-century rectangular edging tile with a similar design to **444**. Size: ? x 67 x 7mm (rectangular); ? x ? 6–8mm (square).

Fig 61 Detail of late 17th- (decorated) and possible 19th-century (plain) Dutch tiles, panel over fireplace, Waxwell Farm (decorated tile size 124–131mm square)

WAXWELL FARM, 125 WAXWELL LANE, PINNER, HA5, HARROW (MIDDLESEX)

The house has been examined by Patricia Clarke who has kindly provided the following information. The plan and detail of the present building indicated a period of construction sometime in 1580–1640. The building was originally a yeoman's house or farmhouse but had been converted to purely residential use in the last quarter of the 19th century. In 1891 Edward Trotter took a nine and a half year lease during which the house was considerably enlarged. The building is currently in private ownership (Fig 7).

The tiles are in a panel of alternating plain and decorated tiles set in a panel four tiles high by 23 tiles wide placed above a fireplace. The decorated tiles, which are both blue on white (44 tiles) and blue and purple on white (four tiles), measure 124–131mm square, whilst the 44 plain white tiles are 130–131mm square. All the decorated tiles have spider head corners but are painted in a variety of styles, suggesting they are from a number of different batches, perhaps even from different pothouses (Fig 61).

The blue on white decorated tiles comprise mainly landscape scenes, with others showing dogs, figures in isolation (cf **316–321**), a flower, a bird, a cherub and a horse. The blue and purple on white tiles show dogs, a rabbit and a horse. Dutch landscape tiles painted in similar style with closely matching spider head corners are illustrated by van Dam, who dates them to the period 1660–1700 (1991, 79, no. 88).

The plain white tiles are clearly later in date than the decorated examples; this suggests that the tile panel may have been installed during the occupancy of Edward Trotter. What is not certain is the original setting of the decorated Dutch tiles. It is possible that they were located somewhere else in Waxwell Farm before the building was altered during the 19th century, or they may have been brought in from elsewhere when the tile panel was installed.

7 DESIGN CATALOGUE

The fireplace was an old one, built by some Dutch merchant long ago, and paved all round with quaint Dutch tiles designed to illustrate the Scriptures.

A Christmas carol, Charles Dickens

The early tiles found in London, those principally used before 1666, are arranged in approximate chronological order. Where appropriate, tiles of similar design have been grouped together, such as the medallion-style tiles of the late 16th and early 17th centuries. Post-1666 tiles are grouped by subject matter and chronology, with the exception of the biblical tiles. Following the convention used elsewhere (eg Ray 1973; Horne 1989) they are arranged by the order in which the scenes depicted appear in the Bible.

Additional London material is illustrated in Britton (1987, 170–86) and Tyler et al (2008, 52–9, 84–92, 100–4, 109).

ATTRIBUTION

Investigation of London production sites has allowed various tile designs to be attributed to a specific pothouse. In particular, many floor tile designs can now be linked with the pothouses at Aldgate, Rotherhithe and Pickleherring. Certain wall tile designs made at Norfolk House, Glasshouse Street, Gravel Lane, Hermitage and Mortlake can also now be identified.

Even when a specific design can be linked to a specific pothouse, it is clear that certain designs were made at more than one production centre. The Tudor rose floor design, for example (**108–111**), was made at Aldgate, Pickleherring and Rotherhithe whilst very similar flower vase patterns (**421**, **422**) are present on blue on white wall tiles made at Norfolk House and Gravel Lane, and polychrome tiles made at Vauxhall (**423**).

When it comes to the identification of Dutch tiles, we are fortunate in having an extensive literature on individual design types. It is clear from published Dutch catalogues that many English floor tiles are close copies of designs used in the Netherlands. In some cases, even after extensive study, it is still not possible to state with any confidence whether certain tiles are English or Dutch, so both attributions are given in the catalogue.

DATING

Where possible specific dates are given in the catalogue, such as '1670–1700', but where there are major uncertainties more general dates such as 'early–mid 16th century' are given. The dating of individual designs can be problematic. The situation is made more difficult by authors proscribing different dates to tiles of the same design or painted in similar decorative styles. Where possible the dating in the catalogue has been adjusted to cover that given by each author, although the information from published sources has on occasions been modified based on various attributes of the tiles themselves, particularly their thickness.

The early–mid 16th-century tiles made at Antwerp tend to be slightly thicker than later floor tiles made in the Netherlands and London. The thickness of Dutch tiles gradually decreases from around 19mm in 1570 to about 12mm in the 1630s, with a further decline to about 7–8mm between 1640 and 1680 (Pluis 1997, 71).

Length and breadth tends to be less useful, although this gradually decreases from around 140mm square to 130mm square up to the third decade of the 17th century (Pluis 1997, 71). After 1850 a larger size of tile was made in the Netherlands for the English market (Pluis 1997, 41). Examples of these larger tiles, which were made to a standard size of 6 inches square (around 150mm square), can be found in a fireplace at Charlton House (Chapter 6, Greater London).

The main published sources used for dating and attribution in the catalogue are as follows (see bibliography for other references): for English tiles, Archer (1997), Horne (1989) and Ray (1973); for Dutch tiles, van Dam (1991), Pluis (1997), van Sabben and Hollem (1987) and Schaap (1984).

CATALOGUE ENTRIES

All the catalogue entries follow the same convention:

Line 1: design number (Spanish tiles, and later copies, are lettered **A–R**, all others numbered **1–505**); location found.
The precise location of many tiles found before the 1940s is unknown, but no English or Low Countries tin-glazed tiles from sites outside London are present in the Museum of London collections. It seems reasonable, therefore, to assume that the English and Low Countries tin-glazed tiles in the MOL with their location recorded as 'unknown' were found somewhere in London.

Line 2: country of origin and production centre (if known); date.

Line 3: comments

Line 4: colour; size in millimetres. For the majority of tiles colour is denoted as follows:
blue = blue on white
purple = purple on white
blue and purple = blue and purple on white
poly = polychrome (multicoloured)

Line 5: museum accession number or, for archaeological material, site code, context and accessioned find number (for details see Chapter 1, Textual conventions used in this volume), scientific analysis, additional publication references. All tiles are in the Museum of London unless stated otherwise.

TILE COLOUR

Tiles of purple colour are sometimes referred to as manganese rather than purple, Manganese is not actually a colour but a pigment used to produce a variety of paint colours from dark purple to pale amethyst. The original Dutch name (dating back to at least 1686) for tiles of this colour was *paars* (purple) (Pluis 1997, 103–4). The term 'purple' has therefore been used in preference to manganese.

The blue colour present on most tiles came from cobalt, yellow from antimony, copper for green and orange from iron rust. Iron oxide was used to produce a red colour (Schaap 1984, 40; Archer 1997, 19).

TILE ILLUSTRATIONS

Tiles illustrating the designs are shown at 1:2 unless specified otherwise. Examples of six complete designs are reproduced from Pluis (1997) at 1:4 and shown alongside the illustrations for designs **76**, **78**, **81**, **89**, **127** and **128**, and **133**.

PUBLISHER'S NOTE

Designs **12**, **14** and **15** were thought to be Flemish but have recently been identified as Spanish (Valencia region) (see above, page 11). Their reattribution occurred too late to change the design catalogue series numbering and they appear (identified as Spanish) under 'English and Low Countries' (pages 92–3).

EARLY TILE DESIGNS (1500–*c* 1666)

The tiles are those believed to have been made before the Great Fire of 1666.

SPANISH

Anthony Ray

Cuerda seca *tiles*

A; All Hallows church, 54 Lombard Street, EC3, City of London
Seville; 1500–25
Particoloured tiles in green and white were widely used to cover large areas. Niculoso himself supplied quantities of such tiles for the dome of Seville Cathedral in 1511 (Ray 2000, 310), though these may have been tiles called *de cartabón*, divided diagonally into two triangles rather than four as on this tile, which appears to be an unusual survival.
Green; 133 x 132 x 22–23mm
15647; Fig 4, no. 11

B; All Hallows church, 54 Lombard Street, EC3, City of London
Seville; 1510–30
This is also an unusual survival. The decoration – a self-contained motif that does not link with an adjacent tile – appears to be a device of some kind, possibly a merchant's mark. It is a good example of how precise outlines can be achieved using the *cuerda seca* technique, seen to impressive effect in the inscription on the tomb of León Enríquez in Santa Paula, Seville, contemporary with Niculoso's magnificent painted doorway, also in Santa Paula.
Poly; 134 x 133 x 23–24mm
15648; Fig 4, no. 11

Arista *tiles*

C; Monument House, 30–35 Botolph Lane, 29–31 Monument Street, EC3, City of London
Seville; 1500–25
The interlace design is very much in the Islamic tradition but the effect is very different – looser and more refined. No precisely similar tiles are recorded.
Poly; ? x 137 x 27–28mm
BPL95 [107] <57>; Blair and Sankey 2007

D; probably London
Seville; 1500–30
The design – four radiating thistle-heads enclosed in a diamond frame of chevrons, with the corners forming a trompe-l'oeil 'nail-head' – is related to one found on a number of tiles in the Mayor's Chapel, Bristol (Gloucestershire): cf the example in the Victoria and Albert Museum, London, from that source (Ray 2000, 368, no. 910). Others are to be found in the parish church of Haccombe in Devon. Commenting on four similar tiles in the Carranza Collection, Pleguezuelo (1996, 31, fig 10) proposes a late 15th-century date and classifies them as *cuerda seca mixta*, with a shallow ridge painted with grease, but the Victoria and Albert Museum example appears to be a normal *arista* tile.
Poly; ? x ? x 25mm
NN15784

E; All Hallows church, 54 Lombard Street, EC3, City of London
Seville; 1510–30
The design can be associated with Niculoso since a virtually complete waster was found in the Calle Pureza, Spain, together with many other fragments. There are several tiles of this type mixed with the painted tiles signed by Niculoso and dated ?1520 in the Rosary Chapel in the parish church of Flores de Ávila, Spain. Others can be seen in the floor of the Mayor's Chapel in Bristol (Gloucestershire) – and one found in the River Frome, Dorset, is now in the Victoria and Albert Museum (Ray 2000, 369 no. 917) – and an even greater number in Coimbra Cathedral, Portugal.
Poly; ? x 136 x 24mm
15646a; Fig 4, no. 11

F; Monument House, 30–35 Botolph Lane, 29–31 Monument Street, EC3, City of London
Seville; 1510–30
Although no corresponding fragment is among the wasters from the Calle Pureza, a tile with this design was excavated in the church of El Carmen in Seville, where many tiles associable with Niculoso, including some magnificent painted tiles, were found. As with **E**, the pattern, spread over four tiles, creates alternating large diamond shapes enclosing a radial motif of leaves and fruits and smaller diamonds with a star-like quatrefoil.
Poly; ? x ? x 23–30mm
BPL95 [+] <361> and [119] <63>; Blair and Sankey 2007; analysed by ICP; Hughes 2005a

G; probably London
Seville; 1510–30
This damaged fragment has an unusual corner motif which is found on tiles still *in situ* in the Cartuja de las Cuevas, Seville, and on other fragments excavated in the church of El Carmen, Seville, both sites having known connections with Niculoso. The same design can also be seen on a tile in the late 19th-century porch of 1 Cadogan Gardens (Chapter 6, City; Fig 12). This fragment may well come from a similar tile.
Poly; ? x ? x 25mm
NN15783

H; 68 Lombard Street, EC3, City of London
Seville; 1520–40
Almost certainly from All Hallows church (Fig 4, no. 11). Biscuit wasters and tiles of very similar design were found in the Calle Pureza (Pleguezuelo 1992, 183, no. 1). There appear to be at least four variants of this design with a central quatrefoil linked to adjacent tiles by a circle interlace and a strong floral counter-pattern in the corners – eg the four in the Carranza Collection (Pleguezuelo 1996, 41, fig 15). A tile very similar to **H**, excavated in the Convento de San Francisco, Dominican Republic, is illustrated by Goggin (1968, pl 8e). The glazes on this tile are in places remarkably thick, a feature common on the tiles in the Casa de Pilatos, Seville.
Poly; 150 x 149 x 15mm
L237/1

I; 27–29 Whitechapel High Street, 2–4 Colchester Street, E1, Tower Hamlets
Seville; 1510–30
This is a typical example of a design that requires 16 tiles to establish the complete pattern. The central motif with a quarter flower enclosed in a 'sun' corresponds with the biscuit-fired waster from the Calle Pureza, and the corner may also have created an alternating pattern of smaller quatrefoil leaves. The floor of the chapel of The Vyne, Hampshire, includes eight panels of four similar tiles (Blanchett 2000, 21).
Poly; ? x ? x 24–26mm
WCEO1 [111] <44>

A

B

C

D

F

E

G

H

I

J; 54 Lombard Street, EC3, City of London
Seville; 1510–30
Almost certainly from All Hallows church (Fig 4, no. 11; see Fig 1 for a reconstruction of the design). A further tile with this design was recovered from 112–116 Lower Thames Street, EC3, City of London (MOL site code PEN79 [102] <261>).

A corresponding fragment was found in the Calle Pureza. Among the painted tiles signed by Niculoso and dated ?1520 in the Rosary Chapel, in the parish church of Flores de Ávila, are several tiles of this type. Fragmentary examples were excavated in the church of El Carmen in Seville together with tiles painted by Niculoso. Other published examples are in the Museo de Artes y Costumbres Populares in Seville (Pleguezuelo 1989, 83, 132, no. 71) and in the Carranza Collection (Pleguezuelo 1996, 60, fig 64). On tiles in the Museo de Pontevedra, Spain, the flower in the corner is inverted (Casamar 1983, no. 106). Examples recorded elsewhere include the Alcázar and San Isidro del Campo in Seville, Coimbra Cathedral in Portugal and the facade of the university in Santo Domingo, Dominican Republic. This is one of the designs copied by the Pulidos in the Casa de Pilatos (Sancho 1953, pl 71).
Poly; 142 x 141 x 26–27mm
L223/4

K; All Hallows church, Lombard Street, EC3, City of London
Seville; 1510–30
The design shows the durability of interlace designs, here combined with Renaissance scrolls. With its variants it occurs on tiles of two different types.

Wainscot tiles: several examples are to be found with the painted tiles signed by Niculoso and dated ?1520 in the Rosary Chapel in the parish church of Flores de Ávila, forming large panels, with 16 tiles completing the pattern. A tile showing the central part of the design, but with a different corner, is in the Museo de Pontevedra (Casamar 1983, no. 59).

Ceiling tiles: these are similar to **R**, with half the design on a rectangular tile with unglazed ends, as can be seen on a ceiling in the Cartuja de las Cuevas, Seville – a site also associated with Niculoso – though here there are variations in the detail of the corners and there are fewer rosettes on the circle: cf the corresponding pair of tiles in the Victoria and Albert Museum (Ray 2000, 364, no. 893). Unfortunately the fragment does not show from which type it comes, but it is probably from a wall tile.
Poly; ? x 138 x 23–24mm
15645; Fig 4, no. 11

L; All Hallows church, 54 Lombard Street, EC3, City of London
Seville; 1510–30
It is a pity that the tile is incomplete, since it is impossible to visualise the overall pattern created, though clearly the emphasis was on the curving bands separating the leaf-scrolls, alternating with some kind of interlace design. In style it has a great affinity with the material from the Calle Pureza.
Poly; ? x 138 x 23–25mm
15649; Fig 4, no. 11

Olambrillas

These tiles, found in Hurstpierpoint, West Sussex (Sussex), rather than London, are included here to complete the catalogue of Spanish tiles in the Museum of London.

These small tiles were used in conjunction with plain red floor tiles of various shapes to create pattern in a floor. They were made in huge quantities and the repertoire of designs is considerable: it includes 'portraits', grotesque heads, animals, monsters, birds and fish together with vegetal and geometric motifs and emblems. A few fired blanks and wasters with such designs were recovered in the Calle Pureza.

M; Hurstpierpoint, West Sussex (Sussex)
Seville; 1510–30
A virtually identical figure occurs on a *cuerda seca* dish in the Instituto Valencia de Don Juan, Madrid, which has been dated 1490–1510 on the basis of the costume. A tile of the same design is in the Victoria and Albert Museum (Ray, 2000, 370, no. 921).
Poly; 72 x 73 x 13mm
16027

N; Hurstpierpoint, West Sussex (Sussex)
Seville; 1510–40
The hare is a very common motif on Spanish pottery generally. A tile in the late 19th-century porch of 1 Cadogan Gardens (Chapter 6, City) is a variant.
Poly; 72 x 73 x 13mm
16028

O; ? Hurstpierpoint, West Sussex (Sussex)
Seville; 1510–40
Another tile depicting what appears to be a wild boar is in the Victoria and Albert Museum (Ray 2000, 370, no. 923).
Poly; 74 x 74 x 14mm
16029

LATER COPIES OF SPANISH TILES

P; probably London
?Flemish, ?Antwerp; ? early–mid 16th century
A very unusual tile with broad ridges separating the areas of colour. The tile is not Spanish, but it may be an Antwerp copy of a Spanish *arista* tile. A tile with the same design was found on the Thames foreshore near Cannon Street station bridge (M Paros, pers comm).
Poly; 134 x 131 x 17–19mm
A4645

Q; Vine Lane, Tooley Street, SE1, Southwark
English, London; 1881–90
A Victorian copy of a 16th-century Spanish *arista* tile, probably made by Garrard at his Millwall factory in the 1870s or 1880s. It has a scored mark in the form of a letter H in the base, perhaps a batch mark. A second probable Victorian copy was found at Mortlake (MOL site code HSL96 [+] <30>).
Poly; ? x 139 x 15–18mm
VIN88 [+] <37>; analysed by ICP (Hughes 2005a)

R; 68 Lombard Street, EC3, City of London
Seville or English, London; late 19th century
Almost certainly from All Hallows church (Fig 4, no. 11).

There was a revival in interest in *arista* tiles in Seville in the second half of the 19th century, and these were also exported; there is, for example, a notable fireplace with such tiles in Waddesdon Manor, Buckinghamshire. Alternatively, it could have been made by Garrard at his Millwall factory in the 1870s or 1880s.

Design **R** is a copy of a design created by the Pulidos in 1535 for the ceiling of the Cenador de la Álcoba in the Alcázar, Seville, and a tile in the Museo de Pontevedra shows a variant of the design (Casamar 1983, no. 64). In Seville these tiles were only used on ceilings (**K**), and if this tile is from All Hallows church it is hard to imagine the setting: a ceiling of this type would have been a very unusual architectural feature in England at the time.
Poly; 306 x 136 x 25mm
L237/2

J

K

M

L

N

O

P

Q

R

ENGLISH AND LOW COUNTRIES

1; Coleman Street, EC2, City of London
Flemish, Antwerp; 1520–40
Two tiles with closely related designs were used to pave the chapel of The Vyne (Rackham 1926, 10, pl 4; Britton 1987, 170, no. 180). The Coleman Street tile is the same size as certain of the square tiles used at The Vyne (Blanchett 2000, 11).
Poly; 133 x 133 x 20mm
6927; analysed by NAA (Chapter 5)

2; Aldgate, EC3, City of London
Flemish, Antwerp, probably National Museum of Navigation pothouse; early–mid 16th century
Rackham (1926, 40, pl 18a) illustrates a tile found in Antwerp with a similar bearded figure wearing a hat. The size of the Aldgate tile is similar to a number of square tiles at The Vyne (Blanchett 2000, 9, SS2 a–c) suggesting that it may have been used with elongated hexagonal tiles in a mosaic pavement. The tile may have come from a mansion house owned by the Duke of Norfolk, situated within the former precinct of Holy Trinity Priory, known as Duke's Place (Schofield 1995, 155; Schofield and Lea 2005; Fig 4, no. 1). The tile is not from the house of Protector Somerset which Britton (1987, 171) incorrectly states was built on the site.
Poly; ? x ? x 20–23mm (reconstructed *c* 106mm square)
A25388; analysed by NAA (Chapter 5)

3; Ministry of Defence, Horse Guards Avenue, Whitehall, SW1, Westminster
Flemish, Antwerp; 1520–40
Duck in landscape. The border area and flowers are closely paralleled on a tile with another kind of bird found at The Vyne (Blanchett 2000, 13, n). Found on the site of Whitehall Palace, for other designs from this site see **7**, **11**, **17**, **18**, **20**, **40** (Fig 4, no. 15).
Blue and brown; ? x ? x 20–21mm
WIH01 [+] <1>

4; Idol Lane, EC3, City of London
Flemish, Antwerp; 1520–40
The design is fairly similar to Antwerp tiles from Herkenrode and The Vyne (Britton 1987, 171).
Poly; 114 x 114 x 20mm
11902; analysed by NAA (Chapter 5)

5; 90–94 Old Broad Street, EC2, City of London
Flemish, Antwerp; 1520–40
Rackham (1926, 28, pl 12) illustrates an Antwerp tile with the same pattern from The Vyne.
Poly; ? x ? x 21–22mm
BRO90 [239] <128>

6; Billingsgate Market Lorry Park, Lower Thames Street, EC3, City of London
Flemish, Antwerp; 1520–40
There are a number of designs in the Herkenrode pavement combining a circular pattern with lines radiating from a central point (Rackham 1926, 36, pl 16; Schaap 1984, 42, fig 13). The design on the Billingsgate tile cannot be matched, but the close similarity including the style of the corner decoration indicates an Antwerp origin.
Poly; ? x ? x 17mm (reconstructed *c* 98mm square)
BIG82 [424] <772>

7; Banqueting House, Whitehall, SW1, Westminster
Flemish, Antwerp; 1520–40
The original size matches the small square tiles used at The Vyne (Blanchett 2000, 8), but the design is very similar to tiles in the Herkenrode pavement (Dumortier 2002, 20, fig 4).
Poly; ? x ? x 19mm (reconstructed *c* 97mm square)
Historic Royal Palaces

8; Royal Mint, East Smithfield, E1, Tower Hamlets
Flemish, Antwerp, probably National Museum of Navigation kiln site; early–mid 16th century
Blue and yellow; ? x ? x 19mm
MIN86 [7514] <4122>; analysed by NAA (Chapter 5)

9; London
Flemish, Antwerp; 1530s
The design is similar to tiles ordered for Herkenrode Abbey in 1532 (Dumortier 2002, 20, fig 4).
Poly; 202 x 83–86 x 15–17mm
6946

10; Preachers Court, Charterhouse Mews, EC1, Islington
Flemish, Antwerp; 1530s
Probably from the Charterhouse in Smithfield which housed the Carthusian monastic order (Fig 4, no. 4). Rackham (1926, 38, pl 17) illustrates some Herkenrode-type tiles with a fairly similar design.
Poly; ? x ? x 17mm
PCC92 [+] <5>; Barber and Thomas 2002; Betts 2002

11; Banqueting House, Whitehall, SW1, Westminster
Flemish, Antwerp; 1530s
Similar to tiles used at Herkenrode Abbey.
Poly; ? x 89 x 18mm
Historic Royal Palaces

12; Royal Naval College (King Charles Quarter), Romney Road, Greenwich, SE10, Greenwich
Valencia region, Spanish; mid–late 15th century
Part of a elongated hexagonal tile with the end of a scroll inscription surrounded by foliage. A complete tile with a very similar design is in the British Museum (1959,1001.1). The tile almost certainly came from Greenwich Palace (Fig 5).
Blue on pale blue and white; ? x 120 x 14mm
RNK00 [5] <1>

13; 2–3 Trig Lane, Upper Thames Street, EC4, City of London
Flemish, Antwerp; 1520–40
Blue; ? x ? x 19–20mm
TL74 [1072] <2976>

14; 51–53 City Road, EC1, Islington
Valencia region (Manises), Spanish; late 15th century
The middle of a elongated hexagonal tile with a floral pattern. The design is almost identical to a complete tile in the British Museum (1905,1030.10) measuring 212 x 108 x 17–19mm.
Blue and purple; ? x ? x 20–22mm
CIO01 [21] <5>

15; Fleet Valley Project, Holborn Viaduct Station to Blackfriars, EC4, City of London
Valencia region (Manises), Spanish; late 15th century
A possible variant of **14** with an area of white in the centre of each flower. A complete tile of this variant design was found during repair in the chancel of Temple church, City of London (Brown 2005, 82, fig 80; Fig 4, no. 9). A further complete tile from the Vatican is in the British Museum (1904,0706.10), but this has partly flat ends (Wallis 1902, 78, fig 84). This tile comes from apartments decorated by Pope Alexander VI in the early years of his reign (1492–1503) (González Martí 1952, 458, 621–44, pl XXIV).

1

2

3

4

5

6

7

8

9

10

11

12

13

14

15

16; Royal Naval College, King William Walk, Romney Road, Greenwich, SE10, Greenwich
?Flemish, ?Antwerp; 1520–70
Rectangular-shaped tile with tapered end of unusual design, probably from Greenwich Palace (Fig 5). Excavations at the palace during the early 1970s produced another tile with a curious circular design in blue on white (with a small central area in green) which may be related. It was found with what appears to be the corner of an interlocking strapwork pattern (cf **83**, **84**; D Gaimster, pers comm). ICP analysis indicates the clay chemistry is close to an Antwerp tile from Guildford (Hughes 2009).
Blue; ? x 73 x 15–18mm
RNW00 [56] <1>; analysed by ICP

17; Banqueting House, Whitehall, SW1, Westminster
Flemish, Antwerp; 1520–40
An edging tile used in conjunction with square and elongated hexagonal tiles. Such tiles are common in the tile pavement at The Vyne, which also contains square tiles with flower petal designs (Blanchett 2000, 25–31).
Poly; ? x ? x 23mm
Historic Royal Palaces

18; Banqueting House, Whitehall, SW1, Westminster
Flemish, Antwerp; 1520–40
An edging tile. The central diaper pattern is also present on a small square tile at The Vyne (Blanchett 2000, 8, f).
Poly; ? x ? x 23mm
Historic Royal Palaces

19; Crutched Friars, EC3, City of London
Flemish, Antwerp; 1520–40
Corner area from a tin-glazed mosaic pavement. A very similar corner tile is illustrated by Horne (1989, 16, no. 10).
Poly; 95 x 48 x 19mm
A12440

20; Banqueting House, Whitehall, SW1, Westminster
Flemish, Antwerp; 1520–40
A small square tile cut diagonally in the base. It was originally intended to split this tile into two triangular shapes, but this never took place.
Blue; 63 x 63 x 23mm
Historic Royal Palaces

21; Charter Quay, Market Place High Street, KT1, Kingston, Surrey
Flemish, Antwerp; probably 1520–40
Part of a rectangular tile with a red clay body rather than the more normal white and cream colour of 16th-century tiles. The wreath design is slightly reminiscent of that found on Italian maiolica pottery and on certain elongated hexagonal tiles from The Vyne and similar tiles are present at Herkenrode (Blanchett 2000, 10, g; Dumortier 2002, 88, fig 27). The Charter Quay tile may have been used in a border in the same manner as the tiles in The Vyne pavement.
Poly; ? x 81 x 21mm
CQD88 [1015] <563>; analysed by NAA (Chapter 5)

22; probably London
Flemish, Antwerp; 1545–70
The top line of the inscription reads 'AN', the last stoke of the letter 'N' extending upwards to form a cross. This is probably an abbreviation of the Latin words 'Anno Domini' (the year of our Lord). On the line beneath is the figure '23', which could represent the date 1523. Perhaps, the tile was made for a specific patron to commemorate some sort of anniversary.

The Fries Museum catalogue (1971, 69, cat no. 110) shows a similar Antwerp tile, whilst another tile with the same corner dated to 1545–70 has been recovered from Anjum, Northern Netherlands (Schaap 1984, 18, fig 2; van Dam 1991, 12, no. 4), and a further example in van Dam (1991, 12, fig 4) is dated 1545–70.
Poly; 115 x ? x 15mm
26122; analysed by NAA (Chapter 5)

23; 62–64 Aldgate High Street, EC3, City of London
English, London, Aldgate, or Flemish, Antwerp; mid–late 16th century
This tile may have been made at the nearby Aldgate pothouse, or it could have been brought in from Antwerp.
Blue; ? x ? x 20mm
AL74 [+] <911>

24; Monument House, 30–35 Botolph Lane, 29–31 Monument Street, EC3, City of London
Flemish, Antwerp; mid 16th century
The tile shows a marked similarity with a mid 16th-century tile from Antwerp (Fries Museum 1971, 79, cat no. 124).
Poly; ? x 133 x 21–22mm
BPL95 [104] <119>; Blair and Sankey 2007

25; Spital Square, 280 Bishopsgate, E1, Tower Hamlets
Flemish, Antwerp; mid 16th century
Probable square tile showing edge of a curving wreath, or similar design to those seen on elongated hexagonal tiles from The Vyne. Similar tiles are also present at Herkenrode (Blanchett 2000, 10, g).
Poly; ? x ? x 21mm
SRP98 [16920] <2037>

26; Great Queen Street, WC2, Camden
Flemish, Antwerp; *c* 1520–50
Tiles with an identical design have been found on the site of a manor house at Place Farm, Bletchingley, Surrey, dated *c* 1520–50 (Gaimster and Nenk 1997, 184–5). Claire Dumortier, an expert on Antwerp maiolica, suggests a date of about 1540 (T Wilson, pers comm). A tile with this design may have been used in a substantial house known as Warwick Inn (Central Criminal Court, Old Bailey, Warwick Square, EC4, City of London: MOL site code GM131 [ER1155] <1>; Fig 4, no. 17).
Poly; ? x 118 x 20mm
32.9/1; analysed by NAA (Chapter 5)

27; probably London
Flemish, Antwerp; *c* 1550
Geometric pattern with elaborate floral decoration in three colours. Antwerp tiles with the same design are illustrated in Dumortier (2002, 188, cat no. 34).
Poly; 135 x 135 x 15mm
26314

28; Bishopsgate, EC2, City of London
Flemish, Antwerp; *c* 1550
Another version of **27**, but with thick blue, rather than yellow lines around the decorative areas. Probably from the same pothouse as **27**.
Poly; 135 x 134 x 16mm
14544

29; Bull Wharf Lane, 16–21 Queenhithe, 66 Upper Thames Street, EC4, City of London
Flemish, Antwerp; *c* 1550
A third version of **27**, but painted using different colours.
Poly; ? x ? x 16mm
BUF90 [+] <606>

16

17

18

19

20

21

22

23

24

25

26

27

28

29

30; 36–41 Scotswood Street, EC1, Islington
Flemish, Antwerp; *c* 1550
Another design painted in the same distinctive style as **27–29**. The complete design is illustrated by Dumortier (2002, 188, cat no. 35). The Scotswood Street tile is probably from Newcastle House (Fig 4, no. 2) built in the ruins of St Mary Clerkenwell nunnery.
Poly; 129 x ? x 20mm
SCT87 [174] <34>

31; Caxton Hall, Caxton Street, SW1, Westminster
?Flemish, ?Antwerp; *c* 1550
The overall pattern would probably have been similar to a Dutch tile in Pluis (1997, 203, A.01.02.36) although the style of decoration is very different.
Poly; ? x ? x 19–21mm
CXH04 [80] <4>

32; 34 Allfarthing Lane, SW18, Wandsworth
?Flemish, ?Antwerp; *c* 1550
Similar in style to the Antwerp tiles with **27–30**.
Poly; 139 x 136 x 19mm
Wandsworth Museum, ANN I, WM 968-01/502

33; Norfolk House, 113–129 Lambeth Road, SE1, Lambeth
?Flemish, ?Antwerp; *c* 1550
Not a Dutch or English design, again painted in similar style to certain Antwerp tiles.
Poly; ? x ? x 15–16mm (reconstructed 126mm square)
NOR90 [1804] <443>, [2643] <891>

34; Billingsgate Market Lorry Park, Lower Thames Street, EC3, City of London
Flemish, Antwerp, Schoytestraat pothouse; 1575–1625
Its chemical composition closely matches the pottery made at the Schoytestraat pothouse in Antwerp (Gaimster and Hughes 1999, 179, fig 16.3) which, according to the typology of the pottery wasters, can be dated to the period 1575–1625 (Veeckman 1999, 115). Designs **35** and **36** are almost certainly from the same source.
Blue and yellow; ? x ? x 14mm
BIG82 [721] <999>; analysed by NAA (Chapter 5)

35; Billingsgate Market Lorry Park, Lower Thames Street, EC3, City of London
Flemish, Antwerp, Schoytestraat pothouse; 1575–1625
Blue and yellow; ? x ? x 14mm
BIG82 [721] <1017>

36; Billingsgate Market Lorry Park, Lower Thames Street, EC3, City of London
Flemish, Antwerp, Schoytestraat pothouse; 1575–1625
Possibly part of a rectangular border tile *c* 77mm wide. An unstratified tile from the same site shows another part of the same design (BIG82 [+] <1792>).
Blue and yellow; ? x ? x 14mm
BIG82 [721] <1313>

37; Central Criminal Court, Old Bailey, Warwick Square, EC4, City of London
Flemish, Antwerp; early–mid 16th century
Border of a tile picture. It has a similar corner motif to **26** indicating it is probably from the same pothouse. Probably from a large house known as Warwick Inn (Fig 4, no. 17).
Poly; 123 x 121 x 22mm
GM131 [ER1155] <2>; analysed by NAA (Chapter 5)

38; Tower Postern, Tower Hill, EC3, Tower Hamlets
Flemish, Antwerp, probably National Museum of Navigation pothouse; 16th century
Part of a heraldic shield which probably covered two tiles. If this is correct then the tile must have been quite large originally (*c* 160mm square). The heraldic design, comprising alternate fleur-de-lis and pelican motifs, has been examined by †John Goodall (pers comm) who states that it is typically English of 15th-century or later date, but is unidentified. Presumably the heraldry represents the coat of arms of a prominent London family, although the record of who this family was appears to have been lost.
Poly; ? x ? x 23mm
TOL79 [161] <59>; analysed by NAA (Chapter 5)

39; London
Flemish, Antwerp; mid 16th century
From the border of a tile picture painted in typical Antwerp style (Britton 1987, 171, no. 182).
Poly; 140 x 138 x 16mm
6945

40; Banqueting House, Whitehall, London, SW1, Westminster
?French; mid 16th century
Part of a larger tile picture.
Poly; 116 x 116 x 22–23mm
Historic Royal Palaces

41; probably London
Flemish, Antwerp; 1520–70
A corner of a rather crudely painted tile picture with a landscape scene and scroll corner decoration. The number 10 is painted on the back. The clay chemistry is close to two Antwerp tiles found at the Chateau Rameyen, Belgium (Hughes 2009).
Poly; 136 x 135 x 17mm
79.58; analysed by ICP

30

31

32

34

35

33

36

37

38

39

41

40

42; Aldgate, EC3, City of London
English, London, Aldgate pothouse; 1571–*c* 1615 or *c* 1620
Camel, in blue and purple medallion border. Almost certainly from the Aldgate pothouse near where it was found. A camel set in a medallion border (but in blue and brownish-yellow) was found on the site of the Pickleherring pothouse (Noël Hume 1977, 55, fig I no. 1).
Poly; 137 x 137 x 15mm
A3908

43; 32–35 Jewry Street, EC3, City of London
English, London, Aldgate pothouse; 1571–*c* 1615 or *c* 1620
Bear baiting, in blue and purple medallion border. This tile is recorded as coming from the site of the city ditch. Probably made at the Aldgate pothouse which lay just to the north of Jewry Street.
Poly; 133 x 133 x 20mm
13475

44; Baynards Castle, Upper Thames Street, EC4, City of London
English, London, Aldgate pothouse, or Flemish, Antwerp; late 16th–early 17th century
Grasshopper, in blue and purple medallion border. The grasshopper is the emblem of the Gresham family so it is possible that this design was commissioned by the Greshams (Horne 1989, 14–15).
Poly; 133 x ? x 16–20mm
30.155

45; probably London
English, London, Aldgate pothouse; 1571–*c* 1615 or *c* 1620
Dog, in blue and purple medallion border.
Poly; 133 x 133 x 18mm
6936

46; London
English, London, Aldgate pothouse; 1571–*c* 1615 or *c* 1620
Pig with bird perched on its back, in blue and purple medallion border.
Poly; ? x 135 x 15–18mm
24004

47; Coleman Street, EC2, City of London
English, London, ?Aldgate pothouse; late 16th–early 17th century
Owl, in blue and purple medallion border.
Poly; 134 x 132 x 19–20mm
6928

48; 36–41 Scotswood Street, EC1, Islington
English, London, ?Aldgate pothouse; late 16th–early 17th century
Bird, in blue and purple medallion border. Probably from Newcastle House (Fig 4, no. 2).
Poly; ? x ? x 17–18mm
SCT87 [19] <19>

49; Royal Mint, East Smithfield, E1, Tower Hamlets
English, London, ?Aldgate pothouse; late 16th–early 17th century
Deer, in blue and purple medallion border. A possible Aldgate tile.
Poly; ? x ? x 17mm
MIN86 [1756] <115>

50; Tower Hill West, Tower Hill, EC3, Tower Hamlets
English, London, ?Aldgate pothouse; late 16th–early 17th century
A man with a hat, in blue and purple medallion border. Medallion tiles with figures are rare in London.
Poly; ? x 135 x 18mm
THW85 [+] <95>

51; Gateway House, 1 Watling Street, EC4, City of London
English, London, Aldgate pothouse, Dutch, or Flemish, Antwerp; mid 16th–early 17th century
Chequerboard pattern in blue and purple medallion border. Almost certainly from the former church of St John the Evangelist in Watling Street (Fig 4, no. 12).
Poly; 133 x ? x 17–18mm
GM160 [ER161 A] <1>

52; 118 Minories, EC3, City of London
English, London, Aldgate pothouse; 1571–*c* 1615 or *c* 1620
Chequerboard pattern in blue and purple medallion border. This would appear to be an experimental tile from the nearby Aldgate pothouse (Chapter 3, English tiles). The tile was made with locally available red clay covered in white slip and then crudely painted.
Poly; ? x ? x 21mm
MIO86 [1010] <74>

53; Mitre Square, EC3, City of London
English, London, Aldgate pothouse; 1571–*c* 1615 or *c* 1620
Animal, probably a rabbit, in blue and purple medallion border. Another experimental tile, almost certainly from the Aldgate pothouse as it was found with kiln furniture and waste from pottery manufacture. As with 52 this was made using local red clay which in this case was overlain by a thin layer (1–2mm) of white-firing 'delft' clay (Chapter 3, English tiles).
Poly; ? x 136 x 15–17mm
CQU04 [10] <26>

42

43

44

45

46

47

48

49

50

51

52

53

54; London
Dutch or possibly English, London, Aldgate pothouse; 1570–1600
Chequerboard pattern, in blue and purple medallion border. The border design is Dutch (Pluis 1997, 521, B.02.00.02) but tiles of this type may also have been made in London. A tile with the same design was also found at 5–11 Tudor Street, EC4, City of London (MOL site code BOY86). Most other London tiles with this central pattern have the corner decoration as found on **42–53** (eg a tile from Billingsgate Market Lorry Park, Lower Thames Street, City of London: MOL site code BIG82 [761] <990>) and these may well be from Aldgate, London.
Poly; 135 x 133 x 19mm
6941a

55; Spitalfields Market, Spital Square, Lamb Street, Nantes Passage, Folgate Street, E1, Tower Hamlets
Dutch or possibly English, London, Aldgate pothouse; 1570–1600
Dog, in blue and purple medallion border.
Poly; 130 x 131 x 19–21mm
SQU94 [1213] <250>

56; Central Criminal Court, Old Bailey, Warwick Square, EC4, City of London
English, London, Pickleherring pothouse; *c* 1618–50
Fox, in blue and yellow medallion border. Tiles of this type were made at Pickleherring.
Poly; 138 x 136 x 13–15mm
24367; GM131 [ER1157]

57; Coleman Street, EC2, City of London
English, London, Pickleherring pothouse; *c* 1618–50
Owl, in blue and yellow medallion border. Tiles of this type were made at Pickleherring.
Poly; 132 x 132 x 13–15mm
6943

58; Clements Lane, EC4, City of London
English, London, Pickleherring pothouse; *c* 1618–50
Bear, in blue and yellow medallion border. Almost certainly made at Pickleherring as a tile with a very similar bear design has come from near the manufacturing site (Noël Hume 1977, 55, fig I no. 2).
Poly; 138 x 138 x 15mm
A27809

59; Vine Lane, Tooley Street, SE1, Southwark
English, London, Pickleherring pothouse; *c* 1618–50
Chequerboard pattern, in blue and yellow medallion border. Found on the site of the pothouse.
Poly; ? x *c* 139 x 17–19mm
VIN88 [147] <7>; Tyler et al 2008

60; London
English, London, or Dutch; late 16th–early 17th century
Figure with a Turkish-style head-dress, in blue and yellow medallion border. This tile has a slightly different corner design; the central fleur-de-lis is not dissected by a blue line.
Poly; 135 x 135 x 18mm
6929

61; probably London
Dutch; 1590–1625
The yellow and orange-brown circular border is characteristic of Dutch tiles (eg Schaap 1984, 62, no. 42; Pluis 1997, 116, 8). A Dutch medallion tile with a similar leaping dog is illustrated by van Sabben and Hollem (1987, 15, no. 40).
Poly; 133 x 133 x ?14mm
11903

62; St Matthew's church, Friday Street, EC4, City of London
?English; late 16th–early 17th century
This tile is of unusually small size suggesting that it may have been specially made for a specific area of the church floor. The chequerboard pattern closely resembles that used on medallion tiles which would suggest a similar date.
Blue; 103 x 103 x 17–18mm
6845; Fig 4, no. 18

54

55

56

57

58

59

60

61

62

63; Abbots Lane, Tooley Street, SE1, Southwark
English, London, Pickleherring pothouse; *c* 1618–50
Dog, in brown and blue circular border with oriental Wan Li corner motifs. Similar Dutch tiles with these corners are dated *c* 1620–50 (Pluis 1997, 402, A.04.01.07; 517, B.01.00.02; 519, B.01.00.20).
Poly; 132 x ? x 12mm
ABO92 [553] <1655>; Tyler et al 2008

64; 110–116 Cheapside, EC2, City of London
English, London, Pickleherring pothouse; *c* 1618–50
Hare, in brownish-orange and blue circular border with Wan Li corners. Similar to **63** although the central design is entirely blue.
Blue and yellow; 131 x 128 x 15mm
21686; GM37 [ER317A]

65; 110–116 Cheapside, EC2, City of London
English, London, Pickleherring pothouse; *c* 1618–50
A goat, in brownish-orange and blue circular border with Wan Li corners. Almost certainly from the same pothouse as **64**. Scientific analysis suggests a Pickleherring origin (Hughes 2009).
Blue and yellow; 133 x 133 x 14mm
21685; GM37 [ER317A]; analysed by ICP

66; Sutton House, 2 and 4 Homerton High Street, E9, Hackney
English, London, or Dutch; 1620–50
Central figure in purple and blue border with Wan Li corner.
Blue, purple; ? x ? x 15mm
SUT90; National Trust; Fig 5

67; Anchor Iron Wharf, Lassell Street, Hoskins Street, SE10, Greenwich
Flemish, ?Antwerp; mid–late 16th century
Part of a heraldic shield. Scientific analysis shows the clay chemistry to be similar to an Antwerp-produced Herkenrode tile of the 1530s found at Whitehall Palace (Hurst and Patourel 1999, 181–2, fig 17.1 lower tile). It is also similar in chemistry to **210** (Hughes 2009).
Poly; ? x ? x 14–15mm
LAS01 [152] <20>; analysed by ICP

68; London
English, London, or Dutch; late 16th–early 17th century
Dutch tiles with this design are dated 1560–1600 (Pluis 1997, 212, A.01.03.54). A tile from Norfolk House (MOL site code NOR90 [1024] <14>) has the same design but the bottom-right corner is painted yellow rather than green.
Poly; 137 x 137 x 14mm
P623

69; St Mary's Hospital, Paddington, W2, Westminster
English, London, or Dutch; late 16th–early 17th century
A different coloured version of **68**. This is closer to the example published by Pluis (1997, 212, A.01.03.54).
Poly; 137 x 135 x 16mm
A13155

70; The Old Swan Public House, Battersea Church Road, SW11, Wandsworth
English, London, or Dutch; late 16th–early 17th century
A drawing (of a ?bird) on the back of a tile with design **69**.
Poly; ? x ? x 16–20mm
BTC93 [9] <16>

71; probably London
English, London, or Dutch; late 16th–early 17th century
Dutch tiles with this design are dated 1580–1600 (Pluis 1997, 208, A01.03.25).
Poly; 140 x 140 x 16mm
79.51/1

72; Fleet Valley Project, Holborn Viaduct Station to Blackfriars, EC4, City of London
English, London, or Dutch; late 16th–early 17th century
Another version of **71** with a border area between the green and blue lacking the thick blue line. A further tile painted in similar style, has two blue bands in the border area (Royal Mint, East Smithfield, E1, Tower Hamlets: MOL site code MIN86 [5262] <2189>).
Poly; ? x ? x 20mm
VAL88 [+] <1874>

73; Southbridge House (site of Rose Theatre), 2–10 Southwark Bridge Road, SE1, Southwark
English, London, or Dutch; late 16th–early 17th century
A different coloured version of **71** and **72**. Found on the site of the Rose Theatre, in use 1587–1603 (Fig 4, no. 20).
Poly; 133 x ? x 17 mm
SBH88 [79] <26>

63

64

65

66

67

68

69

70

71

72

73

74; Southbridge House (site of Rose Theatre), 2–10 Southwark Bridge Road, SE1, Southwark
Two blue markings on the back face of **73**.
SBH88 [79] <26>; Fig 4, no. 20

75; 10–13 Carthusian Street, EC1, City of London
English, London/Dutch; late 16th–early 17th century
Another version of **71–73**, with a thick light blue band in the border area. Found on the site of the Red Lion Inn (Fig 4, no. 13), although it is not certain it was used in this building.
Poly; ? x ? x 16mm
CTN86 [65] <31>

76; 7–11 Bishopsgate, EC2, City of London
?Dutch; 1580–1600
The surviving corner area is virtually identical with complete Dutch tiles on display in the Rijksmuseum, Amsterdam, and the same design is shown in Pluis (1997, 207, A.01.03.19) who dates Dutch tiles with this design to 1580–1600.
Poly; ? x ? x 12mm
ETA89 [210] <914>

77; Platform Wharf, Cathay Street, SE16, Southwark
English, London, Rotherhithe pothouse; *c* 1638–50
Part of a geometric floral pattern. The only other tile known in London with this design was found at 15–17 High Street, Uxbridge, UB8, Hillingdon (Middlesex) (MOL site code UX83 IV [+] <240>).
Poly; ? x 135 x 15–16mm
PW86 [1] <135>; Tyler et al 2008

78; Brooke House, Upper Clapton Road, E5, Hackney
English, London, or Dutch; late 16th–early 17th century
The complete design is shown on a Dutch tile published by Pluis (1997, 203, A.01.02.35) dated 1570–1600. Another tile from Brooke House (85.3/195iii) shows the bottom-left corner is painted brown.
Poly; ? x 134 x 18mm
85.3/195iii, 85.3/195iv; Fig 5; Fig 7

79; Norfolk House, 113–129 Lambeth Road, SE1, Lambeth
English, London, or Dutch; late 16th–early 17th century
As **78** but with the colours in the corner reversed.
Poly; 130 x ? x 17–18mm
NOR90 [+] <335>

80; Caxton Hall, Caxton Street, SW1, Westminster
English, London, or Dutch; late 16th–early 17th century
Similar corner decoration to **78** and **79**, but bordering straight blue on white strapwork.
Poly; ? x ? x 18mm
CXH04 [15] <3>

81; Lime Kiln Dock, Three Colt Lane, E14, Tower Hamlets
English, London, Pickleherring pothouse; *c* 1618–50
The complete design is shown in Pluis (1997, 300, A.01.27.43).
Poly; ? x 133 x 15–16mm
LKD94 [8] <40>

82; Vine Lane, Tooley Street, SE1, Southwark
English, or Dutch; 1570–1650
A similar design to **81** but with a different corner motif. A more complete example from London is illustrated by Horne (1989, 14, no. 2). The tile was used as kiln furniture at the Pickleherring pothouse, but ICP analysis suggests it is from another, unknown, source (Hughes 2008, 126; Tyler et al 2008, 54).
Poly; ? x ? x 15mm
VIN88 [+] <20>; analysed by ICP (Chapter 5)

83; probably London
English, London, Pickleherring or Rotherhithe pothouses; *c* 1618–50
A common design in London. An example from Pickleherring published by Noël Hume (1977, 57, fig II no. 6) has light blue and yellowish-green corners with a light blue centre.
Poly; 135 x 132 x 16mm
16025

84; Blossom's Inn, 20–30 Gresham Street, EC2, City of London
English, London; *c* 1618–50
Another version of **83**, but with orange and yellow corners. The light blue central area has run during the firing.
Poly; 135 x 133 x 14mm
GHT00 [4158] <1103>

74

75

76

Pluis (1997)

77

80

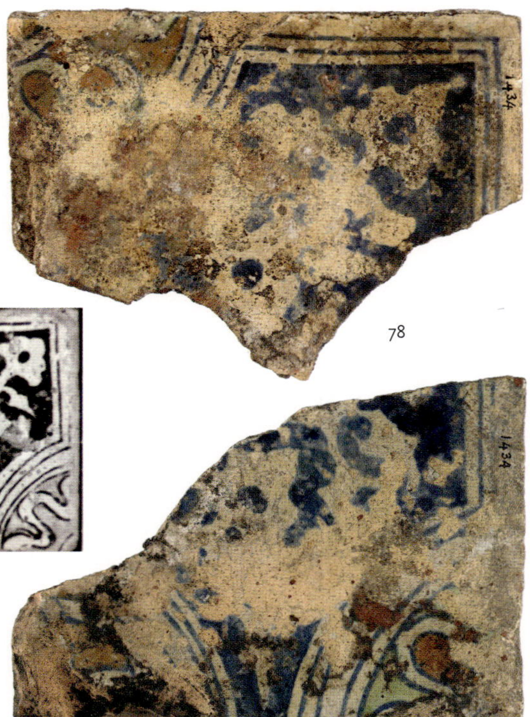

78

Pluis (1997)

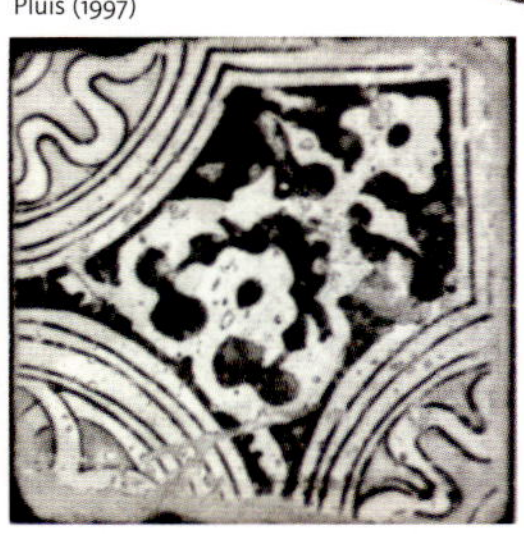

79

81

Pluis (1997)

82

83

84

85; probably London
?English, ?London; late 16th–mid 17th century
Possibly a Pickleherring pothouse product. A Dutch tile of 1570–1600 with similar designs is in Pluis (1997, 331, A.01.70.05).
Poly; 134 x 134 x 18mm
85.59/40

86; Niblett Hall, 4 King's Bench Walk, EC4, City of London
English, London, or Dutch; late 15th–mid 17th century
Perhaps a different coloured version of **85**, although the corner motif is slightly different.
Poly; ? x ? x 19–21mm
KBK92 [49] <135>

87; Vine Lane, Tooley Street, SE1, Southwark
English, London, Pickleherring pothouse; *c* 1618–50
Poly; ? x ? x 13mm
VIN88 [+] <3>; Tyler et al 2008

88; Southbridge House (site of Rose Theatre), 2–10 Southwark Bridge Road, SE1, Southwark
?Dutch; 1570–1600
Similar to a Dutch tile, dated 1570–1600, illustrated by Pluis (1997, 331, A.01.07.06). Found on the site of the Rose Theatre, in use 1587–1603 (Fig 4, no. 20).
Poly; ? x ? x 14mm (reconstructed *c* 130mm square)
SBH88 [40] <695>

89; 10–13 Carthusian Street, EC1, City of London
English, London, or Dutch; late 16th–early 17th century
Found on the site of the Red Lion Inn (Fig 4, no. 13), although it is not certain if it was used in the building. A complete Dutch tile with this design, dated to 1570–1600, is shown in Pluis (1997, 200, A.01.02.16).
Poly; 134 x ? x 18–19mm
CTN86 [65] <32>

90; 10–13 Carthusian Street, EC1, City of London
?English, ?London; late 16th–early 17th century
Similar pattern to **89**, but not the same design.
Poly; 128 x ? x 18mm
CTN86 [65] <21>

91; Thames foreshore near Cannon Street, EC4, City of London
?English, ?London; late 16th–early 17th century
A floral and geometric pattern which if symmetrical is slightly larger than most polychrome tiles used in London.
Poly; ? x *c* 140 x 17–18mm
Private collection, ? Terry Greenwood

92; probably London
English, London; late 16th–mid 17th century
Tiles of this design were made at both the Pickleherring and Rotherhithe pothouses, although it is not certain if the decoration in the brown central area is in the same style as the tile illustrated. A tile of similar design has been found associated with a building known as Honeywood in Carshalton, Sutton (Surrey). However, Honeywood was probably constructed in the 1680s (J Phillips, pers comm), so the tile may be from an earlier building.
Poly; 132 x 130 x 15–17mm
11900

93; probably London
English, London; late 16th–mid 17th century
A different version of **92** with a thicker blue border around the central diamond shape and the two green corners. Probably made in one of the same pothouses as **92**.
Poly; 139 x 135 x 18mm
11898

94; probably London
English, London, ?Pickleherring pothouse; *c* 1618–50
Noël Hume illustrates a fragmentary tile from Pickleherring with the same design (1977, 57, fig II no. 9).
Poly; 138 x 137 x 15–19mm
11897

95; Vine Lane, Tooley Street, SE1, Southwark
English, London, Pickleherring pothouse; *c* 1618–50
The same design as **94** but with yellow replacing brown. The tile was made at Pickleherring pothouse and has a setter attached to the top surface indicating that it was used as kiln shelving during the firing process.
Poly; ? x ? x 18mm
VIN88 [+] <21>; analysed by ICP (Chapter 5); Tyler et al 2008

85

86

87

88

89

Pluis (1997)

90

91

92

93

94

95

96; probably London
English, London, ?Pickleherring pothouse; *c* 1618–50
Another version of **94** and **95** but this time with two thick blue lines in the border between the orangey-brown and blue areas. Other areas of the design are present on the tile from 2 King Edward Street, City of London (MOL site code KEW98 [3051] <1221>). Probably a Pickleherring pothouse product.
Poly; 135 x ? x 16–17mm
79.32/3

97; 2–9, 10–16 Bevis Marks, 15–18 Bury Street, EC3, City of London
?Flemish, or ?English; mid 16th–mid 17th century
Not a Dutch design, the interlocking circular motif is reminiscent of Antwerp tiles (**24**), alternatively it could be English.
Poly; 135 x ? x 17mm
BEV80 [282] <255>

98; 27–29 Whitechapel High St, 2–4 Colchester Street, E1, Tower Hamlets
?Flemish, or ?English; mid 16th–mid 17th century
A further fragment showing more areas of **97**.
Poly; 133 x ? x 16–18mm
WCE01 [+] <45>; Sygrave 2005

99; 62–64 Aldgate High Street, EC3, City of London
?English, or ?Dutch; 1580–1600
One of three tiles with this design from the site (Betts 1999, pl 12). Possibly made at the Aldgate pothouse, although tiles of similar design were made at Rotterdam. Pluis (1997, 306, A.01.30.16) shows a complete tile with this Dutch design.
Poly; ? x ? x 18mm
AL74 [1177] <781>

100; 4 Spital Square, E1, Tower Hamlets
?Dutch; 1600–40
Probably from a large tenanted building, known as the Principal Tenement, on the site of the former priory and hospital of St Mary Spital (Fig 4, no. 8). Pluis (1997, 541, C.01.00.09) illustrates a Dutch tile with the same border and corner design although the central flower pattern is different.
Poly; 130 x ? x 14mm
SPQ88 [+] <432>

101; Gateway House, 1 Watling Street, EC4, City of London
English, London, Rotherhithe pothouse; *c* 1638–50
Almost certainly from the former church of St John the Evangelist in Watling Street (Fig 4, no. 12). Tiles with this design have been found in the vicinity of the Rotherhithe pothouse (Platform Wharf, Cathay Street, SE16, Southwark: MOL site code PW86 [+] <133>, [1] <98>).
Poly; 131 x 129 x 15mm
GM160 [ER191 A] <1>–<4>

102; probably London
?English, or ?Dutch; early–mid 17th century
Another tile with this design, from the site of Bermondsey Abbey (Fig 4), has the central leaves painted in brown rather than green (Bermondsey Abbey, Abbey Street, Long Walk, SE1, Southwark: MOL site code BA84 [1138] <772>). The latter may have come from a large mansion house built on the site of the abbey by Sir Thomas Pope.
Poly; 139 x 137 x 16–19mm
6930

103; Tower Hill West, Tower Hill, EC3, Tower Hamlets
?English, or ?Dutch; early–mid 17th century
Another version of **102**, again painted using different colours.
Poly; ? x ? x 18mm
THW85 [7] <101>

104; Royal Exchange, Threadneedle Street/Cornhill, EC2, City of London
English, London, ?Pickleherring pothouse; early–mid 17th century
There are Pickleherring-made tiles painted in a similar pattern.
Poly; 133 x 132 x 16–18mm
6931

105; Stothard Place, 284–294 Bishopsgate, EC2, Tower Hamlets
?English, ?London; early–mid 17th century
Similar to **104** but with a different arrangement of flowers.
Poly; ? x ? x 17mm
STO86 [109] <171>

106; Threadneedle Street, EC2, City of London
?English, ?London; early–mid 17th century
A version of design **104** with two thicker lines bordering the floral decoration.
Poly; 132 x ? x 22mm
79.51/6

107; Lime Kiln Dock, Three Colt Lane, E14, Tower Hamlets
?English, ?London; early–mid 17th century
Another version of **104** this time with three lines bordering the floral decoration.
Poly; ? x 130 x 16mm
LKD94 [8] <41>

96

97

98

99

100

101

102

103

105

106

104

107

108; probably London
English, London, ?Rotherhithe pothouse; *c* 1638–50
Tudor rose. A popular London design made at both Pickleherring (Noël Hume 1977, 57, fig II no. 2) and Rotherhithe pothouses (Tyler et al 2008). Based on the application and location of the colours, **108** is probably from Rotherhithe.
Poly; 136 x 136 x 14–15mm
A22937

109; Morgan's Lane, Tooley Street, SE1, Southwark
English, London, Pickleherring pothouse; *c* 1618–50
Tudor rose. Another example of **108** showing slight differences in the colours used.
Poly; ? x 136 x 15mm
MOR87 [343] <336>; Tyler et al 2008

110; Monument House, 30–35 Botolph Lane, 29–31 Monument Street, EC3, City of London
English, London, ?Pickleherring pothouse; *c* 1618–50
Tudor rose. Blackened corner area of **108** showing addition of orange paint, perhaps an attempt to improve a poorly made product.
Poly; ? x ? x 16mm
BPL95 [104] <55>; Blair and Sankey 2007

111; probably London
English, London, Pickleherring or Rotherhithe pothouse; *c* 1618–50
Tudor rose. A common blue and white version of **108**, also made at both Pickleherring (Noël Hume 1977, 57, fig II no. 1) and Rotherhithe pothouses (Tyler et al 2008). The same design is present on a tile believed to have been made at Aldgate in 1571–*c* 1615 or *c* 1620, but this is distinctly thicker (19–20mm; Betts 1999, pl 11). Additionally, there are two tile fragments with design similar to **111** from 8–13 Clerkenwell Close, 33–36 Clerkenwell Green, EC1, Islington (MOL site code ENG84 [111] <98>) and 8–13 Sans Walk, EC1, Islington (MOL site code SNS87 [1] <139>).
Blue; 128 x 126 x 14mm
6924a

112; 7–8 (formerly 3–8) King Street, EC2, City of London
?English, or ?Dutch; early–mid 17th century
An unusually large tile showing many similarities in design to **108–111**.
Poly; 138 x 140 x 19mm
15216

113; 62–64 Aldgate High Street, EC3, City of London
English, London, Aldgate pothouse; 1571–*c* 1615 or *c* 1620
Probably from the pothouse at Aldgate.
Poly; 134 x 134 x 13mm
AL74 [+] <276>

114; 62–64 Aldgate High Street, EC3, City of London
English, London, Aldgate pothouse; 1571–*c* 1615 or *c* 1620
A more crudely painted version of **113**. The tile, presumably made at Aldgate, shows a blurred pattern as a result of the glaze running during firing.
Poly; 131 x 130 x 15–17mm
AL74 [+] <277>

115; 16–21 St John's Lane, EC1, Islington
English, London; late 16th–mid 17th
Another version of **113**. Possibly from Aldgate, although equally it could have come from the Rotherhithe or Pickleherring pothouses which made blue on white versions of this design (**116**).
Poly; 129 x 129 x 16–18mm
BRI86 [21] <20>

116; probably London
English, London; 1571–*c* 1650
A blue on white version of **113–115**, made at both the Pickleherring (Noël Hume 1977, 57, fig II no. 3) and Rotherhithe pothouses (Tyler et al 2008), and probably Aldgate as well.
Blue; 135 x 135 x 16mm
P622

108

109

110

111

112

113

114

115

116

117; Leadenhall Street, EC3, City of London
English, London, Pickleherring pothouse; *c* 1618–50
A tile from Bishopsgate Goods Yard (East London Line Extension, Bethnal Green Road, Shoreditch High Street, E1, Hackney (Middlesex): MOL site code BGX05 [522] ‹1498›) with a similar design was analysed by ICP and shown to be of probable Pickleherring origin (Hughes 2009).
Poly; 135 x 135 x 18–19mm
A16598

118, 1–6 Milk Street, 5–6 Russia Row, EC2, City of London
English, London, Pickleherring pothouse; *c* 1618–50
Another version of **117** with a different corner decoration. Pluis (1997, 216, A.01.05.07) shows a Dutch tile with a similar design although in reverse.
Poly; 135 x ? x 17–18mm
MLK76 [3030] ‹1135›

119; Billingsgate Market Lorry Park, Lower Thames Street, EC3, City of London
English, London, Pickleherring pothouse; *c* 1618–50
This is a reverse of **117** and **118**. Horne (1989, 14, no. 4) shows a complete tile with the same reverse design.
Poly; ? x ? x 18mm
BIG82 [721] ‹1005›

120; probably London
English, London, Pickleherring or Rotherhithe pothouse; *c* 1618–50
Grapes with fleur-de-lis corners. The design on this tile is very similar to an example made at Pickleherring pothouse. Alternatively, it may have been made at Rotherhithe as the associated design showing a pomegranate (**123**, **124**) has been found near the Thames in the vicinity of the production site (J Kent, pers comm). A further small fragment (Platform Wharf, Cathay Street, SE16, Southwark: MOL site code PW89 [1457] ‹163›), which could have either grapes or pomegranates, has also been found in the pothouse waste dumps at Rotherhithe.
Poly; 135 x 134 x 17–20mm
6934

121; London
English, London, Pickleherring or Rotherhithe pothouse, or Dutch; *c* 1618–50
Another version of **120**. Similar to a Dutch design (Pluis 1997, 227, A.01.05.76) dated 1620–50, but probably English.
Poly; 140 x 140 x 13mm
13462

122; Spitalfields Market, E1, Tower Hamlets
English, London, Pickleherring or Rotherhithe pothouse; *c* 1618–50
A further version of **120**.
Poly; 129 x 129 x 14–15mm
11991

123; probably London
English, London, Pickleherring or Rotherhithe pothouse; *c* 1618–50
Pomegranate, fleur-de-lis corners. Similar Dutch tiles are in Schaap (1984, 58, nos 35–36).
Poly; 131 x 130 x 15–17mm
P624

124; Cherry Garden Project, Bermondsey Wall East, SE16, Southwark
English, London, Pickleherring or Rotherhithe pothouse; *c* 1618–50
A blue on white version of **123**. A blue on white tile with this design has been found in the vicinity of Rotherhithe pothouse (J Kent, pers comm).
Blue; 130 x ? x 13mm
CG87 [+] ‹192›

125; 4 Spital Square, E1, Tower Hamlets
English, London, Pickleherring pothouse; *c* 1618–50
Probably from a large tenanted building known as the Principal Tenement on the site of the former priory and hospital of St Mary Spital (Fig 4, no. 8). A Pickleherring pothouse product, Noël Hume (1977, 57, fig II no. 7) shows a more complete example from near the manufacturing site.
Poly; ? x ? x 15–16mm
SPQ88 [+] ‹377›, ‹446›; Thomas et al 1997

126; Platform Wharf, Cathay Street, SE16, Southwark
English, London, Rotherhithe pothouse; *c* 1638–50
Leaf and grape design.
Blue and green; ? x ? x 14mm
PW86 [2335] ‹528›; Tyler et al 2008

127; Platform Wharf, Cathay Street, SE16, Southwark
English, London, Rotherhithe pothouse; *c* 1638–50
The complete design on a Dutch tile is illustrated by Pluis (1997, 301, A.01.28.04).
Poly; ? x ? x 13mm
PW90 [2198] ‹482›; Tyler et al 2008

128; Platform Wharf, Cathay Street, SE16, Southwark
English, London, Rotherhithe pothouse; *c* 1638–50
A blue on white version of **127**.
Blue; ? x ? x 13mm
PW90 [2321] ‹490›; Tyler et al 2008

117

118

119

120

121

122

123

124

125
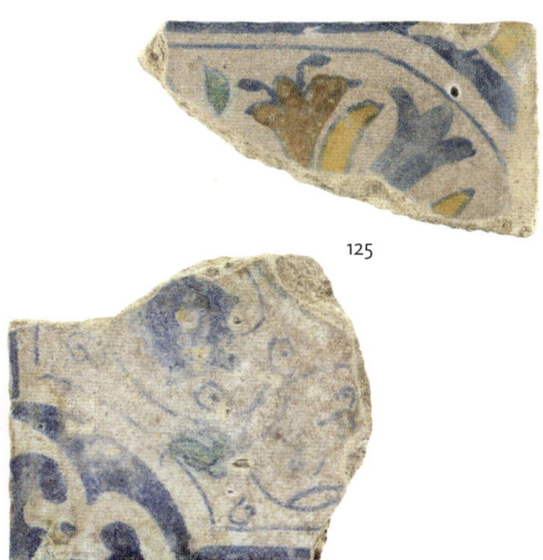

126

127

Pluis (1997)

128

129; probably London
English, London, ?Pickleherring pothouse; *c* 1618–50
Very similar to an example from the Pickleherring pothouse. Tiles painted with this design were also made at Rotherhithe (**132**). Dutch tiles with this design are dated 1610–40 (Pluis 1997, 250, A.01.11.83).
Poly; 133 x 133 x 14–15mm
6948

130; probably London
English, London, ?Pickleherring pothouse; *c* 1618–50
Another version of **129**. The colour scheme is similar, although not identical, to a tile from Pickleherring pothouse published by Noël Hume (1977, 57, fig II no. 5).
Poly; ? x ? x 15mm
79.50/3

131; 8–13 Clerkenwell Close, 33–36 Clerkenwell Green, EC1, Islington
English, London, ?Pickleherring or ?Rotherhithe pothouse; *c* 1618–50
A further version of **129**.
Poly; 132 x 131 x 14mm
ENG84 [+] <97>

132; Platform Wharf, Cathay Street, SE16, Southwark
English, London, Rotherhithe pothouse; *c* 1638–50
A blue on white version of **129**, also made at Pickleherring.
Blue; 135 x ? x 13mm
PW86 [1] <128>; Tyler et al 2008

133; Bull Wharf, Bull Wharf Lane, 66 Upper Thames Street, 16–21 Queenhithe, EC4, City of London
?English, ?London; 1600–50
Flower vase design with quarter rosette corner. Probably English, as a tile with a similar corner motif has been found near the Pickleherring pothouse (Morgan's Lane, Tooley Street, SE1, Southwark: MOL site code MOR87 [+] <397>). Pluis shows a complete Dutch tile with a similar design dated 1600–40 (1997, 422, A.05.08.07).
Poly; ? x ? x 15–16mm
BUF90 [1876] <604>

134; Lime Street, EC3, City of London
Dutch; 1570–1600
Flower vase, flower petal corners. Pluis illustrates an almost identical tile (1997, 421, A.05.08.01).
Poly; 135 x ? x 18–21mm
23929

135; Vine Lane, Tooley Street, SE1, Southwark
English, London, Pickleherring pothouse; *c* 1618–50
Flowers in diamond border. Tiles with similar borders were made at the Rotherhithe pothouse, although here the border is brown rather than yellow.
Poly; ? x 133 x 16mm
VIN88 [+] <38>; Tyler et al 2008

136; Cannon Street Station, Cannon Street, Dowgate Hill, Bush Lane, EC4, City of London
English, London, Pickleherring or Rotherhithe pothouse; *c* 1618–50
A landscape version of **135** with the hind legs of an animal (?dog).
Poly; ? x ? x 14mm
LYD88 [10] <901>

137; Bethel Estate, Vine Lane, SE1, Southwark
English, London, Pickleherring pothouse; *c* 1618–50
Flower vase in diamond border. Another tile from Pickleherring, showing more of the right edge, is illustrated by Noël Hume (1977, 57, fig II no. 4).
Poly; ? x 135 x 18mm
BTH88 [585] <190>; Tyler et al 2008

138; Platform Wharf, Cathay Street, SE16, Southwark
English, London, Rotherhithe pothouse; *c* 1638–50
Flower in diamond border, with large barred ox-head corners.
Poly; ? x ? x 13–14mm
PW86 [2335] <530>; Tyler et al 2008

139; Platform Wharf, Cathay Street, SE16, Southwark
English, London, Rotherhithe pothouse; *c* 1638–50
Tulip in diamond border, barred ox-head corners
Poly; 131 x ? x 13–14mm
PW86 [+] <531>; Tyler et al 2008

140; probably London
English, London, ?Rotherhithe pothouse; *c* 1638–50
A similar blue on white version of **139**, probably also from Rotherhithe.
Blue; 130 x 130 x 14–16mm
11896

129

130

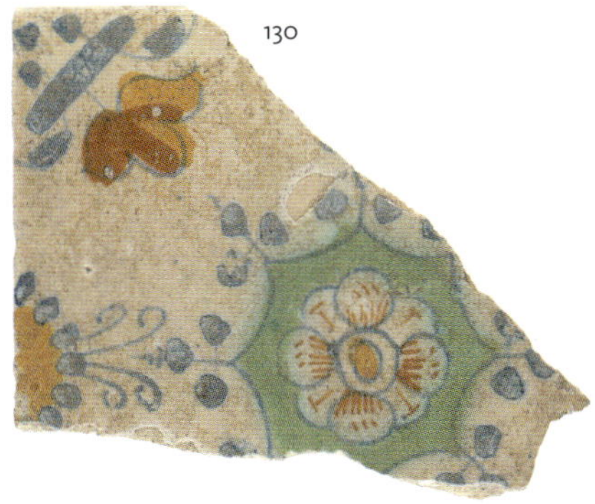

131

132

133

Pluis (1997)

134

135

136

137

138

139

140

141; Billingsgate Market Lorry Park, Lower Thames Street, EC3, City of London
English, London, Rotherhithe pothouse; *c* 1638–50
A similar design to **139** but with three blue lines forming the diamond border. Almost certainly a Rotherhithe pothouse product.
Poly; 131 x 130 x 14mm
BIG82 [42] <465>

142; Platform Wharf, Cathay Street, SE16, Southwark
English, London, Rotherhithe pothouse; *c* 1638–50
A blue on white version of **141**.
Blue; ? x ? x 13mm
PW90 [2247] <514>; Tyler et al 2008

143; Vine Lane, Tooley Street, SE1, Southwark
English, London, Pickleherring pothouse; *c* 1618–50
Flowers in curved lozenge-shaped border, barred ox-head corners. For base of this design see Hinton et al (1988, 334, fig 144 no. 1412, note drawing is upside down).
Poly; ? x ? x 14mm
VIN88 [84] <5>; Tyler et al 2008

144; Cannon Street Station, Cannon Street, Dowgate Hill, Bush Lane, EC4, City of London
English, London, Pickleherring or Rotherhithe pothouse; *c* 1618–63
Flowers in crenulated diamond border, barred ox-head corners. Probably from Rotherhithe pothouse, although Pickleherring is also a possibility.
Poly; 135 x 135 x 14mm
LYD88 [10] <245>

145; Tower Hill West, Tower Hill, EC3, Tower Hamlets
English, London, ?Pickleherring pothouse; *c* 1618–50
Flowers in crenulated diamond border, fleur-de-lis corners. The crudity of the painting suggests that it is English. It appears to be a blue and white version of **146**, which would indicate manufacture at Pickleherring.
Blue; 136 x ? x 13mm
THW85 [9] <100>

146; Morgan's Lane, Tooley Street, SE1, Southwark
English, London, Pickleherring pothouse; *c* 1618–50
This tile has a very similar fleur-de-lis corner design to cat no. **145**, and the small area surviving inside the diamond border is similar.
Poly; ? x ? x 14mm
MOR88 [+] <14>; Tyler et al 2008

147; probably London
Dutch; 1640–70
Flowers in diamond border, fleur-de-lis corners. Van Dam (1991, 69, no. 77) illustrates Dutch tiles of similar design dated 1640–70, although the corner motifs are not quite identical. Similar tiles were evidently made at Rotherhithe where two small pieces of tile with a diamond-shaped border and similar corner motifs have been found in pothouse waste dumps (Tyler et al 2008, 87, fig 141 D12).
Poly; 131 x 130 x 12–13mm
6935

148; probably London
Dutch; 1640–70
Tulip in diamond border, fleur-de-lis corners. The tile has certain similarities in design to Pluis design B.10.00.07 (1997, 527). It also has the same border and corners as a thicker (earlier) tile in Pluis (1997, 542, C.02.00.05).
Blue; 127 x 126 x 10mm
NN15809

149; probably London
Dutch; 1630–60
Flowers in diamond border, modified fleur-de-lis corners. There are Dutch tiles with similar borders and corner motifs in Pluis (1997, 544, C02.00.17–18) and Lunsingh Scheurleer (1986, 5, no. 6) shows another Dutch tile with a similar central flower and the same border and corner arrangement.
Poly; 133 x 132 x 15–16mm
Z3382

150; probably London
Dutch; mid 17th century
Flowers in small diamond border, fleur-de-lis corners. Van Sabben and Hollem (1987, 65, no. 204) illustrate an almost identical Dutch tile with this design.
Blue; 126 x 126 x 11mm
16011

141

142

143

144

145

146

147

148

149

150

151; probably London
Dutch; 1620–70
Three-headed tulip. Identical Dutch tiles are illustrated in Schaap (1984, 87, no. 87) and Pluis (1997, 417, A.05.04.01). The London example is so similar it is possible that it was decorated by the same tile-painter.
Poly; 126 x 126 x 10mm
7104

152; probably London
Dutch; 1620–40
Flower, fleur-de-lis corners. An almost identical Dutch tile with this design is shown by Pluis (1997, 119, fig 13) dated 1620–40.
Poly; 131 x 130 x 12–13mm
Z3406

153; Brooke House, Upper Clapton Road, E5, Hackney (Middlesex)
Dutch; 1640–60
Flowers with crude barred ox-head corners. The skill of the flower painting compared to that shown for the corners shows that this is the work of two different tile-painters. This twin combination of painting styles is seen on a number of Dutch flower tiles with similar barred ox-head corners dated to 1640–60 (van Dam 1991, 66, 70, nos 72, 78).
Poly; ? x 133 x 14mm
EH 1695; Fig 5; Fig 7

154; probably London
?Dutch; mid 17th century
Floral tile painted in an unusual combination of colours, with barred ox-head corners.
Poly; 124 x 123 x 12mm
6947

155; 2–9, 10–16 Bevis Marks, 15–18 Bury Street, EC3, City of London
?English, ?London; *c* 1630–90
Flowers, barred ox-head corners. The open flower closely matches those on London plates dated to *c* 1670–90 (Archer 1997, 90, A30, A32, pl 16). Designs **156–158** are almost certainly from the same pothouse.
Poly; 129 x ? x 13mm
BEV80 [+] <61>

156; 2–9, 10–16 Bevis Marks, 15–18 Bury Street, EC3, City of London
?English, ?London; *c* 1630–90
Flowers, barred ox-head corners.
Poly; 126 x 125 x 12–13mm
BEV80 [4] <54>

157; 2–9, 10–16 Bevis Marks, 15–18 Bury Street, EC3, City of London
?English, ?London; *c* 1630–90
Flowers, barred ox-head corners.
Poly; 129 x 129 x 13mm
BEV80 [+] <63> and <64>

158; 2–9, 10–16 Bevis Marks, 15–18 Bury Street, EC3, City of London
?English, ?London; *c* 1630–90
Flower, barred ox-head corners.
Poly; 127 x 127 x 12mm
BEV80 [4] <53>

159; Guildhall Art Gallery, Guildhall Yard, EC2, City of London
?English, ?London; mid 17th century
Flower, barred ox-head corners. This design has similarities with **161** from the Rotherhithe pothouse. The tile may have been used in the vicarage of St Lawrence Jewry church which formerly occupied part of the west end of what is now Guildhall Yard (Fig 4, no. 10).
Poly; 132 x 132 x 14mm
GAG87 [3082] <1206>; Bowsher et al 2007

151

152

153

154

155

156

157

158

159

160; Platform Wharf, Cathay Street, SE16, Southwark
English, London, Rotherhithe pothouse; *c* 1638–60
Flower, large barred ox-head corners.
Blue and orange; ? x ? x 13–15mm
PW86 [1] <137>; Tyler et al 2008

161; Platform Wharf, Cathay Street, SE16, Southwark
English, London, Rotherhithe pothouse; *c* 1638–60
Flower, barred ox-head corners.
Blue; 135 x 134 x 15mm
PW90 [2283] <479>; Tyler et al 2008

162; probably London
English, London, Pickleherring or Rotherhithe pothouse; *c* 1618–60
Flower vase, barred ox-head corners. Tiles with this design were made at both Pickleherring and Rotherhithe. They were also used in Ham House, Richmond upon Thames (Surrey) (Currie 1996, 109, fig 1 no. 5; Fig 5).
Blue; 136 x 135 x 14–15mm
A4632

163; Braidwood Street, Tooley Street, SE1, Southwark
English, London, Pickleherring or Rotherhithe pothouse; *c* 1618–60
Another version of **162** with a larger vase of flowers. Barred ox-head corners.
Blue; 128 x 128 x 12mm
BRA88 [13] <20>

164; 89–97 St John's Street, EC1, Islington
English, London, Pickleherring or Rotherhithe pothouse; *c* 1618–60
Flower design, barred ox-head corners.
Blue; 128 x ? x 13mm
SAJ98 [177] <45>

165; probably London
Dutch; 1650–75
Central flower with spider head corners. The latter are dated to 1650–75 by Pluis (1997, 555, C.08.00.05).
Blue; 130 x 130 x 11mm
Z3404

166; 12–14 Cooper's Row, EC3, City of London
English, ?London, or Dutch; 1620–60
Fruit bowl, barred ox-head corners. Van Sabben and Hollem show Dutch tiles with similar fruit bowls with a variety of corner decoration (1987, 46, nos 122–127, 48, nos 131–136). There is another similar Dutch tile in Pluis dated 1620–60 (1997, 430, A.06.01.06). The quality of painting on the Cooper's Row tile is less accomplished than on these Dutch examples suggesting it may be a London copy, perhaps made at Pickleherring or Rotherhithe.
Blue; 138 x 137 x 14–16mm
L-P: Archaeology CPQ03 [763] <134>

167; probably London
Dutch; 1630–50
Bird in foliage, barred ox-head corners (see **168–171**). Tiles with the same corner and border arrangement are dated 1630–50 by Pluis (1997, 551, C.07.00.18). Bird tiles with similar borders and corners are in Schaap (1984, 75, no. 65).
Poly; 125 x 128 x 10mm
A20294

168; probably London
Dutch; 1630–50
Bird on foliage, barred ox-head corners.
Poly; 127 x 127 x 10mm
A20293

160

161

162

163

164

165

166

167

168

169; probably London
Dutch; 1630–50
Bird on foliage, barred ox-head corners.
Poly; 130 x 126 x 10mm
A20295

170; probably London
Dutch; 1630–50
Bird on foliage, barred ox-head corners.
Poly; 129 x 128 x 10mm
A20296

171; probably London
Dutch; 1630–50
Bird and foliage, barred ox-head corners.
Poly; 128 x 126 x 10mm
A20292

172; probably London
Dutch; 1640–70
Bird on foliage, barred ox-head corners. Similar bird tiles are in Schaap (1984, 76, no. 66).
Poly; 129 x 131 x 10mm
16023

173; Duke Street, Aldgate, EC3, City of London
English, ?Pickleherring pothouse, or Dutch; mid 17th century
Bird, barred ox-head corners. Animal tiles with slightly different barred ox-head corners were made at Pickleherring (**175**), but the bird has similarities to that found on a Dutch tile in Schaap (1984, 74, no. 64-B).
Blue; 134 x 134 x 10–11mm
A20389

174; Bermondsey Abbey, Abbey Street, Long Walk, SE1, Southwark
English, London, ?Pickleherring pothouse; mid 17th century
Horned animal, probably made at the Pickleherring pothouse (see **175**). Possibly from Bermondsey House a large mansion house built on the site of the abbey by Sir Thomas Pope in the 1540s (Steele et al in prep; Fig 4, no. 3).
Blue; 130 x ? x 10–11mm
BA84 [242] <773>

175; Bethel Estate, Vine Lane, SE1, Southwark
English, London, Pickleherring pothouse; *c* 1618–50
Horned animal. A further tile from this pothouse has what appears to be a dog (Vine Lane, Tooley Street, SE1, Southwark: MOL site code VIN88 [338] <102>).
Blue; ? x ? x 13mm
BTH88 [+] <257>; Tyler et al 2008

176; Stave Wharf/Rosings Wharf, Cathedral Street (Clink Street), SE1, Southwark
English, London, Pickleherring pothouse; *c* 1618–50
Small dog.
Blue; 127 x ? x 13mm
WP83C [57] <867>

177; 11–11A Pudding Lane, 121–127 Lower Thames St, EC3, City of London
Dutch; 1640–70
Seal, small barred ox-head corners. The same animal is depicted on a Dutch tile illustrated in Schaap (1984, 151, no. 196-E). This has spider head corners, but similar tiles depicting mythical sea creature have barred ox-head corner motifs (Schaap 1984, 151, no. 195). The distinctive small barred ox-head corners are present on Dutch tiles showing crustaceans which Pluis dates to 1640–70 (1997, 408, A.04.05.02–03).
Blue; 127 x 127 x 9mm
PDN81 [3062] <592>

178; Probably found at Platform Wharf, Cathay Street, SE16, Southwark
English, London, Rotherhithe pothouse; 1650–60
Landscape with small barred ox-head corners. Probably an English copy of a contemporary Dutch wall tile design.
Blue; ? x ? x 14mm
PW86/PW89/PW90/PW91 [+] <138>; analysed by ICP (Chapter 5); Tyler et al 2008

169

170

171

172

173

174

175

176

177

178

179; probably London
Dutch; 1625–70
House with a foliated circle, and elaborate floral corners. Pluis (1997, 522, B.03.00.03) dates Dutch tiles with this border to 1625–70. Four tiles with the same border and isolated buildings painted in the same style are in van Dam (1991, 72, no. 84) dated 1650–70.
Blue and yellowish-brown; 128 x 129 x 9mm
7102

180; Bethel Estate, Vine Lane, SE1, Southwark
English, London, Pickleherring pothouse; *c* 1618–50
Flower in oval border. A complete Dutch tile with the same border and corner arrangement is shown in Pluis (1997, 523, B.04.00.02) dated 1620–50. Four polychrome Dutch examples are in Schaap (1984, 88, no. 89).
Blue; ? x ? x 14mm
BTH88 [469] <238>; Tyler et al 2008

181; probably London
Dutch; 1630–60
Chinese-style pattern, the design is fairly similar to a Dutch tile in Pluis (1997, 436, A.08.03.02). Decorators copied almost directly from the thousands of dishes imported from China by the Dutch East India Company (Lang 2004, 120).
Blue; 130 x 130 x 14mm
10205

182; Platform Wharf, Cathay Street, SE16, Southwark
English, London, Rotherhithe pothouse; 1638–60
Tudor rose, stylised fleur-de-lis corners.
Blue; ? x 127 x 14mm
PW86 [+] <122>; Tyler et al 2008

183; probably London
Dutch; 1620–50
Vase of flowers. A similar tile is shown in Pluis (1997, 423, A.05.08.11). Dutch tiles with this border decoration are dated 1620–50 (Pluis 1997, 531, B.13.00.01).
Blue; 137 x 133 x 15–16mm
Z3414

184; probably London
Dutch; 1625–50
Vase of flowers. Pluis illustrated a tile with a flower vase and similar corner decoration (1997, 551, C.07.00.15). Van Sabben and Hollem (1987, 94, no. 320) show a further Dutch tile with the same border and corner arrangement, although with a rabbit in the centre.
Blue; 134 x 133 x 11mm
10201

185; Platform Wharf, Cathay Street, SE16, Southwark
English, London, Rotherhithe pothouse; *c* 1638–50
Vase of flowers, crenulated oval border.
Blue; ? x ? x 12mm (reconstructed *c* 134mm square)
PW86 [1] <123>; Tyler et al 2008

186; probably London
Dutch; 1620–50
Vase of flowers, fleur-de-lis corners. Pluis has a number of tiles with fairly similar flower-filled vases. He dates the corner motif to 1620–50 (Pluis 1997, 424–5, 542, A.05.08.19, A.05.08.27, C.02.00.06).
Blue; 132 x 132 x 12–13mm
Z3379

187; Tower Hill West, Tower Hill, EC3, Tower Hamlets
Dutch; 1620–50
Soldier in barbed circular border. Two parts of what are almost certainly the same tile. The border is typically Dutch (van Dam 1991, 61, no. 65; Pluis 1997, 525, B.07.00.01).
Blue; ? x ? x 10–11mm
THW85 [10] <103>, <104>

188; Southwark
Dutch; 1620–60
Male figure in scalloped circular border with Wan Li corner motifs. This border, and corner motif, is dated to 1620–60 by Pluis (1997, 549, C.06.00.03).
Blue; 133 x 133 x 14mm
A11253

179

180

181

182

183

184

185

186

187

188

189; probably London
Dutch; 1620–60
Three-headed tulip in barbed circular border with Wan Li corners. This tile is almost identical to Dutch tiles illustrated by van Dam (1991, 53, no. 54) and Pluis (1997, 417, A.05.04.04).
Blue; 127 x 127 x 7mm
73.138/15

190; probably London
Dutch; 1650–80
Flower vase in circular border with Wan Li corner motifs. Pluis (1997, 141, no. 66, bottom left) illustrates an almost identical Dutch tile which may well have come from the same pothouse as the London example.
Blue; 132 x 130 x 12mm
Z3401

191; Guildhall Bollards, Guildhall Yard, EC2, City of London
Dutch; 1630–80
Part of the same three-headed tulip design as **189**, but with unusual leaf-head corner decoration. From a pit fill dated by the associated pottery to 1630–80. The tile may have been used in an apartment above a gatehouse formerly situated in what is now the southern entrance to Guildhall Yard east of St Lawrence Jewry church.
Blue; ? x ? x 11mm
GUD99 [1] <51>

192; Monument House, 30–35 Botolph Lane, 29–31 Monument Street, EC3, City of London
Dutch; 1650–66
Sea creature, small barred ox-head corner. From Great Fire of 1666 destruction debris, possibly derived from a wealthy merchant's house known as Lombards Place. Similar tiles are illustrated by Schaap (1984, 148–51, nos 186–196).
Blue; ? x ? x 10mm
BPL95 [119] <68>; Blair and Sankey 2007

193; Monument House, 30–35 Botolph Lane, 29–31 Monument Street, EC3, City of London
Dutch; 1645–66
Sailing ship, barred ox-head corners, similar to van Dam (1991, 80, no. 89). Another tile from 1666 destruction debris (see **192**).
Blue; ? x 128 x 10mm
BPL95 [104] <80>; Blair and Sankey 2007

194; Platform Wharf, Cathay Street, SE16, Southwark
English, London, Rotherhithe pothouse; 1650–60
Boat, spider head corners. Possibly an English copy of a contemporary Dutch wall tile design, such as those shown in van Sabben and Hollem (1987, 52–3, nos 144–160).
Blue; ? x 128 x 14mm
PW86 [1] <124>; Tyler et al 2008

195; Monument House, 30–35 Botolph Lane, 29–31 Monument Street, EC3, City of London
Dutch; 1660–6
Part of a landscape tile, similar in style to those in van Dam (1991, 79, no. 88). From a masonry wall incorporating reused pre-1666 building material.
Blue; 125 x ? x 9–10mm
BPL95 [123] <106>; Blair and Sankey 2007

196; Bermondsey Abbey, Abbey Street, Long Walk, SE1, Southwark
?English, ?London, ?Rotherhithe pothouse; mid 17th century
Landscape with large spider head corners. Possibly from Bermondsey House (Fig 4, no. 3; see **174**).
Blue; 134 x ? x 11mm
BA84 [242] <3745>

197; probably London
?English, ?London, ?Rotherhithe pothouse; mid 17th century
Tower with two boats, spider head corners. The thickness suggests that this is another English tile attempting to imitate the designs found on thinner Dutch wall tiles (see **178**, **194**).
Blue; 127 x 125 x 14–15mm
79.54/1

198; probably London
Dutch; 1625–50
Man in cape, ox-head corners. The figure is outlined in dark blue, along with the bars on the ox-head corners. The rest of the design is painted in a lighter shade of blue. Figurative tiles with similar barred ox-head corners are illustrated in Pluis (1997, 350, A.02.04.04–05) and van Sabben and Hollem (1987, 68, nos 211–19).
Blue; 128 x 130 x 10mm
7079

199; probably London
Dutch; 1625–50
Pikeman, same barred ox-head corners as **198**. Nine pikemen are illustrated on a series of Dutch tiles with slightly different barred ox-head corners in Schaap (1984, 128, no. 159).
Blue; 129 x 129 x 10mm
7080

189

190

191

192

193

194

195

196

197

198

199

200; Monument House, 30–35 Botolph Lane, 29–31 Monument Street, EC3, City of London
Dutch; 1635–60
Mounted soldier, similar to a tile in Pluis (1997, 356, A.02.07.03). This tile, and **201**, are from Great Fire of 1666 destruction debris.
Blue; 127 x 127 x 9–10mm
BPL95 [104] <86>; Blair and Sankey 2007

201; Monument House, 30–35 Botolph Lane, 29–31 Monument Street, EC3, City of London
Dutch; 1635–60
Mounted soldier.
Blue; 127 x 127 x 10mm
BPL95 [104] <85>; Blair and Sankey 2007

202; probably London
Dutch; 1650–75
Soldier on horseback. A tile with similar spider head corners is dated by Pluis to 1650–75 (1997, 556, C.08.00.09).
Blue; 127 x 127 x 9–10mm
7114

203; probably London
Dutch; 1625–50
Musketeer with variant of barred ox-head corner. A tile with similar corner motif is shown in Pluis (1997, 547, C.04.00.02).
Blue; 130 x 129 x 11–12mm
A4628

204; probably London
Dutch; 1640–60
Male figure holding a pot, variant of barred ox-head corner. The corners are almost identical to those in Pluis (1997, 347, A.02.02.04).
Blue; 128 x 129 x 10–11mm
A4637

205; probably London
Dutch; 1640–60
Female figure carrying tapered container similar to those used by water-carriers. Variant of barred ox-head corner. Same corners as **204**.
Blue; 129 x 130 x 11mm
A4627

206; Fleet Valley Project, Holborn Viaduct Station to Blackfriars, EC4, City of London
English, or Dutch; early–mid 17th century
Part of a tile panel with a heraldic crest.
Blue; ? x ? x 17mm
VAL88 [789] <5043>

207; Fleet Valley Project, Holborn Viaduct Station to Blackfriars, EC4, City of London
English or Dutch; mid–late 17th century
Combed slip tile cut down after firing to a width of only 48mm. A 19th-century tile in Pluis (1997, 579, D.08.00.03) shows how **207** may have looked when complete.
Purple; ? x ? x 16mm
VAL88 [+] <1082>

208; Billingsgate Market Lorry Park, Lower Thames Street, EC3, City of London
Dutch; 1650–66
Two parts of what are probably the same tile, with a white diamond and mock marbling in each corner. This is a Dutch design dating to 1650–1700 (Pluis 1997, 329, A.01.60.08). The tiles were found associated with a property which is believed to have been built by Thomas Soane in 1645–7 or by his widow Elizabeth who leased the building in her own name in 1652 (Schofield and Pearce 2009). The property was destroyed in the Great Fire of 1666, which would account for the slight burning on one of the fragments.

A pre-1666 tile with a diamond pattern was found at nearby Monument House, 30–35 Botolph Lane, 29–31 Monument Street, EC3, City of London (BPL95 [119] <69>), although on this example the diamond pattern is outlined in blue and there are purple corners.
Blackish-purple; ? x ? x 10mm
BIG82 [41] <459>

209; 2–9, 10–16 Bevis Marks, 15–18 Bury Street, EC3, City of London
Dutch; mid–late 17th century
Pluis (1997, 264, A.01.13.03) illustrates a Dutch tile with a slightly larger diamond pattern in powdered purple and white dated 1660–1700.
Blue and purple; ? x ? x 12mm
BEV80 [5] <56>

210; 2 King Edward Street, EC1, City of London
Flemish, Antwerp; 1520–70
A highly unusual counter-relief design in blue on a white background based on a 15th-century Valencian Hispano-Moresque design (H van Lemmen, pers comm). Another tile with this design is from an unknown London location (36.144/3). Scientific analysis suggests an Antwerp origin (Hughes 2009). It would appear to be a rather crude copy of a 15th- to 16th-century Spanish tile design known from Valencia (Coll 2009, 40, fig 3, bottom-middle).
Blue; ? x 131 x 19mm
KEW98 [652] <352>; analysed by ICP; Betts 2007b

200

201

202

203

204

205

206

207

208

209

210

LATER TILE DESIGNS (1666–*c* 1930)

Tiles believed to have been made after the Great Fire of 1666.

LANDSCAPE AND FIGURATIVE DESIGNS

Designs **211–225** lack borders and corners, **226–250** have spider head corners, whilst **251–265** are of barred ox-head type. For other types see individual design entries.

211; 2 King Edward Street, EC1, City of London
English, Liverpool; 1750–75
For similar Liverpool landscape tiles see Horne (1989, 39, nos 167–175).
Blue on pale blue; 126 x 126 x 7mm
KEW98 [1479] <863>; Betts 2007b; Fig 6, no. 15

212; 2 King Edward Street, EC1, City of London
English, Liverpool; 1740–75
The dark band at the base and the swans are echoed in a Liverpool tile in Ray (1973, 174, no. 306).
Blue; ? x 129 x 6mm
KEB92 [33] <125>; Betts 2007b; Fig 6, no. 15

213; 34–46 Albert Embankment, SE1, Lambeth
English, London, Glasshouse Street pothouse; 1740–60
Found with biscuit-fired tiles on the site of the Glasshouse Street pothouse. For a similar tile see Horne (1989, 37, no. 148).
Blue; ? x 126 x 8mm
L54/80 [1013]

214; 2 King Edward Street, EC1, City of London
Dutch; 1700–1800
The same winter scene, but set on a circular border is shown in **251**.
Blue; 130 x ? x 7mm
KEB92 [33] <83>; Betts 2007b; Fig 6, no. 15

215; probably London
Dutch; 1700–1800
Blue; 130 x 130 x 7mm
7093

216; probably London
English, London; 1700–60
There is a slightly different version of this scene in Archer (1997, 441, N52) dated 1700–25. Horne dates tiles of this style to 1710–60 (1989, 26, nos 64, 66–68).
Blue; 128 x 128 x 9mm
11894

217; probably London
Probably Dutch; 1700–1800
Blue; 126 x 126 x 7mm
7009

218; probably London
Probably Dutch; 1700–1800
Blue; 127 x 127 x 8mm
7043

219; probably London
Dutch; 1700–1800
Blue; 128 x 128 x 7mm
7056

211

212

213

214

215

216

217

218

219

220; probably London
Dutch; 1700–1800
Blue; 126 x 126 x 8mm
7044

221; probably London
Dutch; 1700–1800
Blue; 127 x 127 x 7mm
7050

222; probably London
Dutch; 1700–1800
For the same design but in purple with a circular border and barred ox-head corners see **263**.
Blue; 128 x 127 x 7mm
7046

223; probably London
Dutch; 1700–1800
Blue; 127 x 127 x 7mm
7049

224; probably London
Dutch; 1700–1800
Blue; 128 x 128 x 7mm
11895

225; probably London
Dutch; 1700–1800
Church and ship.
Blue; 127 x 127 x 7mm
7057

226; probably London
Dutch; 1700–50
This tile (together with **227–229**) is similar to eight landscape tiles shown in van Dam (1991, 101, no. 112).
Blue; 126 x 126 x 8mm
10206

227; probably London
Dutch; 1700–50
Blue; 130 x 129 x 8mm
7074

228; probably London
Dutch; 1700–50
Blue; 127 x 127 x 6mm
79.54/2

220

221

222

223

224

225

226

227

228

229; probably London
Dutch; 1700–50
Blue; 129 x 129 x 8mm
7075

230; 2 King Edward Street, EC1, City of London
Dutch; 1750–1800
Landscape tile with unusual spider head corner motif. Pluis (1997, 132, no. 38) has a series of purple Dutch landscape designs with a similar corner motif, although a little larger, whilst Schaap (1984, 113, no. 138) has two tiles with the same corner.
Blue; 124 x ? x 7mm
KEW98 [1479] <959>; Betts 2007b; Fig 6, no. 15

231; 172–188 Regent Street, W1, Westminster
Dutch; 1700–1800
Blue; 126 x ? x 7mm
RGN92 [371] <30>

232; Norfolk House, 113–129 Lambeth Road, SE1, Lambeth
Probably Dutch; 1680–1800
Blue; ? x ? x 8mm
NOR90 [1088] <54>

233; 12 Colosseum Terrace, Albany Street, NW1, Camden
Dutch; 1700–50
The same design is shown on two Dutch tiles in van Sabben and Hollem (1987, 118, no. 386).
Blue; ? x 129 x 8mm
CTA94 [+] <8>; Fig 6, no. 7

234; 2 King Edward Street, EC1, City of London
Dutch; 1700–50
Similar landscape tiles are illustrated in van Dam (1991, 115, no. 139) and Pluis (1997, 366, A.03.01.17).
Blue; 127 x 126 x 6–7mm
KEW98 [1479] <862>; Betts 2007b; Fig 6, no. 15

235; The Globe, 14–24 Great Dover Street, SE1, Southwark
Dutch, Rotterdam; 1700–50
This closely resembles other landscape tiles illustrated by van Dam (1991, 115, no. 139).
Blue; ? x ? x 7mm
GTD02 [26] <5>

236; 2 King Edward Street, EC1, City of London
Dutch; 1780–1820
Similar in style to late Dutch landscape tiles illustrated in van Sabben and Hollem (1987, 128, no. 397).
Blue; 127 x 127 x 6–7mm
KEW98 [1479] <841>; Betts 2007b; Fig 6, no. 15

237; probably London
English, London; *c* 1700
Blue and purple; 130 x 130 x 7–8mm
7037

229

230

231

232

233

234

235

236

237

Two similar landscape tiles from the same pothouse as **238**, **239**, **241–247** were analysed by ICP which revealed that they are typical of the range of chemical composition for Gravel Lane tin-glazed ware. In particular they are consistent with the biscuit and glazed tiles analysed from Gravel Lane and a tin-glazed ware bowl (M Hughes, pers comm). Horne (2005, 33) shows a number of blue on white tiles with similar landscape scenes set in circular borders with spider head corners. Design **240** was originally believed to be part of the same group but is now thought to be Dutch.

238; 38–46 Albert Embankment, SE1, Lambeth
London, Gravel Lane pothouse; 1700–30
Designs **238–247** formed part of the same decorative scheme.
Purple; 126 x 126 x 7–8mm
38ALB89 [5] <37>

239; 38–46 Albert Embankment, SE1, Lambeth
London, Gravel Lane pothouse; 1700–30
A landscape tile with a similar figure, but in blue on white, is illustrated by Horne (2005, 33, E4).
Barred ox-head corners.
Purple; 124 x 126 x 7mm
38ALB89 [5] <45>

240; 38–46 Albert Embankment, SE1, Lambeth
Dutch; 1700–50
The corners are smaller than the other tiles in the group and the flag is Dutch, suggesting the tile is Dutch (H van Lemmen, pers comm). The same scene, minus the Dutch flag, is on a London tile with barred ox-head corners shown in Horne (1989, 27, no. 71).
Purple; 125 x 125 x 6–8mm
38ALB89 [5] <63>

241; 38–46 Albert Embankment, SE1, Lambeth
English, London, Gravel Lane pothouse; 1700–30
The same scene, but in blue on white, is illustrated by Horne (2005, 33, G1).
Purple; 125 x 126 x 6–7mm
38ALB89 [5] <2>

242; 38–46 Albert Embankment, SE1, Lambeth
English, London, Gravel Lane pothouse; 1700–30
The same scene, but again in blue on white, is illustrated by Horne (2005, 33, D4).
Purple; 125 x 125 x 7mm
38ALB89 [5] <15>

243; 38–46 Albert Embankment, SE1, Lambeth
English, London, Gravel Lane pothouse; 1700–30
Same scene as **242**, but the building does not have a spire.
Purple; 123 x 123 x 7–8mm
38ALB89 [5] <11>

244; 38–46 Albert Embankment, SE1, Lambeth
English, London, Gravel Lane pothouse; 1700–30
A similar scene in blue on white is shown in Horne (2005, 33, C5).
Purple; 125 x 124 x 7mm
38ALB89 [5] <52>

245; 38–46 Albert Embankment, SE1, Lambeth
English, London, Gravel Lane pothouse; 1700–30
A blue on white version of this scene is also shown in Fig 19 and in Horne (2005, 33, A3).
Purple; 126 x 125 x 8mm
38ALB89 [5] <23>

246; 38–46 Albert Embankment, SE1, Lambeth
English, London, Gravel Lane pothouse; 1700–30
The same design in blue on white is illustrated by Horne (2005, 33, A2).
Purple; 125 x 125 x 7mm
38ALB89 [5] <38>

247; 38–46 Albert Embankment, SE1, Lambeth
English, Gravel Lane pothouse; 1700–30
Purple; 125 x 125 x 8mm
38ALB89 [5] <34>

238

239

240

241

242

243

244

245

246

247

248; probably London
Dutch; 1760–1810
This is in a similar style to van Dam design 140 (1991, 115).
Purple; 127 x 128 x 7mm
10204

249; probably London
Dutch; 1660–1800
This is in a similar style to Pluis design A.03.03.04 (1997, 378). Two similar tiles showing shepherds are illustrated in Schaap (1984, 113, no. 138).
Purple; 120 x 120 x 8–9mm
7110

250; probably London
Dutch; 1780–1820
The same scene is in van Dam (1991, 116, no. 141, top second left).
Blue; 120 x 120 x 7mm
7072

251; probably London
Dutch; 1680–1760
This is the same scene as **214**. Similar corner motifs are in Pluis (1997, 553–4, C.07.00.34, C.07.00.48) and van Dam (1991, 91, no. 124).
Blue; 130 x 130 x 9mm
7112

252; probably London
Dutch; 1700–1800
Blue; 125 x 125 x 7mm
7070

253; probably London
Dutch; 1700–1800
Blue; 128 x 128 x 8mm
7111

254; 2 King Edward Street, EC1, City of London
English or Dutch; 1700–1800
Blue; 127 x 127 x 8–9mm
KEW98 [1479] <854>; Betts 2007b; Fig 6, no. 15

255; 2 King Edward Street, EC1, City of London
Dutch, ?Rotterdam; 1740–80
The same dashed sea is present on **274**.
Blue; 127 x 126 x 6–7mm
KEW98 [1479] <846>; Betts 2007b; Fig 6, no. 15

256; Norfolk House, 113–129 Lambeth Road, SE1, Lambeth
English, London, Norfolk House or Lambeth High Street pothouse; 1770–90
The same central scene is illustrated by Ray (1973, 131, no. 109) set in an octagonal border with carnation-head corners. The Norfolk House tile has no mortar, so may have been made at the pothouse. Alternatively, it could be a Lambeth High Street product as landscape and biblical tiles with the same corner motif have been found in the vicinity of this pothouse (Ray 1973, 99, figs 22a–c, 25f).

The design and duck-egg blue background suggests a date later than 1770 (J Horne, pers comm). Four landscape tiles with similar corner decoration on a pale blue background are in Horne (1989, 30, nos 89–92).
Blue on pale blue; 123 x ? x 7mm
NOR90 [1284] <173>; Tyler et al 2008

248

249

250

251

252

253

254

255

256

257; Norfolk House, 113–129 Lambeth Road, SE1, Lambeth
English, London, Norfolk House pothouse; 1760–90
Similar barred ox-head corners to **256**. A possible waster with a scarred corner. There is mortar on the back so it was evidently used, although perhaps somewhere on the walls of the pothouse.
Blue on pale blue; ? x ? x 6mm
NOR90 [1024] <1>; analysed by ICP (Chapter 5); Tyler et al 2008

258; 40–41 Furnival Street, EC4, City of London
English, Liverpool; 1750–75
Designs **258–262**, **345** and **346** were found in a tiled niche in a brick cellar (Fig 6, no. 11; Fig 22). They are typical of Liverpool tiles made in great numbers between 1750 and 1775. Nine similar tiles are in Horne (1989, 36, nos 138–146).
Blue; 126 x 126 x 7mm
FUR87 [38]/[84]

259; 40–41 Furnival Street, EC4, City of London
English, Liverpool; 1750–75
Found next to a white and blue edging tile (**450**).
Blue; 126 x 127 x 7mm
FUR87 [38]/[84]; Fig 6, no. 11

260; 40–41 Furnival Street, EC4, City of London
English, Liverpool; 1750–75
The same design is in Horne (1989, 36, no. 140).
Blue; 130 x 130 x 7mm
FUR87 [38]/[84]; Fig 6, no. 11

261; 40–41 Furnival Street, EC4, City of London
English, Liverpool; 1750–75
Blue; 127 x 126 x 7mm
FUR87 [38]/[84]; Fig 6, no. 11

262; 40–41 Furnival Street, EC4, City of London
English, Liverpool; 1750–75
Blue; 127 x 128 x 6mm
FUR87 [38]/[84]; Fig 6, no. 11

263; 2 King Edward Street, EC1, City of London
Dutch; 1700–1800
Another version of this scene is shown in **222**.
Purple; ? x ? x 7mm
KEW98 [1479] <850>; Betts 2007b; Fig 6, no. 15

264; Stave Wharf/Rosings Wharf, Cathedral Street (Clink Street), SE1, Southwark
Dutch; 1700–1800
A common theme on Dutch tile, for example those in van Dam which have certain similarities with this tile (1991, 113, no. 136).
Blue; 128 x 130 x 7mm
WP83C [287] <900>

265; Stave Wharf/Rosings Wharf, Cathedral Street (Clink Street), SE1, Southwark
English, Liverpool; 1750–80
Landscape tile with foreground swans painted in typical Liverpool fashion. For similar landscape scenes see Horne (1989, 42, nos 196, 200) and for similar foreground detail see Ray (1973, 171, nos 282, 284).
Blue; 128 x 127 x 7mm
WP83C [287] <902>

258

259

257

260

261

262

263

264

265

266; 2 King Edward Street, EC1, City of London
Dutch, ?Amsterdam; 1720–90
Landscape tiles with carnation-head corners are rare in London. The example illustrated has a similar carnation head to that found on a Dutch tile illustrated by Pluis (1997, 567, C.17.00.06).
Blue; ? x ? x 7mm
KEW98 [1414] <534>; Betts 2007b; Fig 6, no. 15

267; The Mitre Hotel, Hampton Court Bridge, East Molesey, KT8, Richmond upon Thames (Surrey)
English, London; 1760–90
Landscape with tree and house and diaper corners, found with **268**. Four landscape tiles with the same border are in Horne (1989, 30, nos 93–96).
Blue; 130 x ? x 9mm
MHL92 [+] <19>

268; The Mitre Hotel, Hampton Court Bridge, East Molesey, KT8, Richmond upon Thames (Surrey)
English, London; 1760–90
Cow and man in landscape, diaper corners.
Blue; 128 x ? x 7mm
MHL92 [+] <20>

269; Fleet Valley Project, Holborn Viaduct Station to Blackfriars, EC4, City of London
Dutch, Rotterdam; 1700–50
Landscape scene in octagonal border with fleur-de-lis corners. Pluis shows a landscape tile of similar type (1997, 374, A.03.01.57) although the corner motif is closer to that on another tile (Pluis 1997, 543, C.02.00.11).
Blue; 126 x 126 x 7mm
VAL88 [1499] <794>

270; 38–46 Albert Embankment, SE1, Lambeth
Dutch, Rotterdam; 1740–1800
Typical Dutch landscape scene with couple in walled garden, octagonal border, foliage corners. Tiles with fairly similar corners and octagonal borders are illustrated in Pluis (1997, 568, C.18.00.01–03) together with another tile with the same central scene without a border or corners (Pluis 1997, 381, A.03.05.03). Other walled landscape scenes set within octagonal borders with fairly similar corners are illustrated by van Dam (1991, 106, no. 127).

This landscape design was copied by English tile-painters; a London tile with the same garden scene is in Horne (1989, 26, no. 64).
Blue; 125 x 125 x 8mm
38ALB89 [5] <82>

271; probably London
Dutch, Rotterdam; 1740–80
River with boats in narrow octagonal border with quarter flower-head corners.
Blue; 127 x 127 x 8mm
6989

272; probably London
Dutch, Rotterdam; 1740–80
River with bridge in narrow octagonal border with quarter flower-head corners.
Blue; 126 x 126 x 8mm
7039

273; probably London
Dutch, Rotterdam; 1740–80
River and houses in narrow octagonal border with quarter flower-head corners.
Blue; 128 x 128 x 9mm
6993

274; probably London
Dutch, Rotterdam; 1740–80
Harbour with boats in narrow octagonal border with quarter flower-head corners.
Blue; 127 x 127 x 10mm
7038

266

267

268

269

270

271

272

273

274

275; 2 King Edward Street, EC1, City of London
Dutch, Rotterdam; 1730–60
Landscape tile with Dutch border design see Pluis (1997, 376, A.03.01.69).
Blue; 127 x 126 x 6mm
KEW98 [1479] <867>; Betts 2007b; Fig 6, no. 15

276; probably London
Dutch, Rotterdam; 1730–60
Landscape, church to the left, with boats and swans, scalloped octagonal frame and carnation-head corners. For similar landscape tiles see Pluis (1997, 531, B.12.00.17–18).
Blue; 125 x 125 x 8mm
6998

277; 2 King Edward Street, EC1, City of London
Dutch; 1730–1800
Landscape tile with ice skating scene. A Dutch tile with the same distinctive border decoration is illustrated by Pluis (1997, 530, B12.00.15). A similar winter scene is illustrated on a Dutch tile in van Dam (1991, 104, no. 121, top right).
Blue; 126 x 127 x 7mm
KEW98 [1479] <861>; Betts 2007b; Fig 6, no. 15

278; 2 King Edward Street, EC1, City of London
Dutch, Rotterdam; 1750–70
Figures in landscape, the stone palisade is typical of Dutch tiles (see **270**). Pluis (1997, 381, A.03.05.05) shows a Dutch tile with the same scene. The scene was also copied by London tilemakers (see Horne 1989, 26, no. 65, but with position of figures reversed), but the corner motif is exclusively Dutch (see Pluis 1997, 559, C.12.00.10).
Blue; 127 x 126 x 6mm
KEW98 [1479] <845>; Betts 2007b; Fig 6, no. 15

279; 2 King Edward Street, EC1, City of London
Dutch; *c* 1750–1800
Mounted figure in landscape with different flower-head corner motif.
Blue; 127 x 126 x 7mm
KEW98 [1479] <858>; Betts 2007b; Fig 6, no. 15

280; probably London
Dutch; 1730–*c* 1800
Fisherman in a boat within an octagonal border and quarter flower-head corners. A long-lived Dutch border and corner design dating to 1730–1920 (Pluis 1997, 370, A.03.01.37–39, 530, B.12.00.14), although **280**, and similar designs nos **281–284**, are probably 18th century.
Blue; 128 x 128 x 8mm
7004

281; probably London
Dutch; 1730–*c* 1800
Landscape with milkmaid and cow, octagonal border and quarter flower-head corners.
Blue; 128 x 128 x 7mm
P652

282; Stave Wharf/Rosings Wharf, Cathedral Street (Clink Street), SE1, Southwark
Dutch; 1730–*c* 1800
Skaters on frozen canal, octagonal border and quarter flower-head corners. A similar design can be found on Liverpool tiles (Horne 1989, 45, no. 217).
Blue; 126 x 126 x 7mm
WP83C [57] <870>

283; 19–20 College Hill, EC4, City of London
Dutch; 1730–*c* 1800
Couple by moat with castle and church, octagonal border and quarter flower-head corners.
Blue; 127 x 127 x 7mm
COL81 [+] <47>

275

276

277

278

279

280

281

282

283

284; 2 King Edward Street, EC1, City of London
Dutch; 1730–*c* 1800
Landscape with harbour, octagonal border and quarter flower-head corners.
Purple; 127 x 126 x 7–8mm
KEW98 [1479] <878>; Betts 2007b; Fig 6, no. 15

285; 12 Colosseum Terrace, Albany Street, NW1, Camden
Dutch; 1890–1920
Church and houses within an elaborate frame. Tiles with the same border are dated by Pluis to 1770–1800 and 1890–1920 (1997, 528, B.11.00.05). The presence of Dutch biblical tiles dated 1890–1920 in the same fireplace suggests that the Colosseum Terrace tile is late 19th or early 20th century (Chapter 6, City; Fig 6, no. 7).
Blue; 131 x 132 x 7mm
CTA94 [+] <6>

286; probably London
Dutch; 1700–50
People in landscape, Louis XV border with diaper corners. This design is in van Dam (1991, 100, no. 107, bottom right).
Purple; 132 x 131 x 8mm
7096

287; probably London
Dutch; 1740–1800
People in a landscape, Louis XV border with diaper corners. This has larger petal decoration midway along each edge than **286**.
Purple; 124 x 122 x 8mm
7097

288; 2 King Edward Street, EC1, City of London
English, ?Liverpool; *c* 1770
Landscape scene with house and church set within Louis XV border with diaper corners. This is a Liverpool design but similar tiles were made at the Mortlake pothouse (**496**). The King Edward Street tile has a pale blue glaze more characteristic of certain Liverpool tiles. For similar Liverpool tiles see Horne (1989, 45, nos 209–217).
Blue; 126 x 126 x 7–8mm
KEW98 [1479] <866>; Betts 2007b; Fig 6, no. 15

289; Mill Road/Merton High Street, Merton, SW19, Surrey
English, Liverpool; 1750–80
Building by a waterside with two swans, a characteristic feature of Liverpool landscape tiles, Louis XV border with diaper corners.
Blue; ? x 128 x 8mm
MIS92 [1] <35>

290; probably London
English, Liverpool; 1750–80
Landscape scene, Louis XV border with buttercup corners. The complete design can be seen on a Liverpool tile in Ray (1973, 173, no. 294) which has the same border but with diaper corners.
Purple; 125 x 125 x 7mm
26121

291; 2 King Edward Street, EC1, City of London
English, Liverpool; 1750–80
Landscape scene, Louis XV border with buttercup corners. For similar tiles see Horne (1989, 44, nos 205–208).
Blue on pale blue; ? x ? x 8mm
KEW98 [1479] <555>; Betts 2007b; Fig 6, no. 15

292; 2 King Edward Street, EC1, City of London
English, Liverpool; 1750–75
Landscape with figure in elaborate floral ground border. This border design is exclusive to Liverpool (Horne 1989, 41, nos 185, 186).
Blue; ? x 121 x 6mm
KEW98 [1479] <843>; Betts 2007b; Fig 6, no. 15

293; 2 King Edward Street, EC1, City of London
English, London; 1740–60
Harbour scene in octagonal border with carnation corners. Horne illustrates a London tile with a similar harbour scene (but in blue) with the same border (1989, 23, no. 51).
Purple; 125 x 125 x 8mm.
KEW98 [1479] <879>; Betts 2007b; Fig 6, no. 15

284

285

286

287

288

289

290

291

292

293

294; probably London
English, London; 1720–50
Figure in landscape, octagonal border with very rare strap and flower petal corners. A landscape tile with the same border and corner is in Archer (1997, 442, N58).
Purple; 127 x 127 x 9mm
7021

295; probably London
English, London; 1720–50
Figure in landscape, octagonal border with unusual strap and flower petal corners.
Purple; 125 x 125 x 7mm
11883

296; Stave Wharf/Rosings Wharf, Cathedral Street (Clink Street), SE1, Southwark
English, Liverpool; 1750–75
Landscape tile with unusual octagonal cherub border. For similar tiles see Horne (1989, 41, nos 187–188). The dark blue areas of the pattern have a metallic gold finish. It is not certain if this was a deliberate effect or an accident of firing.
Blue and gold; 129 x 129 x 7mm
WP83C [287] <910>

297; probably London
English, London; 1740–50
Blue landscape with woman and child in powdered purple octagonal frame with blue quarter rosette corners (see also **298–301**, **420**). The same scene is shown on a similar blue and purple tile in Horne (1989, 22, no. 34) although this has carnation corners. Horne also shows a landscape tile with a very similar corner (1989, 21, no. 31).
Blue and purple; 128 x 128 x 9mm
7017

298; probably London
English, London; 1740–50
Blue landscape with a man in a boat talking to a woman on shore.
Blue and purple; 128 x 128 x 8mm
11881

299; probably London
English, London; 1740–*c* 1750
Blue landscape with two people.
Blue and purple; 128 x 129 x 8mm
7015

300; probably London
English, London; 1740–50
Blue landscape with man fishing on a river bank.
Blue and purple; 129 x 128 x 8mm
7018

301; probably London
English; 1740–50
Blue landscape with church, milkmaid and cow.
Blue and purple; 129 x 129 x 9mm
7014

302; 2 King Edward Street, EC1, City of London
Dutch; 1700–50
Fleur-de-lis corner motif, for dating see Pluis (1997, 544, C.02.00.16).
Blue and purple; ? x ? x 7mm
KEW98 [1479] <1627>; Betts 2007b; Fig 6, no. 15

303; probably London
?Dutch; 1720–60
Shepherd asleep under a tree with scallop-edged, powdered purple border and quarter rosette corners. Dutch tiles with fairly similar corners are shown in Pluis (1997, 559, C.12.00.09–10). The corner motif is also not too dissimilar to that found on certain English tiles attributed to Bristol (Ray 1973, 133, nos 110, 111; Horne 1989, 21, nos 25–30), but as Bristol tiles are currently unknown in London **303** is likely to be Dutch.
Blue and purple; 127 x 127 x 8mm
7099

294

295

296

297

298

299

300

302

301

303

304; Jacob's Island, Bermondsey Wall West, SE1, Southwark
Probably English; 1720–60
Landscape with a shepherd woman walking. This scene is similar to that found on both English and Dutch tiles. For similar Dutch tiles see Schaap (1984, 113, no. 136) and van Dam (1991, 90, no. 119).
Blue and purple; 125 x 124 x 9mm
JAC96 [32] <141>

305; 2 King Edward Street, EC1, City of London
Dutch; 1700–70
Heart-shaped corner motif, for dating see Pluis (1997, 562, C.13.00.02).
Blue and purple; ? x ? x 8mm
KEW98 [1479] <1625>; Betts 2007b; Fig 6, no. 15

306; 25 West Tenter Street, E1, Tower Hamlets
Dutch; 1670–1750
For dating of this corner motif see Pluis (1997, 557, C.09.00.04).
Blue and purple; ? x ? x 8mm
WSN00 [21] <2>

Not illustrated; 10 Bowling Green Lane, EC1, Islington
Dutch; 1700–50
Scalloped powdered purple border (as **303–306**), with blue on white fleur-de-lis corners. Tile may have Pluis design A.08.01.03 (1997, 435), dated 1700–50.
Blue and purple; ? x ? x 7mm
BGQ06 [43]

Not illustrated; Bishopsgate Goods Yard (East London Line Extension), Bethnal Green Road, Shoreditch High Street, E1, Hackney (Middlesex)
Dutch, Rotterdam; 1720–70
Scalloped, powdered purple border (as **303–306**) with blue on white leaf corners. Present on a Dutch landscape tile. This border and corner arrangement is dated 1720–70 (Pluis 1997, 565, C.15.00.11).
Blue and purple; ? x ? x 7mm
BGX05 [2050]

307; 1 Poultry, EC2, City of London
Dutch; 1670–1700
Two tiles showing a landscape with people in border with hearts. Pluis (1997, 517, B.01.00.09) shows a landscape tile with the same distinctive border design.
Blue and purple; ? x ? x 9mm
ONE94 [16004] <6458> (right) <6564> (left)

308; Guildhall Art Gallery, Guildhall Yard, EC2, City of London
Dutch; 1660–80
Landscape tile with distinct open-box-type border in powdered purple. Pluis (1997, 520, B.01.00.34) illustrates a complete tile with this border.
Blue and purple; ? x ? x 10mm (reconstructed *c* 126mm square)
GAG87 [3076] <1215>; Bowsher et al 2007

309; probably London
Dutch; 1680–1730
Kneeling figure within octagonal powdered purple and white border. This border arrangement, present on **309–311**, was used on Dutch tiles from 1650 to 1800 (Pluis 1997, 530, B.12.00.10). Design **309** is probably late 17th or early 18th century as the same kneeling figure is present on a Dutch tile with eight-petal powdered purple border and quarter rosette corners dated by van Dam to 1680–1725 (1991, 103, no. 118, bottom left). He also illustrates four landscape tiles with the same distinctive octagonal border dated to the period 1680–1730 (van Dam 1991, 102, no. 116).
Blue and purple; 128 x 128 x 7mm
7098

310; Abbot's Lane, Tooley Street, SE1, Southwark
Dutch; 1680–1730
Buildings within octagonal powdered purple and white border. The buildings are similar to those shown in one of the four landscape tiles mentioned above (Pluis 1997, 102, no. 116, bottom left).
Blue and purple; ? x ? x 9mm (reconstructed *c* 132mm square)
ABO92 [234] <852>

311; 1 Poultry, EC2, City of London
Dutch; 1680–1730
Buildings within octagonal powdered purple and white border (see comments for **309**).
Blue and purple; ? x ? x 8mm
ONE94 [16004] <6462>

312; Modern foreshore, River Thames, EC3 to EC4, City of London
Dutch; 1670–1730
Well within powdered purple diamond border. Tiles with this border were made from 1650 until 1920 (Pluis 1997, 527, B.10.00.02) although **312** is probably late 17th–early 18th century. Similar well scenes are present on a number of tiles without corners and borders dated by van Sabben and Hollem to 1650–1700 (1987, 125, no. 393).
Blue and purple; 130 x 130 x 8mm
MFS76 [1] <284>

313; Platform Wharf, Cathay Street, SE16, Southwark
English, London; *c* 1675–1700
Blue glaze with central floral motif and spider head corner in white, a style known as *bleu persan* or *bleu de Nevers* (see **443** for example of plain blue glaze). Noted as a decorative technique used at Pickleherring, Norfolk House and probably also the Bear Garden pothouse (Archer 1997, 248). Britton shows a London-made mug of late 17th-century date painted in this style (1987, 90, pl L) and two others are illustrated by Archer (1997, 247–8, C12–C13). The decorative patterns on pottery vessels suggests that the use of *bleu persan* was restricted to the last quarter of the 17th century.
White on blue; ? x ? x 8mm
PW86 [1] <95>

304

305

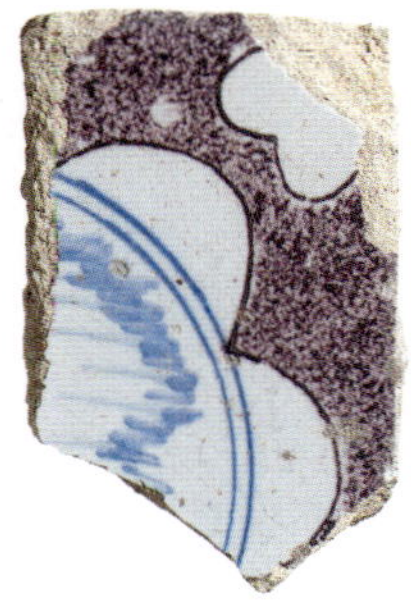

306

307

308

309

310

311

312

313

Designs **314–323** are typical of many similar Dutch tiles showing children playing and scenes from everyday life (see also Schaap 1984, 109, no. 129; van Sabben and Hollem 1987, 81, nos 284–285; van Dam 1991, 101, no. 113). Corner decoration, where present, is often of small size.

314; probably London
Dutch; 1660–1700
Blue; 130 x 130 x 10mm
Z3398

315; probably London
Dutch; 1640–1700
Similar small spider head corners are illustrated in Pluis (1997, 348, 360, A.02.02.08, A.02.12.03) and van Dam (1991, 79, no. 88).
Blue; 121 x ? x 8mm
7117

316; probably London
Dutch; 1640–1700
Blue; 129 x 130 x 9–10mm
Z3393

317; probably London
Dutch; 1640–1700
Blue; 126 x 125 x 9mm
Z3389

318; probably London
Dutch; 1670–1700
A tile with a similar small spider head corners is in Pluis (1997, 556, C.08.00.14).
Blue; ? x 133 x 10mm
Z3388

319; probably London
Dutch; 1640–1700
Blue; 127 x 127 x 10mm
Z3385

320; probably London
Dutch; 1640–1700
Blue; 128 x 125 x 10mm
Z3386

321; 2 King Edward Street, EC1, City of London
Dutch; 1680–1750
Blue; 122 x 121 x 8mm
KEW98 [1479] <562>; Betts 2007b; Fig 6, no. 15

322; London
Dutch; 1640–80
These small barred ox-head corners are typical of Dutch tiles dating to the second half of the 17th and early 18th century (see van Dam 1991, 80–1, 85, nos 89–94; Pluis 1997, 126, no. 27, 383, A.03.06.08).
Blue; 127 x 127 x 10mm
7078

323; probably London
Dutch; 1640–80
Blue; 125 x 125 x 10mm
7116

314

315

316

317

318

319

320

321

322

323

324; Bishopgate Goods Yard (East London Line Extension), Bethnal Green Road, Shoreditch High Street, E1, Hackney (Middlesex)
Dutch; 1650–80
Man or boy sitting on a large bird. The complete design is shown in Pluis which shows fairly small barred ox-head corners (1997, 397, A.03.12.03).
Blue; ? x ? x 10mm
BGX05 [+] <173>

325; Norfolk House, 113–129 Lambeth Road, SE1, Lambeth
Dutch; late 17th–18th century
An unusually large tile showing boys playing, with fern corners. A Dutch tile showing the same children's game (known in one of the authors' (IB) Yorkshire childhood as 'finger, thumb or dum') as illustrated in Schaap (1984, 105, no. 123). The game is also shown on one of the large Dutch tiles used to decorate Queen Mary's apartments at Hampton Court, Richmond upon Thames (Middlesex), *c* 1694 (Graves 2002, 86, fig 4.20).
Blue; 178 x 179 x 15mm
NOR90 [1260] <153>

326; Norfolk House, 113–129 Lambeth Road, SE1, Lambeth
The reverse of **325** showing a shooting star.
NOR90 [1260] <153>

327; 2 King Edward Street, EC1, City of London
English, Liverpool; 1750–75
Chinese figure in black, blue, green, yellow and brown, with Michaelmas daisy corners. Similar tiles are in Horne (1989, 58, nos 309–310) and Archer (1997, 501–2, N363–N380, pls 313–15).
Poly; 126 x 126 x 7mm
KEW98 [1475] <569>; Betts 2007b; Fig 6, no. 15

MILITARY FIGURES

328; probably London
Dutch; 1670–1750
Soldier on horseback in classical costume, spider head corners.
Blue; 130 x 130 x 7mm
7083

329; Priory of St John, Clerkenwell, EC1, Islington
Dutch; 1700–50
Cavalier, spider head corners. This design, and others showing mounted soldiers (**330–332**), have similar corners to examples illustrated in Pluis (1997, 356, A.02.07.06) and van Dam (1991, 86, no. 100) although the latter are thicker.
Blue; 123 x 122 x 7mm
17799

324

325

326

327

328

329

330; probably London
Dutch; 1700–50
Soldier on horseback, spider head corners.
Purple; 126 x 127 x 7mm
7047a

331; probably London
Dutch; 1700–50
Soldier on horseback, spider head corners.
Purple; 126 x 127 x 7mm
7047c

332; probably London
Dutch; 1700–50
Soldier on horseback, spider head corners.
Purple; 126 x 127 x 7mm
7047b

333; Lime Kiln Dock, Three Colt Lane, E14, Tower Hamlets
Dutch; 1700–50
Rider in hat, spider head corner motifs.
Purple; ? x ? x 8–9mm
LKD94 [8] <38>

334; Southwark
Dutch; 1680–1750
Knight on horseback, with fleur-de-lis corners. The latter are similar to that used on a Dutch tile showing a child with a spinning top dated 1630–60 (Pluis 1997, 382, A.03.06.05). However, the smaller thickness of **334** suggests a slightly later date.
Blue; 127 x 127 x 7mm
A11238

335; Southwark
Dutch; 1680–1750
Soldier fallen from horseback, same fleur-de-lis corners as **334**.
Blue; 127 x 127 x 7mm
A11235

336; Southwark
Dutch; 1680–1750
Soldier on horseback. Two of fleur-de-lis corners have been distorted due to movement of the glaze during firing. Very similar distorted fleur-de-lis corners are present on a series of Dutch tiles depicting pikemen and Saracen bowmen illustrated in Schaap (1984, 127, no. 157), but these are thicker and earlier in date.
Blue; 127 x 127 x 7mm
A11239

337; probably London
Dutch; 1650–1700
Soldier, fleur-de-lis corners. Tiles with similar corners and soldiers are in Schaap (1984, 126, 155) dated 1625–50, but again these are thicker and probably earlier in date.
Blue; 129 x 129 x 9mm
Z3400

338; 12 Colosseum Terrace, Albany Street, NW1, Camden
Dutch; 1650–1700
Soldier, spider head corners. Part of the glaze has moved during firing giving the design a blurred appearance. Pluis dates the corner decoration to 1650–75 (1997, 556, C.08.00.09), whilst van Dam shows three tiles with mounted soldiers and similar corners dated 1675–1725 (1991, 86, no. 100). Similarly dressed military figures and the same corners are present on two 17th-century tiles in van Sabben and Hollem (1987, 69, no. 220).
Blue; 125 x 125 x 10mm
CTA94 [+] <5>; Fig 6, no. 7

330

331

332

333

334

335

336

337

338

SAILING SHIPS AND BOATS

339; 2–3 Windsor Street, Uxbridge, UB8, Hillingdon (Middlesex)
English, London; 1680–1700
Warship, spider head corners. One of six ship designs from Windsor Street, Uxbridge (see **340**, **341**). Horne (2005, 30–6) illustrated a series of London-made landscape and biblical tiles of similar late 17th-century date.
Blue; 125 x 125 x 9mm
UX83i [15] <122>

340; 2–3 Windsor Street, Uxbridge, UB8, Hillingdon (Middlesex)
English, London; 1680–1700
Warship, spider head corners.
Blue; 125 x 125 x 9mm
UX83i [15] <120>

341; 2–3 Windsor Street, Uxbridge, UB8, Hillingdon (Middlesex)
English, London; 1680–1700
Warship, spider head corners.
Blue; 126 x 125 x 8mm
UX83i [15] <121>

342; 2 King Edward Street, EC1, City of London
?Dutch or perhaps English; mid–late 17th century
Sailing ship, spider head corners. Dutch tiles of the same thickness showing sailing ships (but with different corners and no border) are dated 1645–75 (van Dam 1991, 80, no. 89). A landscape tile in blue and purple with the same corner motif is known from 38–46 Albert Embankment, SE1, Lambeth (MOL site code 38ALB89 [288]).
Blue and purple; ? x ? x 13mm
KEW98 [1479] <954>; Betts 2007b; Fig 6, no. 15

343; probably London
Dutch; 1645–80
Coastal vessel, barred ox-head corners. Van Dam has a number of Dutch ship tiles with similar corners (1991, 80, nos 89–91).
Blue; 130 x 130 x 12mm
7081

344; probably London
Dutch; 1650–80
Coastal vessel, barred ox-head corners.
Blue; 129 x 130 x 12mm
7082

345; 40–41 Furnival Street, EC4, City of London
English, Liverpool; 1750–75
Coastal vessel, barred ox-head corners.
Blue; 125 x 127 x 7mm
FUR87 [38]/[84]; Fig 6, no. 11

346; 40–41 Furnival Street, EC4, City of London
English, Liverpool; 1750–75
Coastal vessel with English merchant flag, barred ox-head corners.
Blue; 124 x 126 x 7mm
FUR87 [38]/[84]; Fig 6, no. 11

339

340

341

342

343

344

345

346

BIBLICAL TILES

Designs **347–387** show a series of biblical scenes from the Old and New Testaments and from the Apocrypha. These are arranged by the order in which they appear in the Bible: eg the Crucifixion (John 19 v. 18) is placed chronologically before the Ascension (Luke 24 v. 51).

347; probably London
English, London; 1720–50
The Temptation and Fall (Genesis 3 v. 6), barred ox-head corners. The design is very similar to a tile illustrated by Horne (1989, 76, no. 436) dated 1720–50.
Blue; 129 x 129 x 8mm
6952

348; Norfolk House, 113–129 Lambeth Road, SE1, Lambeth
English, London, Norfolk House pothouse; *c* 1720–50
Another version of the Temptation and Fall (Genesis 3 v. 6), barred ox-head corners. It was found with kiln waste suggesting it is a Norfolk House product.
Purple on light blue; ? x ? x 6–7mm
NOR90 [1024] <20>; Tyler et al 2008

349; Norfolk House, 113–129 Lambeth Road, SE1, Lambeth
English, London, Norfolk House pothouse; 1720–50
A further version of the Temptation and Fall (Genesis 3 v. 6), ox-head corners. Made at Norfolk House as other blue on white biblical tiles with the same border were found associated with kiln waste (**370**), or their provenance was confirmed by ICP analysis (**354**). Tiles with the same distinctive corner motifs are dated by Horne to 1720–50 (1989, 27, nos 70–71).
Blue; ? x ? x 9mm
NOR90 [1494] <637>; Tyler et al 2008

350; probably London
Dutch; 1680–1760
The expulsion from Eden (Genesis 3 v. 24), barred ox-head corners.
Blue; 126 x 126 x 8mm
6954

351; Stave Wharf/Rosings Wharf, Cathedral Street (Clink Street), SE1, Southwark
Dutch; 1680–1760
The Flood (Genesis 7 v. 19), barred ox-head corners. A similar scene is found on both Dutch and English tiles.
Blue; 129 x 130 x 7–8mm
WP83C [287] <896>

352; probably London
Dutch; 1680–1760
Animals leaving the ark (Genesis 8 vv. 13–19), barred ox-head corners.
Blue; 130 x 130 x 7mm
79.53/1

353; 2 King Edward Street, EC1, City of London
Probably English; 1680–1720
Abraham dismissing Hagar and Ishmael (Genesis 21 v. 14), painted in an unusual combination of colours. A similar scene in blue on white is shown in Horne (1989, 78, no. 450).
Blue and pale bluish-purple; ? x ? x 8mm
KEB92 [5] <59>; Betts 2007b; Fig 6, no. 15

354; Norfolk House, 113–129 Lambeth Road, SE1, Lambeth
English, London, Norfolk House pothouse; 1720–50
Probably Abraham dismissing Hagar and Ishmael (Genesis 21 v. 14), ox-head corners. ICP analysis confirms that this tile was made at Norfolk House (Chapter 5). It has the same barred ox-head corners as **349**.
Blue; ? x ? x 8mm
NOR90 [1054] <62>; analysed by ICP (Chapter 5)

355; Norfolk House, 113–129 Lambeth Road, SE1, Lambeth
English, London, Norfolk House pothouse; late 17th–early 18th century
The expulsion of Hagar and Ishmael (Genesis 21 v. 14), spider head corners. The spider head corner is more commonly a Dutch decorative motif; its use at Norfolk House may reflect the influence of Dutch potters who are known to have been involved with wall tile production in London during the late 17th and early 18th centuries (Chapter 4, London tiles). The tile was found with kiln waste and ICP analysis has confirmed it was made at Norfolk House.
Blue; ? x ? x 7–8mm
NOR90 [1024] <26>; analysed by ICP (Chapter 5); Tyler et al 2008

356; Stave Wharf/Rosings Wharf, Cathedral Street (Clink Street), SE1, Southwark
Dutch; 1680–1700
Joseph and Potiphar's wife (Genesis 39 v. 12).
Blue; 129 x 130 x 8mm
WP83C [287] <882>

357; probably London
Dutch; 1670–1720
Joseph in Pharaoh's chariot (Genesis 41 v. 43). The same scene is shown on a Dutch tile in van Sabben and Hollem (1987, 111, no. 371). Biblical tiles of similar style in van Dam are dated 1670–1720 (1991, 87, no. 98).
Blue; 123 x 120 x 10mm
6984

358; 1–7 Albion Place, EC1, Islington
Dutch; 1680–1750
The gathering of manna (Exodus 16 vv. 11–36). The same scene is shown on a Dutch tile in Huijg (1978, 57). Horne shows three English versions of this scene (1989, 83, nos 486–488).
Blue; 130 x 130 x 7mm
JAN90 [1] <22>; Fig 6, no. 1

347

348

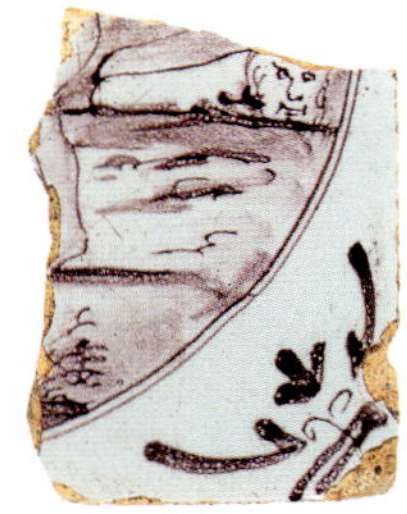

349

350

351

352

353

354

355

356

357

358

359; 19–20 College Hill, EC4, City of London
Dutch; 1680–1760
Moses about to smash the Ten Commandments (Exodus 32 v. 19), barred ox-head corners. Dutch tiles with similar corners, showing a different version of this scene, are in Schaap (1984, 119–20, nos 147, 1-B, 148, 3-A, 5-A).
Blue; 131 x ? x 6mm
COL81 [+] <7>

360; 1–7 Albion Place, EC1, Islington
English, Liverpool; 1740–75
Balaam and the ass (Numbers 22 v. 27). The unusual small powdered purple octagonal border is found on Liverpool biblical and landscape tiles (Archer 1997, 435, 456–7, N27, N148–150). The same scene, but in reverse, is shown on a Dutch tile in van Dam (1991, 87, 98, middle) and on English tiles in Ray (1973, 121, no. 41) and Horne (1989, 84, no. 492).
Purple; ? x ? x 7mm
ABP94 [255] <404>; Fig 6, no. 1

361; probably London
English, London; 1730–60
Samson killing the lion (Judges 14 v. 6), barred ox-head corners. A similar scene is in Horne (1989, 85, no. 501) dated 1730–50, whilst the corner motif is similar to that on London biblical tiles dated 1740–60 (Horne 1989, 76–7, 108, nos 441, 448, 654).
Blue; 128 x ? x 8–9mm
11892

362; The German Hospital, Dalston Lane, E8, Hackney (Middlesex)
Dutch; 1680–1760
The shearing of Samson (Judges 16 v. 19), barred ox-head corners.
Purple; ? x 130 x 8mm
GMN93 [+] <6>

363; Mansell Street, E1, City of London
English, London; 1740–60
David returning with Goliath's head (1 Samuel 17 v. 54), barred ox-head corners. For other versions of this scene see Horne (1989, 87, no. 512) and Ray (1973, 120, no. 48).
Blue; 127 x 127 x 8mm
12616

364; 12 Colosseum Terrace, Albany Street, NW1, Camden
Dutch, Utrecht; 1890–1920
King Soloman praying to God to bless the temple (1 Kings 8). The caption at the base reads in Dutch 'Judges, 3 v. 14' which is clearly a mistake. Two further biblical tiles from the same series are illustrated by van Lemmen (1986, 24). The distinct ox-head corner motif dates these tiles to 1890–1920 (Pluis 1997, 553, C.07.00.36); they were made by Westraven (formerly Ravesteyn) in Utrecht.
Blue; 129 x 129 x 7mm
CTA94 [+] <10>; Fig 6, no. 7

365; Norfolk House, 113–129 Lambeth Road, SE1, Lambeth
English, London, Norfolk House pothouse; 1720–50
Elijah fed by ravens (1 Kings 17 v. 6). This tile has an unusual ox-head corner design similar to **349** and **370**, and was found with kiln waste at Norfolk House.
Blue; ? x ? x 7–8mm
NOR90 [1024] <21>; Tyler et al 2008

366; 1 Poultry, EC2, City of London
Dutch; 1670–1720
Shadrach, Meshach and Abednego in the fiery furnace (Daniel 3 vv. 21–6). A complete version of this scene is shown on a Dutch tile in Huijg (1978, 101). Found dumped in the cellar of a building along with pottery of 1665–1730. Biblical tiles of similar type and thickness, dated 1670–1720, are illustrated in van Dam (1991, 87, no. 98).
Blue; ? x ? x 9mm
ONE94 [16004] <6459>

367; probably London
Dutch; 1670–1720
Jonah and the whale (Jonah 2 v. 10), spider head corners. Van Dam shows a number of Dutch biblical tiles painted in similar style (1991, 87, no. 98).
Blue; 127 x 127 x 8mm
6965

368; probably London
English, London; 1700–50
An English version of Jonah and the whale (Jonah 2 v. 10), barred ox-head corners. The same scene is in Archer (1997, 437, N40), Horne (1989, 92, no. 539) and Ray (1973, 123, no. 60).
Blue; 130 x 130 x 9mm
6964

359

360

361

362

363

364

365

366

367

368

369; probably London
English, London; 1740–60
Tobias with a fish and the Angel (Tobit 6 vv. 3–4; see Ray 1973, 123, no. 63; Britton 1987, 183, no. 211).
Purple; 125 x 125 x 6mm
P633

370; Norfolk House, 113–129 Lambeth Road, SE1, Lambeth
English, London, Norfolk House pothouse; 1720–50
Tobias catching the fish (Tobias 6 vv. 3–4), barred ox-head corners. This has the same ox-head corner design as **349** and was found with kiln waste at Norfolk House.
Blue; 127 x 128 x 9mm
NOR90 [1025] <15>; Tyler et al 2008

371; Norfolk House, 113–129 Lambeth Road, SE1, Lambeth
English, London, ? Norfolk House pothouse; late 17th–early 18th century.
Judith and the head of Holfernes (Judith 13 v. 15), spider head corner. See comments for **355**.
Blue; ? x ? x 8mm
NOR90 [1088] <53>; Tyler et al 2008

372; 2 King Edward Street, EC1, City of London
English, London; *c* 1680–1700
The women and the Angel at the Tomb (Matthew 28 vv. 1–6), spider head corners. Jonathan Horne (pers comm) believes this could be a rare early English tile (see **355**, **371**). There are four other probable early English biblical tiles with similar corners from the same site (KEW98 [667] <400>, [1479] <538> <956>, [1554] <519>). Others tiles believed to be from the same series are illustrated by Horne (2005, 35).
Blue; 125 x 124 x 7–8mm
KEW98 [1479] <842>; Betts 2007b; Fig 6, no. 15

373; 2 King Edward Street, EC1, City of London
Dutch; 1680–1760
Salome with the head of John the Baptist (Mark 6 v. 28), barred ox-head corners. The same scene is shown on English (Horne 1989, 99, no. 584) and Dutch tiles (Huijg 1978, 125; Schaap 1984, 120, no. 2-A).
Blue; 125 x 125 x 8mm
KEB92 [38] <129>; Betts 2007b; Fig 6, no. 15

374; 1–7 Albion Place, EC1, Islington
English, London; 1720–70
Christ and the tribute money (Mark 12 vv. 13–17). The same scene in reverse is shown in Horne (1989, 103, no. 617).
Blue; 127 x 127 x 8mm
JAN90 [1] <5>; Fig 6, no. 1

375; Platform Wharf, Cathay Street, SE16, Southwark
Dutch; 1680–1760
The Circumcision (Luke 2 v. 21).
Blue; ? x 129 x 7mm
PW86 [1] <113>

376; Stave Wharf/Rosings Wharf, Cathedral Street (Clink Street), SE1, Southwark
Dutch; 1680–1760
The Circumcision (Luke 2 v. 21).
Blue; ? x ? x 8mm
WP83C [287] <907>

377; probably London
English, London; 1740–60
Christ in the house of Martha and Mary (Luke 10 vv. 38–42).
Purple; 125 x 125 x 7mm
P632

378; Billingsgate Market Lorry Park, Lower Thames Street, EC3, City of London
Dutch; 1670–*c* 1700
Probably a biblical scene showing the prodigal son in misery (Luke 15 v. 16). The animals and kneeling figure show similarities to an English biblical tile in Ray (1973, 127, no. 83). It was found with tiles showing pastoral scenes so it would appear that the subject matter could also be interpreted as a pastoral scene (Betts 1991). Tiles with a similar style of spider head corner are illustrated by van Dam (1991, 86, no. 100) and Pluis (1997, 556, C.08.00.11).
Blue; 125 x 127 x 8–9mm
BIG82 [721] <997>

369

370

371

372

373

374

375

376

377

378

379; probably London
English, London; 1740–60
Jesus and the woman of Samaria at Jacob's well (John 4 vv. 4–15).
Purple; 125 x 125 x 6mm
P630

380; Steward Street, Brushfield Street E1, 240–276 Bishopsgate EC2, Tower Hamlets
Dutch; 1680–1800
Jesus and the woman of Samaria at Jacob's well (John 4 vv. 4–15), spider head corners. The complete scene is shown by Huijg (1978, 145).
Purple on pale blue; ? x ? x 8mm
STE95 [523] <130>

381; probably London
English, London; 1740–60
Christ healing the blind man (John 9 vv. 6–7). The same tile is illustrated by Britton (1987, 183, no. 214) where the scene is mistakenly identified as 'The woman healed of an issue of blood' (Matthew 9 vv. 21–2). For tiles showing the latter see Horne (1989, 98, nos 579–580).
Purple; 124 x 125 x 7mm
P626

382; 2 King Edward Street, EC1, City of London
Dutch; 1670–1720
Christ healing the blind man (John 9 vv. 6–7), spider head corners. Similar in style to Dutch biblical tiles in van Dam (1991, 87, no. 98).
Blue; 127 x 127 x 7mm
KEW98 [1479] <841>; Betts 2007b; Fig 6, no. 15

383; probably London
English, London, ? Norfolk House pothouse; 1720–50
Christ bound to the column (John 19 v. 1). The design is almost identical to that on a biblical tile from the Norfolk House pothouse, although this has a circular border and barred ox-head corners (Norfolk House, 113–125 Lambeth Road, SE1, Lambeth: MOL site code NOR88 [341] <25>), as has a very similar tile in Horne (1989, 105, no. 628).
Blue; 127 x 127 x 8mm
6976

384; probably London
Dutch; 1680–1760
Christ carrying the Cross (John 19 v. 17), barred ox-head corners. Fairly similar to a Dutch tile in Schaap (1984, 120, no. 1-D). For English versions of this design see Horne (1989, 105, nos 629–633).
Blue; 127 x 127 x 8mm
6977

385; probably London
English, London; 1740–60
Christ carrying the Cross (John 19 v. 18).
Purple; 124 x 125 x 7mm
P631

386; probably London
English, London; 1700–50
The Crucifixion (John 19 v. 18), barred ox-head corners. The lettering INRI is an abbreviation from the Latin: 'Jesus of Nazareth, King of the Jews'. The corners are Dutch in appearance but Horne (1989, 106, nos 635–638) believes this tile was probably made in London. Ray shows a purple on white English biblical tile with similar corners (1973, 117, no. 28).
Blue; 124 x 124 x 7mm
P634

387; probably London
English, London; 1740–60
The Ascension (Luke 24 v. 51).
Purple; ? x 127 x 7mm
P628

379

380

381

382

383

384

385

386

387

MYTHOLOGICAL CREATURES

388; 2 King Edward Street, EC1, City of London
Dutch; 1680–1750
Mythical sea creature, spider head corners. For similar tiles see Schaap (1984, 151, no. 196).
Blue; 126 x 125 x 8mm
KEW98 [1479] <868>; Betts 2007b; Fig 6, no. 15

389; Norfolk House, 113–129 Lambeth Road, SE1, Lambeth
Dutch; *c* 1715
Winged mermaid, spider head corners. Jonathan Horne (pers comm) has suggested a date of *c* 1715 based on the tile's thickness. The distinctive rendering of the sea can be seen on many Dutch tiles (Schaap 1984, 151, nos 195–196) and is also present on a tile with a mythical sea creature from Laurence Pountney Lane, EC4, City of London (MOL site code LPL73 [L1] <77>).
Purple; 126 x 126 x 7mm
NOR90 [1261] <255>

390; 2 King Edward Street, EC1, City of London
Dutch; 1680–1750
Neptune with spear, possibly from the same tile-painter as **389**.
Purple; ? x ? x 6–7mm
KEW98 [1479] <955>; Betts 2007b; Fig 6, no. 15

391; probably London
Dutch, ?Harlingen; 1650–80
Neptune, small barred ox-head corners. Tiles with similar mythical water beasts are illustrated by van Dam (1991, 81, nos 93–94).
Blue; 130 x 130 x 12mm
16018

392; probably London
Dutch; 1640–80
Mythical sea creature with shield and sword, barred ox-head corners. Similar tiles are in the Schaap (1984, 149–51, nos 191–195).
Blue; 126 x 125 x 10mm
Z3384

393; probably London
Dutch, Rotterdam; 1740–80
Mythological scene showing the rape of Europa within an octagonal border with typical Dutch foliate corners. The scene is taken from Ovid's 'Metamorphoses' which tells how Europa was carried away from Tyre by the god Zeus who had transformed himself into a bull. Sixteen blue and white tiles from the same series are illustrated in van Dam (1991, 94, no. 129). Pluis (1997, 129, no. 33, 568, C.08.00.01–02) dates tiles with similar borders and corners to 1740–80.
Blue; 126 x 123 x 8mm
6983

394; probably London
Dutch, Rotterdam; 1740–80
Another scene taken from Ovid's 'Metamorphoses'. The same scene is illustrated in van Dam (1991, 94, no. 129, second row, second from the left).
Blue; 124 x 124 x 7mm
6982

388

389

390

391

392

393

394

BIRDS AND ANIMALS

395; 2 King Edward Street, EC1, City of London
Dutch; 1660–1700
Bird holding fruit in brown, yellow and blue, with fleur-de-lis corners. The corner decoration is similar to certain Dutch tiles dated 1625–60 (Pluis 1997, 543, C.02.00.07), but its thickness would suggest a later date.
Poly; 121 x 120 x 8–9mm
KEW98 [1479] <564>; Betts 2007b; Fig 6, no. 15

396; St Paul's Cathedral, St Paul's Church Yard, EC4, City of London
Dutch; mid–late 17th century
Bird, with slightly different fleur-de-lis corner.
Poly; ? x ? x 9mm
SCP04 [42] <1>

397; 2–9, 10–16 Bevis Marks, 16–18 Bury Street, EC3, City of London
Dutch; 1660–1700
Owl.
Blue; ? x ? x 9–10mm
BEV80 [+] <62>

398; Laurence Pountney Lane, EC3, City of London
Dutch; 1660–1700
Running dog or fox painted on pinkish-white glaze, spider head corners. Animals depicted in a similar pose and with the same corner motif are in van Sabben and Hollem (1987, 102, no. 356).
Blue; 122 x ? x 9–10mm
LPL73 [L1] <66>

399; Laurence Pountney Lane, EC3, City of London
Dutch; 1660–1700
Lizard. An unusual subject matter, but Pluis shows a 17th-century Dutch tile with another type of lizard (1997, 407, A.04.04.02).
Blue; ? x ? x 8mm
LPL73 [L1] <78>

400; probably London
Dutch; 1680–1800
Fox or dog in unusual diamond and circular border, spider head corners.
Blue and purple; 123 x 127 x 7–8mm
7103

FLOWERS

401; probably London
English, Liverpool; 1750–75
Vase of flowers painted in 'Fazackerly colours' (red, blue, yellow, mauve and green) named after a pair of mugs traditionally made for Thomas and Catherine Fazackerly in Liverpool in 1757–8. A similar vase of flower is illustrated by Archer (1997, 489, N306, pl 300).
Poly; 127 x 127 x 9mm
7105

402; 2 King Edward Street, EC1, City of London
Probably Dutch; 1670–1700
Flower vase, barred ox-head corners (cf Pluis 1997, 550, C.07.00.04–05). Dutch flower vase tiles with similar corners are illustrated by van Dam (1991, 70, no. 78). The tile thickness suggests a late 17th-century date.
Blue; ? x 126 x 7mm
KEW98 [1479] <848>; Betts 2007b; Fig 6, no. 15

403; St Stephen Coleman Street church, 36–40 Coleman Street, EC2, City of London
Dutch or English; 1680–1800
Floral device, barred ox-head corners. The tile comes from the site of St Stephen church destroyed by enemy action in 1940.
Blue; ? x ? x 8mm
GM42 [ER561] <2>

404; 2 King Edward Street, EC1, City of London
Dutch; mid–late 17th century
Carnation flower head, barred ox-head corners. Similar to Dutch tiles in van Sabben and Hollem (1987, 38, nos 99–100).
Blue and green; ? x ? x 9–10mm
KEW98 [1479] <952>; Betts 2007b; Fig 6, no. 15

405; 1–7 Albion Place, EC1, Islington
Dutch; 1660–1700
Single tulip, fleur-de-lis corner. The corner motif is similar to that found on Dutch tiles with flower vase decoration dated 1620–60 (Pluis 1997, 423, 425, A.05.08.15, A.05.08.23). Numerous tiles of similar date with single flowers are illustrated in Schaap (1984, 80–5, nos 72–81). The thickness of the Albion Place tile would suggest a slightly later date.
Blue and purple; ? x 127 x 8mm
JAN90 [95] <132>, [100] <133> (joining fragments); Fig 6, no. 1

395

396

397

398

399

400

401

402

403

404

405

406; 2 King Edward Street, EC1, City of London
?Dutch or ?English; late 17th century
Tulip design in diamond border. Painted in a similar style to (thicker) mid 17th-century tiles from the Rotherhithe pothouse. The King Edward Street tile, however, may be Dutch.
Blue; ? x 124 x 7mm
KEW98 [1479] <844>; Betts 2007b; Fig 6, no. 15

407; probably London
Dutch; late 17th century
The paint colours used are very different from those used by English tile-painters suggesting the tile is Dutch. Similar tiles are illustrated by van Dam (1991, 69, no. 77). The tile thickness suggests a later 17th-century date.
Poly; 130 x 130 x 8mm
Z3402

408; Norfolk House, 113–125 Lambeth Road, SE1, Lambeth
English, London, Norfolk House pothouse; 1720–60
Vase of flowers with dotted flower-head corners. ICP analysis has confirmed the tile was made at the Norfolk House pothouse. However, flower vase designs were not exclusive to Norfolk House as floral tiles with similar corners have been found on the site of the Lambeth High Street pothouse (Ray 1973, 99, fig 27a–c) and ICP analysis has also confirmed they were made at the Gravel Lane pothouse (Hughes 2007b). Flower vase tiles with similar corners are illustrated by Horne (1989, 61, 63, nos 332, 346–349).
Blue; 125 x ? x 7–8mm
NOR88 [+] <41>; analysed by ICP (Chapter 5); Tyler et al 2008

409; Norfolk House, 113–129 Lambeth Road, SE1, Lambeth
English, London, Norfolk House pothouse; 1740–70
Vase of flowers with slightly different dotted flower-head corners. The pale duck-egg blue background suggests a slightly later date. See Horne (1989, 63, no. 348) for similar background colour.
Blue on pale blue; ? x 127 x 7mm
NOR90 [2112] <629>; Tyler et al 2008

410; Fleet Valley Project, between Blackfriars and Holborn Viaduct Stations, EC4, City of London
English, London, Norfolk House, Lambeth High Street or Gravel Lane pothouse; 1720–60
Vase of flowers, dotted flower-head corners.
Blue; 127 x 127 x 7mm
VAL88 [1911] <1149>, [1953] <1168>

411; 2 King Edward Street, EC1, City of London
English, London, Norfolk House, Lambeth High Street or Gravel Lane pothouse; 1720–40
Vase of flowers, dotted flower-head corners. Similar polychrome tiles are illustrated by Horne (1989, 60, nos 320–325).
Poly; ? x ? x 8mm
KEB92 [32] <78>; Betts 2007b; Fig 6, no. 15

412; St Philomena's School, Carshalton, SM5, Sutton (Surrey)
Dutch; Rotterdam; 1740–80 or possibly 19th century
Flower vase and bird, flower-head corners. Jan Pluis has seen photographs of tile designs **412–414** and concludes that they are Dutch tiles of 1740–80, but Jonathan Horne thinks they may be 19th-century copies. An 18th-century Dutch tile with a similar design is illustrated by Pluis (1997, 429, A.05.08.46).
Blue; 127 x 128 x 7mm
Private collection, St Philomena's School, Carshalton; Fig 7

413; St Philomena's School, Carshalton, SM5, Sutton (Surrey)
Dutch; Rotterdam; 1740–80 or possibly 19th century
Flower vase with insects, flower-head corners.
Blue; 128 x 128 x 7mm
Private collection, St Philomena's School, Carshalton; Fig 7

414; St Philomena's School, Carshalton, SM5, Sutton (Surrey)
Dutch; Rotterdam; 1740–80 or possibly 19th century
Flower vase with insect, flower-head corners.
Blue; 127 x 127 x 7mm
Private collection, St Philomena's School, Carshalton; Fig 7

406

407

408

409

410

411

412

413

414

415; 2 King Edward Street, EC1, City of London
English, Liverpool; *c* 1750–75
Stylised flower vase decoration (Archer 1997, 498, N347).
Blue; 127 x 128 x 6mm
KEW98 [1479] <936>; Betts 2007b; Fig 6, no. 15

416; 2 King Edward Street, EC1, City of London
English, Liverpool; 1740–70
Stylised flower vase design (Horne 1989, 72, no. 418; Archer 1997, 496, N338).
Blue; 126 x 126 x 7mm
KEW98 [1479] <865>; Betts 2007b; Fig 6, no. 15

417; Brooke House, Upper Clapton Road, E5, Hackney (Middlesex)
Dutch; 1740–1850
Floral arrangement with winged cherubs. Dutch tiles with slight variations of this design can be found in van Sabben and Hollem (1987, 115, no. 383) and Pluis (1997, 309, A.01.30.35)
Blue; 131 x 130 x 6–7mm
EH 1696; Fig 7

418; Claremont Road, Surbiton, KT6, Kingston upon Thames, Surrey
Dutch, Harlingen or Utrecht; 1880–1920
Part of a geometric floral pattern painted in a rather unusual combination of colours. Complete tiles with a similar design are in Pluis (1997, 148, no. 86b, 267, A.01.13.19). Design **497** shows another late Dutch tile.
Dark purple and yellow; ? x ? x 7mm
CMN98 [109] <3>

419; 2 King Edward Street, EC1, City of London
English, London; 1730–50
Flower vase and two birds with cherub-head corners. A complete tile with the same design is in Horne (1989, 62, no. 339).
Blue and purple; ? x 126 x 7mm
KEB92 [38] <126>; Betts 2007b; Fig 6, no. 15

420; probably London
English, London or Bristol; 1725–50
Flower vase design in powdered purple octagonal frame, blue quarter rosette corners. The same design is in Ray (1973, 215, no. 495) where it has been attributed to Bristol. However, as there are no Bristol tiles currently known from London, a London origin would seem a more likely possibility (see **297–301**).
Blue and purple; 122 x 123 x 8mm
79.52

421; 283 Tooley Street, SE1, Southwark
English, London Norfolk House or Gravel Lane pothouse; 1730–50
Vase of flowers with birds, in powdered purple octagonal frame, blue carnation corners. Very similar tiles are illustrated by Horne (1989, 62, no. 334) and Archer (1997, 482, N258, pl 291), and a waster is known from Norfolk House (**422**).
Blue and purple; 124 x 128 x 8–9mm
TOS93 [13] <74>

422; Norfolk House, 113–129 Lambeth Road, SE1, Lambeth
English, London, Norfolk House pothouse; 1730–50
Vase of flowers in powdered purple octagonal frame, blue carnation corners. A waster, confirmed by ICP analysis to have been made at the Norfolk House pothouse. ICP analysis has confirmed the same design was also made at the Gravel Lane pothouse (Hughes 2007b). A similar tile dated 1730–50 is illustrated by Horne (1989, 62, no. 334).
Blue and purple; 130 x ? x 9mm
NOR90 [1024] <12>; analysed by ICP (Chapter 5); Tyler et al 2008

423; Fleet Valley Project, Holborn Viaduct Station to Blackfriars, EC4, City of London
English, London, Vauxhall or Gravel Lane pothouse; 1730–50
Vase of flowers in powdered blue octagonal frame, brownish-red carnation corners. The complete design is shown in Horne (1989, 62, no. 335) and Archer (1997, 479, N245, pl 289) whilst a fragment with a similar design from the Vauxhall pothouse is in Britton (1987, 71, K). ICP analysis has confirmed the same design was also made at the Gravel Lane pothouse (Hughes 2007b).
Poly; ? x ? x 7mm
VAL88 [12113] <5042>

424; 2 King Edward Street, EC1, City of London
English, Liverpool; *c* 1750
Blue flowers set in elaborate purple geometric border. Archer illustrates a complete tile with a similar central floral design set in the same border (1997, 474, N223).
Blue and purple; 125 x ? x 7mm
KEW98 [1479] <1623>; Betts 2007b; Fig 6, no. 15

425; 2 King Edward Street, EC1, City of London
Dutch; 1750–1800
A complex tulip and carnation floral pattern covering the whole tile. A Dutch tile with a very similar design is shown in Pluis (1997, 135, no. 49).
Blue; 127 x 126 x 7mm
KEW98 [1479] <872>; Betts 2007b; Fig 6, no. 15

415

416

417

418

419

420

421

422

423

424

425

426; 2 King Edward Street, EC1, City of London
Dutch; 1740–*c* 1800
Complex floral pattern incorporating a bird.
Purple; ? x ? x 6–7mm
KEW98 [1479] ‹884›; Betts 2007b; Fig 6, no. 15

427; 2 King Edward Street, EC1, City of London
Dutch; 1740–*c* 1800
Pluis shows a Dutch tile with a similar design (1997, 219, A.01.05.29).
Purple; ? x ? x 7mm
KEW98 [1479] ‹885›; Betts 2007b; Fig 6, no. 15

428; Finsbury Avenue Square, EC2, City of London
English, London; ? mid 17th century
Common Tudor rose design found on numerous London-made floor tiles dating from the late 16th to the mid 17th centuries (**108–110**). This tile is only 9mm thick suggesting that it may have been intended as walling, although the worn surface shows it was actually used as flooring. It may represent an attempt by London tilemakers to produce tiles of similar thickness to the wall tiles which were arriving from the Netherlands in the mid 17th century.
Poly; ? x ? x 9mm
FNB02 [1040] ‹38›

DECORATED CORNERS AND GEOMETRIC PATTERNS

429; 2 King Edward Street, EC1, City of London
English, London, ? Lambeth High Street pothouse; 1725–70
Plain, with the quarter rose corners forming the only decoration. Tiles of this design have been found in the vicinity of the Lambeth High Street pothouse (Ray 1973, 99, fig 27 e–f; 235, no. 586) along with tiles with a complete rose in the centre (Horne 1989, 73, no. 422; Archer 1997, 505, N403–N405). A further tile with **429** was found on the site of the Mortlake pothouse (MOL site code HSL96 [1] ‹25›): this tile has mortar on the back showing it was attached to a wall and, therefore, it is not certain if it was made at Mortlake.
Blue; 127 x 126 x 7mm
KEW98 [1479] ‹876›; Betts 2007b; Fig 6, no. 15

430; 38–46 Albert Embankment, SE1, Lambeth
English, London, Glasshouse Street pothouse; *c* 1743–84
Geometric pattern in blue and white. This has the same distinctive flat back and thickness as biscuit-fired tiles from the Glasshouse Street pothouse. There is no exact parallel for this design, the nearest is a Greek key pattern on a rectangular border tile in Horne (1989, 70, no. 399).
Blue; ? x ? x 9mm
38ALB89 [215]; Tyler et al 2008

431; 38–46 Albert Embankment, SE1, Lambeth
English, London; 18th century
Unusual overall diamond pattern.
Blue; ? x ? x 8mm
38ALB89 [5] ‹85›

432; Jacob's Island, Bermondsey Wall West, SE1, Southwark
Dutch, Harlingen, Rotterdam or Utrecht; 1780–*c* 1880
Geometric pattern with hearts in two corners. The full design is shown in Pluis (1997, 224, A.01.05.56).
Blue; ? x 130 x 7mm
JAC96 [32] ‹423›

433; probably London
Dutch; 1760–1920
Geometric pattern, very similar to Pluis (1997, 260, A.01.12.47), but possibly slightly earlier in date.
Purple; 129 x ? x 8mm
7108

434; 2 King Edward Street, EC1, City of London
Dutch; 1750–*c* 1800
Geometric pattern in white on powdered purple ground. A Dutch tile with the same design is in van Sabben and Hollem (1987, 134, no. 415).
Purple; *c* 128 x *c* 128 x 9mm
KEB92 [33] ‹85›; Betts 2007b; Fig 6, no. 15

435; 2 King Edward Street, EC1, City of London
Dutch; 1700–1800
Geometric pattern in white on powdered purple ground. The same central design, although with different corner decoration, is present on a tile in Pluis (1997, 299, A.01.27.37).
Purple; ? x ? x 7–8mm
KEW98 [1479] ‹893›; Betts 2007b; Fig 6, no. 15

426

427

428

429

430

431

432

433

434

435

436; 2 King Edward Street, EC1, City of London
Dutch; 1700–1800
This design is similar to Dutch tiles illustrated in van Sabben and Hollem (1987, 134, no. 417) and Pluis (1997, 263, A.01.12.62).
Purple; ? x ? x 9mm
KEW98 [1479] <935>; Betts 2007b; Fig 6, no. 15

437; Stave Wharf/Rosings Wharf, Cathedral Street (Clink Street), SE1, Southwark
Dutch; 1700–1800
The full design is illustrated by Pluis (1997, 251, A.01.11.86).
Purple; 128 x ? x 8mm
WP83C [51] <873>

438; 2 King Edward Street, EC1, City of London
English, London, Vauxhall pothouse; 1750–70
Geometric and floral pattern. Very similar to complete tiles in Archer (1997, 507, N409–N411, pls 323–4), Horne (1989, 74, no. 434) and Ray (1973, 235, no. 594). A tile of this design was found with kiln waste on the site of the Vauxhall pothouse (Cockell 1974, pl 136a).
Blue and purple; ? x ? x 7mm
KEB92 [5] <45>; Betts 2007b; Fig 6, no. 15

IMITATION MARBLE AND PLAIN TILES

439; probably London
Dutch; 1650–1700
Combed slip-marbled decoration. Very similar tiles are illustrated in Schaap (1984, 158, no. 208) and Pluis (1997, 579, D.08.00.01–02).
Purple and reddish-brown; 130 x 130 x 10mm
7122

440; Westminster
English or Dutch; 1700–1800
Tortoiseshell-marbled decoration. A possible Liverpool tile with a fairly similar marble pattern is shown in Ray (1973, 235, no. 595) and Dutch examples are illustrated in Pluis (1997, 578, D.07.00.01–03).
Purple and light brown; 131 x 131 x 7mm
A13950

441; 40–41 Furnival Street, EC4, City of London
English, possibly Liverpool; 1750–90
Very unusual imitation marble decoration in black and white. The use of black on a white background can be seen on a chequerbroad-style Liverpool tile in Horne (1989, 74, no. 431).
Black; ? x ? x 7mm
FUR87 [38]/[84]; Fig 6, no. 11

442; 38–46 Albert Embankment, SE1, Lambeth
English, London, ? Glasshouse Street pothouse; *c* 1743–84
Plain purple with a blistered border. This tile is a definite waster. The Glasshouse Street pothouse also produced plain tin-glazed tiles in various shades of pale duck-egg blue (Tyler et al 2008, 109).
Dark purple; 129 x 129 x 7mm
38ALB89 [5] <124>

443; Platform Wharf, Cathay Street, SE16, Southwark
English, London; *c* 1675–1700
Plain blue glaze (*bleu persan*), one of the few tiles known from London with this glaze colour. Another was recovered under Cannon Street Station (Upper Thames Street, Cousin Lane, EC4, City of London: MOL site code UTA87 [1031]). For a decorated example see **313**.
Blue; ? x ? x 7mm
PW89 [1001]

436

437

438

439

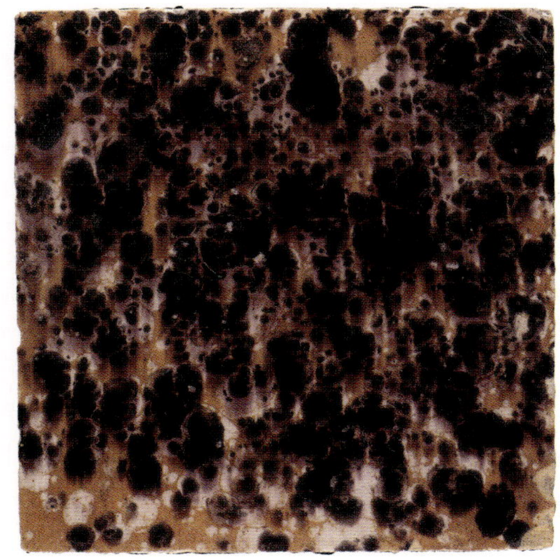
440

441

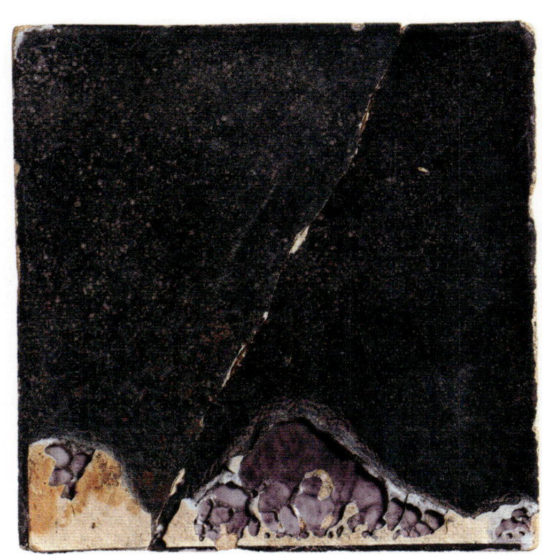
442

443

RECTANGULAR EDGING TILES

444; 40–41 Furnival Street, EC4, City of London
English, ?London; 1750–70
Floral edging tile. An edging tile showing similarities in design to the Furnival Street example is illustrated by Horne (1989, 70, no. 397).
Blue; 125 x 62–63 x 7mm
FUR87 [38]/[84]; Fig 6, no. 11

445; 38–46 Albert Embankment, SE1, Lambeth
English, London, Vauxhall pothouse; 1750–70
Floral edging tile. Horne (1989, 70, no. 398) illustrates an edging tile with the same design, although painted in a different style. This design has been found on the site of the Vauxhall pothouse (Cockell 1974, pl 136e).
Blue; 125 x 64 x 7mm
38ALB89 [5] <81>

446; Platform Wharf, Cathay Street, SE16, Southwark
?English, ?London; 1740–70
Floral edging tile.
Blue; ? x 66 x 8mm
PW86 [+] <109>

447; 2 King Edward Street, EC1, City of London
Dutch, Harlingen or Rotterdam; 1750–1800
Edging tile with floral design with insect. The number 2 is in purple on the back. The same floral pattern complete with winged insect is illustrated in Pluis (1997, 486, A.14.06.47) where the design is dated to 1750–1850, although the example illustrated here is almost certainly 18th century.
Purple; ? x 67 x 7mm
KEW98 [1479] <571>; Betts 2007b; Fig 6, no. 15

448; probably London
Dutch, Harlingen, Makkum or Utrecht; 1750–1800
Floral edging tile. The design is in Pluis (1997, 483, A.14.06.34) dated 1750–1920, although again the illustrated tile is probably 18th century.
Purple; 128 x 63 x 7mm
7119

449; 34–35 Great St Helen's, Bishopsgate, EC3, City of London
Dutch; 1770–*c* 1800
Foliage. The purple leaf decoration on a white background is similar to that found on two Dutch rectangular border tiles dated 1770/80–1930 (Pluis 1997, 481, A.14.06.16–17). The Great St Helen's tile is probably 18th century in date.
Purple; ? x ? x 7mm
SHL90 [+] <35>

450; 40–41 Furnival Street, EC4, City of London
Probably English, London; 1750–80
Floral edging tile with powdered blue ground. The design is similar to that found on square Dutch floral tiles with floral patterns on a blue ground (**425**), but the bluish background and the soft (ie slightly indistinct) decorative pattern suggests this is English (H van Lemmen, pers comm).
Blue; 127 x 67 x 7mm
FUR87 [38]/[84]; Fig 6, no. 11

451; The Mitre Hotel, Hampton Court Bridge, East Molesey, KT8, Richmond upon Thames (Surrey)
Probably English, London; 1750–80
Floral edging tile with powdered blue ground.
Blue; ? x 62 x 8mm
MHL92 [+] <18>

452; Norfolk House, 113–129 Lambeth Road, SE1, Lambeth
English, London, ? Norfolk House pothouse; 1740–60
Edging tile with Greek key pattern. A complete tile with the same design, but in purple on white, is illustrated by Horne (1989, 70, no. 399).
Blue; ? x 62 x 7mm
NOR90 [1569] <398>

444

445

446

447

448

449

450

451

452

TILE PICTURES

For a polychrome example see **498**.

453; probably London
English, London or Dutch; 1700–1800
Diana the huntress between twisted columns surrounded by an arch with animal heads. A row of at least three tiles appears to be missing along the base. Other missing tiles have now been replaced with modern tiles painted in pale purple.
Blue; 127 x 127 x 8mm
6313; Britton 1987, 179

454; probably London
English, London or Dutch; 1700–1800
Matching panel to **453**, but looking right.
Blue; 127 x 127 x 8mm
6314; Britton 1987, 180

The following two tile pictures are from Saffron Walden, Essex (**455**, **456**). They have been included here as both were made in London and can be compared with similar picture panels found in London itself.

455; Old Sun Inn, Saffron Walden, Essex
English, London; *c* 1739
Tile picture commemorating the stay of Oliver Cromwell in Saffron Walden in 1645.
Blue; 126–127 x 126–127 x 7mm
Saffron Walden Museum, Essex

456; Old Sun Inn, Saffron Walden, Essex
English, London; 1739
Tile picture commemorating the birth of Prince Edward, Duke of York in 1739. Signed 'WE 1739'.
Blue; 126–127 x 126–127 x 7mm
Saffron Walden Museum, Essex

453

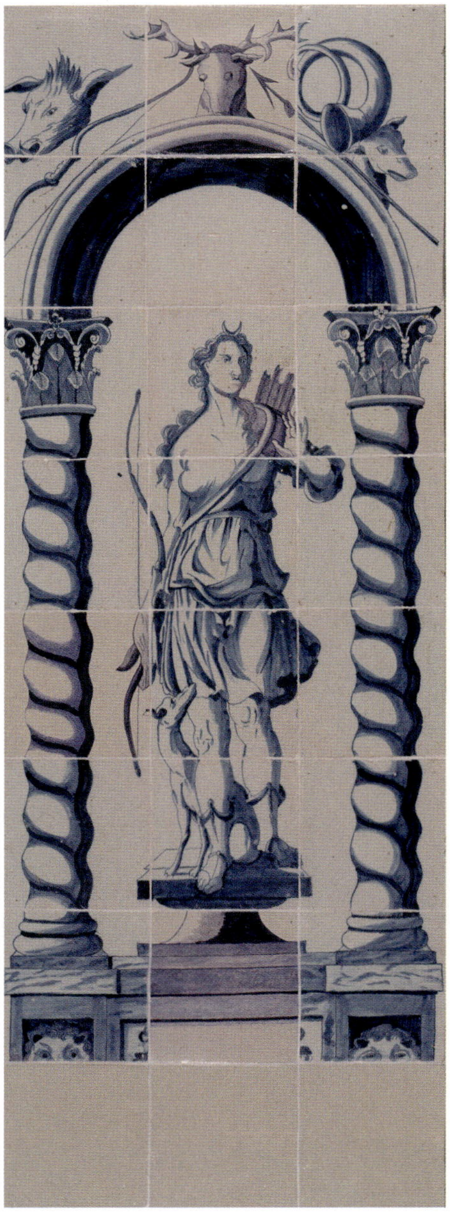

at 1.6

454

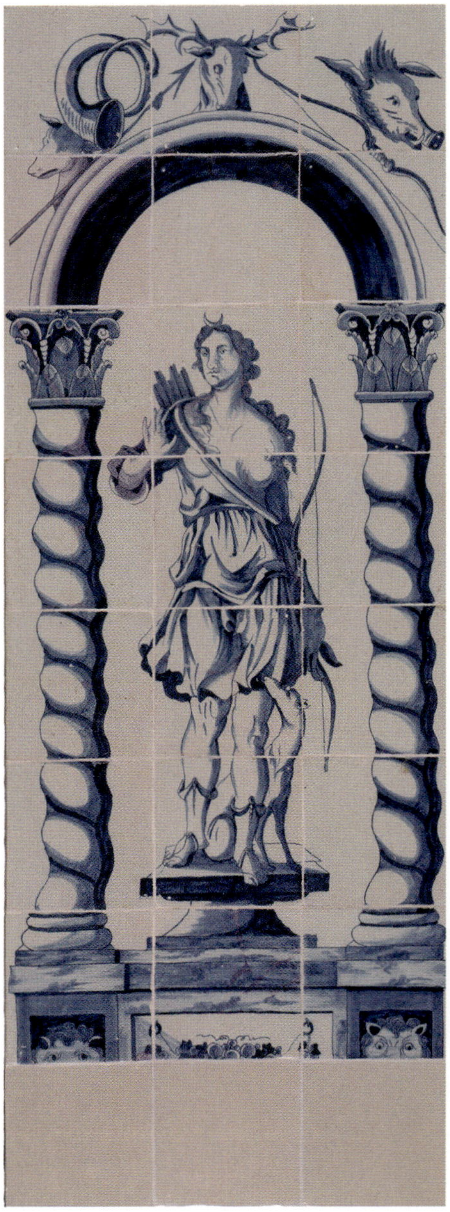

at 1.6

455

at 1.6

456

at 1.6

457; Daun and Vallentin's Distillery, Lambeth Road (formerly Church Street), SE1, Lambeth
English, London, ? Gravel Lane pothouse; 1720–30
Landscape picture panel. One of a series of eight picture panels from the pantry of a dwelling house attached to Daun and Vallentin's distillery located at the western end of Lambeth Road (formerly Church Street). Although adjacent to the Norfolk House pothouse all eight are believed to have been made at Gravel Lane (Chapter 4, Location and decorative use; **464**).
Blue; 125 x 125 x ?mm
10358

458; probably London
English, London; early–mid 18th century
From near the base of a tile picture showing the bottom half of two figures in a landscape scene.
Blue; 126 x 126 x 7mm
11889

459; 2 King Edward Street, EC1, City of London
English or Dutch; mid–late 17th century
Part of a tile picture showing a pair of legs.
Blue; ? x 121 x 8mm
KEW98 [1479] ‹960›; Betts 2007b; Fig 6, no. 15

460; Lime Kiln Dock, Three Colt Lane, E14, Tower Hamlets
Dutch or English; early 18th century
Part of a tile picture with a landscape scene.
Purple; ? x ? x 8mm
LKD94 [8] ‹35›

461; Cock and Bottle Inn, Cannon Street/Laurence Pountney Hill, EC4, City of London
Probably English; 1710–30
Tile picture with cockerel and a bladder onion bottle of 1710–75. The picture is surrounded by rectangular border tiles with small square tiles in each corner. These small square tiles, which were also made in the Netherlands, are very rare in Britain (Horne 1989, 70).
Blue; 124 x 124 x ?mm (square), 124 x 67 x ?mm (rectangular), 67 x 67 x ?mm (small square)
7142

457

at 1.6

458

459

460

461

at 1.6

462; 2 King Edward Street, EC1, City of London
Dutch; 1700–50
Back and tail of a horse from a large decorative picture. In the Netherlands, pictures depicting bounding and prancing horses were frequently mounted over hearths (Schaap 1984, 168, no. 218). Pluis shows a number of tile panels with horses (1997, 593, 613, eg E.02.04.01, E.02.05.01 and E.04.01.04).
Purple; 126 x 126 x 7mm
KEW98 [1479] <939>; Betts 2007b; Fig 6, no. 15

463; 38–46 Albert Embankment, SE1, Lambeth
Dutch; 1700–1800; or English; 1720–40
Part of a tile picture with birds and ship's rigging. Decorative picture panels showing sailing ships are common on Dutch tiles, various examples are illustrated by Pluis (1997, 166–7, 603–7).
Blue; 128 x 128 x 7mm
38ALB89 [5] <76>

464; Daun and Vallentin's Distillery, Lambeth Road (formerly Church Street), SE1, Lambeth
English, London, ? Gravel Lane pothouse; 1720–30
Tile picture showing a flower vase with birds. A further picture panel from the pantry of a dwelling house attached to Daun and Vallentin's distillery (see **457**). A Dutch picture panel with a similar flower vase is illustrated by Pluis (1997, 617, E.05.02.02).
Blue; 125 x 125 x ?mm
10359

462

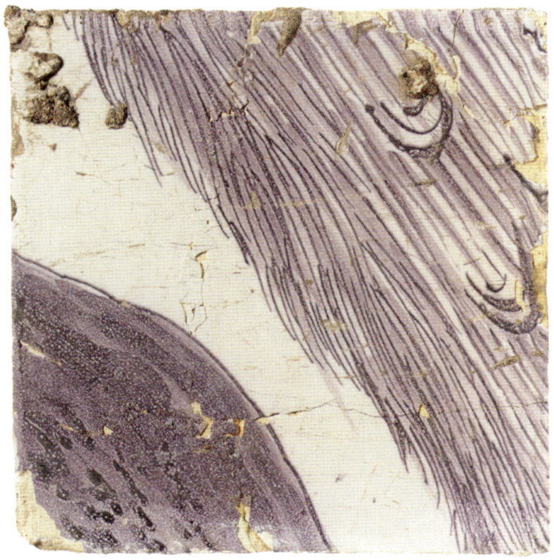

463

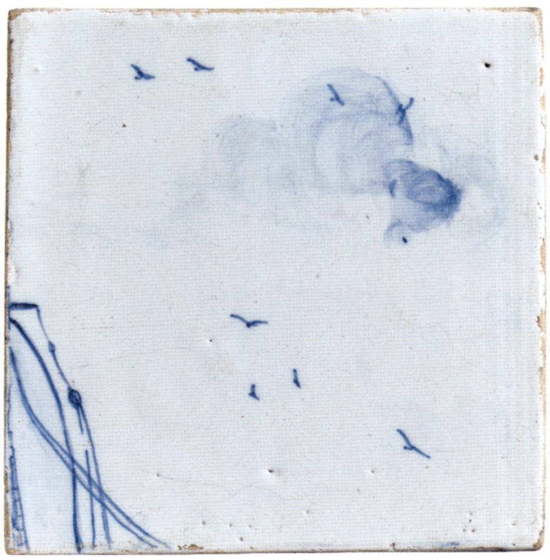

464

at 1.6

Designs **465–468** appear to be part of two complementary tile pictures found in Victorian or later demolition debris.

465; Finsbury Avenue Square, EC2, City of London
English, London; 1720–60
Part of flower vase tile picture, numbered 21 in blue on the back.
Blue on pale blue; 126 x 126 x 8mm
FNB02 [1109] <28>

466; Finsbury Avenue Square, EC2, City of London
English, London; 1720–60
Part of flower vase tile picture, numbered 21 in blue on the back. Part of second tile picture with near-identical design as **465**.
Blue on pale blue; 126 x 126 x 8mm
FNB02 [1109] <33>

467; Finsbury Avenue Square, EC2, City of London
English, London; 1720–60
Part of flower vase tile picture, numbered 13 in blue on the back. Part of same tile picture as **465** or **466**.
Blue on pale blue; 126 x 126 x 8mm
FNB02 [1109] <29>

468; Finsbury Avenue Square, EC2, City of London
English, London; 1720–60
Part of flower vase tile picture adjoining **467**, numbered 14 in blue on the back. Part of same tile picture as **465** or **466**.
Blue on pale blue; 126 x 126 x 8mm
FNB02 [1109] <32>

Designs **469–473** appear to be part of a second pair of complementary tile pictures.

469; 38–46 Albert Embankment, SE1, Lambeth
English, ?London; 1740–60
From a tile picture with foliage, numbered 5B on reverse.
Blue; 125 x 126 x 7mm
38ALB89 [5] <83>

470; 38–46 Albert Embankment, SE1, Lambeth
English, ?London; 1740–60
Tile picture with foliage, numbered 18B on reverse. Probably from same tile picture as **469**.
Blue; 125 x 125 x 7mm
38ALB89 [5] <79>

471; 38–46 Albert Embankment, SE1, Lambeth
English, ?London; 1740–60
Tile picture with foliage, numbered 21B on reverse. Probably from same tile picture as **469**.
Blue; 127 x 126 x 7mm
38ALB89 [5] <77>

472; 38–46 Albert Embankment, SE1, Lambeth
English, ?London; 1740–60
Tile picture with foliage, numbered 16A on reverse. The letter A suggests that this comes from a matching panel to these marked with the letter B.
Blue; 126 x 126 x 7mm
38ALB89 [5] <78>

473; 38–46 Albert Embankment, SE1, Lambeth
English, ?London; 1740–60
Tile picture with bird and foliage, numbered 10 on reverse (letter missing). This could be from either tile picture.
Blue; ? x 125 x 7mm
38ALB89 [5] <80>

465

466

467

468

469

470

471

472

473

474; 2 King Edward Street, EC1, City of London
Probably Dutch; 1700–50
Part of a tile picture with flower head.
Purple; 127 x 126 x 7–8mm
KEW98 [1479] <877>; Betts 2007b; Fig 6, no. 15

475; 2 King Edward Street, EC1, City of London
Probably Dutch; 1700–50
Tile picture with flower and foliage, probably part of same decorative panel as **474**.
Purple; ? x ? x 8mm
KEW98 [1479] <1603>; Betts 2007b; Fig 6, no. 15

476; probably London
Dutch; 1700–50
Tile picture with bird in a twisting vine. There are certain similarities to a Dutch tile picture in Pluis (1997, 625, E.12.02.03). The letter n is painted on the back in the top left corner.
Purple; 128 x 127 x 7mm
11890

TRADE SIGNS

The only other tiles with similar letters to **477–479** are in Saffron Walden Museum, Essex. Horne (1989, 119) mentions the tiles lettered 'OF' and 'SS&' but there are also further tiles with the letters 'ts S' and 'ere'.

477; probably London
English, probably London; *c* ?1718
Trade sign. Letters on the back mark the position of each tile in the panel. This panel is illustrated in Horne (1989, 119, no. 677) with the missing letters reconstructed from a typical trade card of the mid 18th century. Tile panel is mounted to a wall so thickness cannot be currently measured.

A drawing of the same panel recently found in Bristol Museum shows that it contained an original tile dated 1718 instead of the word 'by'. This may refer to the date of the panel or something else (J Horne, pers comm).
Blue; *c* 125 x 125 x ?mm
Private collection, ? J Horne

478; 2 King Edward Street, EC1, City of London
English, London; mid 18th century
The letter R, probably from a similar trade sign to **477**.
Blue on pale blue; 125 x 124 x 7mm
KEW98 [1479] <950>; Betts 2007b; Fig 6, no. 15

479; 2 King Edward Street, EC1, City of London
English, London; mid 18th century
Part of what may be the letter L (or perhaps an E or a T). Probably from a trade sign.
Blue on pale blue; ? x ? x 7mm
KEB92 [5] <51>; Betts 2007b; Fig 6, no. 15

MOSAIC TILES

480; 38–46 Albert Embankment, SE1, Lambeth
English, London, ? Glasshouse Street; 1823–46
Design **480** shows a sample of the 84 small tin-glazed tiles made in 25 individual shapes found unstratified at Albert Embankment. Many are covered by a light blue glaze characteristic of plain glazed tiles made at Glasshouse Street. Others have yellow-, darker blue-, light and dark green- and black-coloured glaze. Their thickness (3–8mm) and shape would suggest they were intended to be used in a wall mosaic. A different set of mosaic tiles from the same site are unglazed, these derive their decorative effect from differences in firing colour.
Blue, green and yellow; various sizes
38ALB89 [+]; Tyler et al 2008

WOODBLOCK TILES

481; 2 King Edward Street, EC1, City of London
English, Liverpool; 1756–7
Woodblock-printed tile, made by John Sadler, showing a girl and a shepherd in octagonal Louis XV border (Ray 1994, 17, A1-6).
Black on pale blue; 126 x 126 x 7mm
KEW98 [1479] <827>; Betts 2007b; Fig 6, no. 15

482; Mill Road, Merton High Street, SW19, Merton, Surrey
English, Liverpool; 1756–7
Woodblock tile, made by John Sadler, showing part of a chinoiserie scene in octagonal Louis XV border. The full design is illustrated in Ray (1994, 19, A4-2).
Purple; ? x ? x 7mm
MIS92 [18] <36>

474

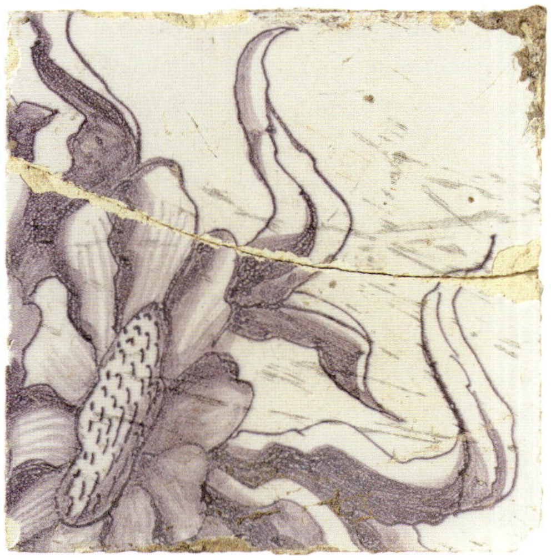

475

476

477

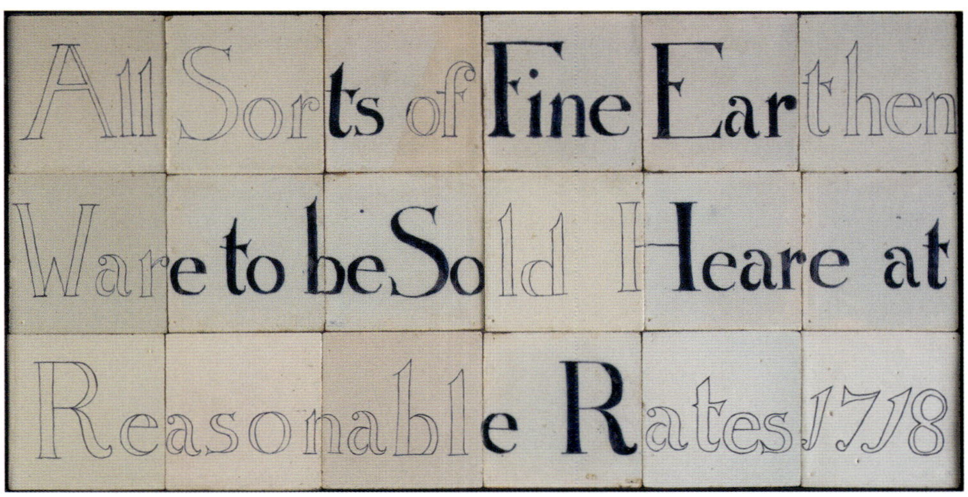

at 1.6

478

479

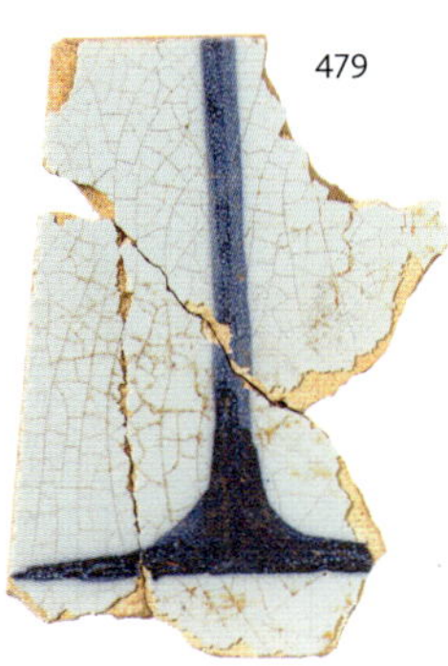

480

481

482

COPPERPLATE TILE

483; probably London
English, Liverpool; 1757–61
A nursemade with two children, one learning to walk, printed from a copper plate (Ray 1994, 26, B4-10). An early tile printed from a copper plate, made in Liverpool by John Sadler. Two later copper plate tiles were found at 2 King Edward Street, City of London, one was made by Sadler's successor Guy Green in 1770–*c* 1780, whilst the other was probably made by Sadler's apprentice Richard Abbey in 1773–*c* 1777 (Betts 2007b, 163, fig 164 <T61>–<T62>).
Red; 126 x 126 x 7mm
7120

TRIAL PIECES

484; 19 Albert Embankment, SE1, Lambeth
English, London, Norfolk House pottery
What appear to be flowers or leaves painted in red on the top of a biscuit-fired tile.
Unglazed; ? x ? x 7mm
ALA88 [109]

485; Norfolk House, 113–125 Lambeth Road, SE1, Lambeth
English, London, Norfolk House pottery
What appear to be flowers or leaves painted in red on the top of a biscuit-fired tile.
Unglazed; ? x ? x 7mm
NOR88 [21] <43>; Tyler et al 2008

HERMITAGE POTHOUSE PRODUCTS

Designs **486–490** were all found on the site of the Hermitage pothouse (*c* 1665–1773) in Wapping together with various biscuit-fired tiles. They represent the first evidence of the designs used at the pothouse, although there are uncertainties concerning the provenance of **486** (Chapter 4, London tiles) and **490** (Chapter 5).

486; Hermitage Basin, corner of Vaughan Way/Stockholm Way, E1, Tower Hamlets
English, London, Wapping, Hermitage pothouse or Liverpool; *c* 1750–73
Landscape, barred ox-head corners painted in Liverpool style.
Blue; ? x ? x 6–7mm (reconstructed *c* 128mm square)
HIT96 [19] <10>

487; Hermitage Basin, corner of Vaughan Way/Stockholm Way, E1, Tower Hamlets
English, London, Wapping, Hermitage pothouse; 1765–*c* 1773
Landscape.
Blue; ? x ? x 8mm
HIT96 [19] <14>

488; Hermitage Basin, corner of Vaughan Way/Stockholm Way, E1, Tower Hamlets
English, London, Wapping, Hermitage pothouse; 1720–*c* 1773
Blue; ? x ? x 7mm
HIT96 [19] <29>

489; Hermitage Basin, corner of Vaughan Way/Stockholm Way, E1, Tower Hamlets
English, London, Wapping, Hermitage pothouse; 1720–*c* 1773
Figure beneath drapes. There have been various interpretations of this design. Smith (1999, 155) suggests the figure is holding a coin at arm's length, whilst one of the authors (RW) believes it may be a biblical scene 'King Belshazar and the writing on the wall' (Daniel 5 vv. 5–9) or depict an actor on stage.
Blue; ? x ? x 8mm
HIT96 [27] <12>; analysed by ICP (Chapter 5)

490; Hermitage Basin, corner of Vaughan Way/Stockholm Way, E1, Tower Hamlets
English; 1740–60
Landscape. This is a much paler blue than the other decorated tiles. It was published as a Hermitage pothouse design (Smith 1999, 155), but subsequent ICP analysis has revealed that it was probably made at an as yet unidentified English pothouse (M Hughes, pers comm).
Blue; ? x ? x 8mm
HIT96 [23] <30>; analysed by ICP (Chapter 5)

483

484

485

486

487

488

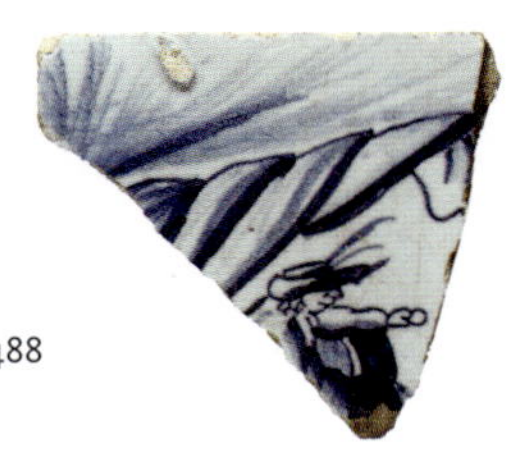

489

490

MORTLAKE POTHOUSE PRODUCTS

Designs **491–496**, some of which are wasters, were found on the site of one of the two pothouses known to have been located along Mortlake High Street (Stephenson 2003, 69). The biggest decorated pieces illustrated here represent the first firm evidence of the designs made at Mortlake. Many closely resemble a series of landscape tiles illustrated by Horne (1989, 38, nos 155–166) which were described as 'London' but can now be firmly attributed to Mortlake. Horne dates these landscape tiles to 1780–1800, but they are unlikely to be later than 1794 when Mortlake switched to concentrating on the production of stoneware (Chapter 4, London tiles).

491; 71–75 Mortlake High Street, SW14, Richmond upon Thames (Surrey)
English, London, Mortlake pothouse; 1780–94
Two tiles fused together in firing (not shown in image). The same design is illustrated by Horne (1989, 38, no. 158).
Blue; ? x ? x 7mm
HSL96 [521] <17>

492; 71–75 Mortlake High Street, SW14, Richmond upon Thames (Surrey)
English, London, Mortlake pothouse; 1780–94
Palm frond trees in dark blue. This is a waster as clay is attached to decorated surface.
Blue; ? x ? x 6mm
HSL96 [523]

493; 71–75 Mortlake High Street, SW14, Richmond upon Thames (Surrey)
English, London, Mortlake pothouse; 1780–94
Landscape.
Blue; ? x ? x 6mm
HSL96 [523] <29>

494; 71–75 Mortlake High Street, SW14, Richmond upon Thames (Surrey)
English, London, Mortlake pothouse; 1780–94
Landscape.
Blue; ? x ? x 6–7mm
HSL96 [521] <13>, [523] <16>

495; 71–75 Mortlake High Street, SW14, Richmond upon Thames (Surrey)
English, London, Mortlake pothouse; 1780–94
Landscape.
Blue; ? x ? x 7mm
HSL96 [521] <18>

496; 71–75 Mortlake High Street, SW14, Richmond upon Thames (Surrey)
English, London, Mortlake pothouse; 1750–94
Landscape set within a Louis XV border with diaper corners. It is possible that some of the dark blue landscape tiles with the same decorative surround published as 'Liverpool' by Horne (1989, 45, nos 212, 214) and Ray (1973, 173, no. 296) are in fact products of the Mortlake pothouse.
Blue; ? x 133 x 7mm
HSL96 [632] <15>

OTHER TILES

497; North House, Great Peter Street, SW1, Westminster
Dutch, Harlingen, Makkum or Utrecht; 1880–1930
Tiles with very similar geometric and floral patterns are shown in Pluis (1997, 139, no. 63, 304, A.01.30.06).
Poly; ? x ? x 7mm
NOU08 [100] <7>

498; probably London
English; mid 18th century
Part of a tile picture. The reverse has what appears to be B7 in dark blue.
Poly; 125 x 125 x 7mm
7107

499; St Bartholomew's Hospital, West Smithfield, EC1, City of London
English, Liverpool; 1750–75
Classical ruin in barbed medallion border with quarter flower-head corners
Blue; 126 x 127 x 6mm
St Bartholomew's Hospital archives and museum; Fig 6, no. 21

491

492

493

494

495

496

497

498

499

500; St Bartholomew's Hospital, West Smithfield, EC1, City of London
English, Liverpool or Bristol; 1750–75
Landscape in very unusual spotted circular border with Michaelmas daisy corners
Blue; 125 x 125 x 6mm
St Bartholomew's Hospital archives and museum; Fig 6, no. 21

501; St Bartholomew's Hospital, West Smithfield, EC1, City of London
English, Liverpool; *c* 1760–80
Blue; 125 x 123 x 7mm
St Bartholomew's Hospital archives and museum; Fig 6, no. 21

502; St Bartholomew's Hospital, West Smithfield, EC1, City of London
English, Liverpool; 1750–75
A Tamarisk tree
Blue; 126 x 125 x 7mm
St Bartholomew's Hospital archives and museum; Fig 6, no. 21

503; St Bartholomew's Hospital, West Smithfield, EC1, City of London
English, London or Liverpool; 1740–60
Biblical tile showing Samson pushing down the philistine temple (Judges 16 v. 29), barred ox-head corners
Blue; 130 x 130 x 7mm
St Bartholomew's Hospital archives and museum; Fig 6, no. 21

504; St Bartholomew's Hospital, West Smithfield, EC1
English, Liverpool; 1750–75
Sheep derived from a book of etchings by Nicolaes Berchem (1620–83).
Blue; 126 x 126 x 7mm.
St Bartholomew's Hospital archives and museum; Fig 6, no. 21

505; St Bartholomew's Hospital, West Smithfield, EC1
Dutch; 1720–50
Landscape set in elaborate wavy circular, powdered purple border with fleur-de-lis corners.
Blue; 125 x 125 x 8mm
St Bartholomew's Hospital archives and museum; Fig 6, no. 21

500

501

502

503

504

505

FRENCH, DUTCH AND GERMAN SUMMARIES

RÉSUMÉ

Tin-glazed tiles from London se penche sur la formidable diversité des motifs décoratifs en faïence stannifère qui existent à Londres depuis plus de 400 ans. En commençant par les motifs d'inspiration mauresque et de renaissance venus d'Espagne, l'ouvrage retrace l'importation de ces faïences décoratives originaires d'Espagne et des Pays-Bas jusqu'à leur fabrication sur place à Londres. Les premières faïences employaient des motifs spectaculaires pour créer des pavements colorés. Plus tard, les faïences furent utilisées comme revêtement décoratif mural, tout particulièrement au niveau des pourtours de cheminée. Ces faïences présentent souvent des motifs bleus sur fond blanc que l'on associe traditionnellement à la ville hollandaise de Delft.

Cet ouvrage est le premier à illustrer et discuter d'un grand nombre de ces motifs en faïence stannifère. Beaucoup de faïences murales et de pavements en faïence ont été retrouvés à Londres et dans ses environs ces 50 dernières années, et ce sont ces découvertes qui servent de base au catalogue illustré de types de motifs individuels. L'ouvrage commence par une vue d'ensemble des méthodes de fabrication de la faïence stannifère (Chapitre 2). Puis il s'intéresse à l'introduction et à l'utilisation de pavements en faïence (Chapitre 3) importés de Séville, en Espagne, au début du XVIe siècle, et aux importations plus tardives en provenance des Flandres (l'actuelle Belgique) à partir du milieu du XVIe siècle. La fabrique de faïence commença à Londres en 1571. Ces pavements en faïence présentent une très grande variété de motifs colorés de formes géométriques et florales. Entre la fin du XVIe et le début du XVIIe siècles, les Londoniens étaient tout particulièrement friands de motifs d'animaux et d'oiseaux entourés d'un pourtour circulaire.

La section suivante s'intéresse à l'utilisation de faïences murales qui arrivèrent pour la première fois à Londres dans les années 1630 d'origine hollandaise (Chapitre 4). Beaucoup des faïences murales utilisées à Londres provenaient des Pays-Bas, même si on fabriquait à Londres ce type de céramique entre 1676 et les alentours de 1800. Ces faïences murales présentent, elles aussi, une formidable variété de motifs, qu'il s'agisse de scènes bibliques ou de figures mythologiques, tout comme des voiliers, des paysages, oiseaux, animaux et fleurs. Les plus spectaculaires restent les immenses tableaux de faïences composés de 66 carreaux individuels. Quatorze poteries ont été identifiées dans Londres et ses alentours qui fabriquaient de la céramique en plus de la faïence fine. Lorsque la production cessa à la fin du XVIIIe siècle, les Néerlandais continuèrent de satisfaire les besoins en faïence stannifère jusque dans les premières années du XXe siècle. L'ouvrage présente les résultats (Chapitre 5) des analyses scientifiques effectuées pour déterminer le lieu de fabrication de dix faïences stannifères découvertes à Londres.

La dernière partie du livre (Chapitre 6) s'intéresse dans plus de détail à des édifices à

Londres et dans ses alentours dont les pavements et les murs sont recouverts de faïence stannifère. La plupart sont d'origine hollandaise, mais on y trouve également quelques exemples fabriqués à Londres et à Liverpool. Un catalogue de plus de 500 faïences illustrant l'immense variété de motifs de faïences murales et de pavements en faïence découverts à Londres constitue la dernière section de l'ouvrage (Chapitre 7).

SAMENVATTING

Tinglazuur Tegels van Londen bespreekt de rijke verscheidenheid van decoratieve tegels die over een periode van 400 jaar in de hoofstad gebruikt zijn. Het boek begint met ontwerpen in the Moorse en Renaissance stijlen uit Spanje en volgt de invoer van decoratieve tegels uit Spanje en de Nederlanden tot de uiteindelijke productie in Londen zelf. De vroege tegels vormden opzienbarende meerkleurige vloerpatronen. Later werden tegels gebruikt als decoratieve muurbedekking, vooral in en rond de haard. Deze tegels hebben vaak de blauw-witte decoraties die traditioneel verbonden worden met de stad Delft in Holland.

Veel van de tinglazuur tegelontwerpen uit Londen worden in dit boek voor de eerste keer afgebeeld en besproken. Tijdens de laatste 50 jaar zijn er grote hoeveelheden muur en vloertegels in Londen en haar omgeving gevonden en het zijn deze tegels die de basis vormen van de geillustreerde catalogus van individuele tegelontwerpen. Het boek begint met een overzicht van de productiemethoden van tinglazuurtegels (Hoofdstuk 2). Dan kijkt het naar de introductie en het gebruik van tinglazuur vloertegels (Hoofdstuk 3) ingevoerd uit Sevilla in Spanje in the vroege 16de eeuw en latere invoer uit Belgie (Vlaanderen) in het midden van de 16de eeuw. Productie begon in Londen in 1571. Deze vloertegels hebben een grote verscheidenheid van kleurrijke geometrische en florale motieven. Dieren en vogels gezet in een ronde omlijsting waren vooral in trek bij de inwoners van Londen gedurende de late 16de en vroege 17de eeuw.

Het gebruik van tinglazuur muurtegels die voor het eerst in Londen aankwamen vanuit Nederland in de jaren 1630 wordt ook besproken (Hoofdstuk 4). Veel muurtegels gebruikt in Londen komen uit Nederland, ondanks de productie van dit soort tegel in Londen zelf tussen 1676 en circa 1800. Deze muurtegels laten een wijde schakering aan onderwerpen zien van bijbelse voorstellingen en mythologische figuren tot zeilschepen, landschappen, vogels, dieren en bloemen. Meer imposant zijn de grote tegeltableaus die tot uit 66 individuele tegels kunnen bestaan. Het is bekend van veertien pottenbakkerijen in Londen dat zij tegels hebben gemaakt naast the productie van tinglazuuraardewerk. Toen productie ophield aan het einde van de 18e eeuw, werd de vraag naar tinglazuur wandtegels bevredigd door Nederlanders die doorgingen met de aanvoer van decoratieve tegels naar Londen tot aan de vroege jaren van de 20de eeuw. De resultaten worden gegeven van wetenschappelijke analyses (Hoofdstuk 5) van tien tinglazuurtegels gevonden in Londen om hun plaats van productie vast te stellen.

In het laatste gedeelte van het boek (Hoofdstuk 6) worden in meer detail gebouwen in Londen besproken waar nog tinglazuur vloer en muurtegels zitten. Dat zijn over het algemeen Nederlandse tegels maar er zijn ook voorbeelden uit Londen en Liverpool. Het boek wordt afgesloten met een catalogus van meer dan 500 tegels die de grote verscheidenheid van vloer and muur tegelontwerpen laten zien die in Londen gevonden zijn (Hoofdstuk 7).

ZUSAMMENFASSUNG

Zinnglasierte Fliesen aus London stellt die große Vielfalt dekorativer Fliesen mit Zinnglasur, auch Fayencefliesen genannt, aus über 400 Jahren Londoner Geschichte vor. Von frühen Beispielen aus Spanien im maurischen und Renaissance-Stil verfolgt das Buch die Einfuhr dekorativer Fliesen aus Spanien und den Niederlanden bis zum Beginn der Herstellung in London selbst. Die frühen Fliesen bildeten eindrucksvolle, vielfarbige Bodenmuster. Später wurden sie auch als dekorative Wandbekleidung verwendet, vor allem zur Kaminumrandung. Diese Fliesen hatten oft das typische blaue Muster auf weißem Hintergrund, das man mit der holländischen Stadt Delft verbindet.

Viele Fayencefliesen-Dekore aus London werden in diesem Buch zum ersten Mal abgebildet und erläutert. Während der letzten 50 Jahre hat man in London zahlreiche Wand- und Bodenfliesen gefunden, und diese bilden die Grundlage des Katalogs einzelner Dekortypen. Das Buch beginnt mit einem Überblick über die Herstellungsmethoden für zinnglasierte Fliesen (Kapitel 2). Anschließend wird die Einführung und Verwendung dieser Fliesen beschrieben, die im frühen 16. Jahrhundert aus dem spanischen Sevilla und später, zur Mitte des Jahrhunderts, aus Belgien (Flandern) in die englische Hauptstadt kamen (Kapitel 3). Die Herstellung in London begann im Jahr 1571. Diese Bodenfliesen weisen eine breite Vielfalt von farbenfrohen geometrischen Mustern und Blumenmotiven auf. Tiere und Vögel in runden Rahmen waren bei Londonern im späten 16. bis zum frühen 17. Jahrhundert besonders beliebt.

Die Verwendung zinnglasierter Wandfliesen, die in den 1630ern erstmals aus den Niederlanden nach London kamen, wird in Kapitel 4 behandelt. Viele in London verwendete Wandfliesen sind holländischer Herkunft, trotz der eigenen Produktion solcher Fliesen in der Stadt zwischen 1676 und ca. 1800. Sie haben ebenfalls eine breite Vielfalt an Mustern, von biblischen Szenen und mythologischen Figuren über Segelschiffe und Landschaften bis zu Vögeln, Tieren und Blumen. Noch eindrucksvoller sind die großen Fliesenbilder aus bis zu 66 einzelnen Fliesen. Man weiß, dass es in London vierzehn Fayencewerkstätten gab, die Fliesen und andere Keramikerzeugnisse anfertigten. Als die Werkstätten zum Ende des 18. Jahrhunderts ihre Produktion einstellten, wurde der Bedarf an zinnglasierten Wandfliesen von den Holländern gedeckt, die London bis in das frühe 20. Jahrhundert hinein weiterhin mit dekorativen Wandfliesen belieferten. Kapitel 5 präsentiert die Ergebnisse wissenschaftlicher Analysen, die durchgeführt wurden, um den Herstellungsort von zehn in London gefundenen Fayencefliesen zu ermitteln.

Im weiteren Verlauf (Kapitel 6) stellt das Buch Gebäude in London und Umgebung vor, die zinnglasierte Boden- und Wandfliesen besitzen – größtenteils holländische Erzeugnisse, aber auch einige englische Exemplare aus London und Liverpool. Ein Katalog von über 500 Fliesen, der die breite Vielfalt der in London gefundenen Boden- und Wandfliesen illustriert, schließt das Buch ab (Kapitel 7).

BIBLIOGRAPHY

MANUSCRIPT SOURCES

GUILDHALL LIBRARY, CITY OF LONDON (GL): MANUSCRIPT DEPARTMENT
MS 366/3 list of glass sellers with City shops, 16 September 1689

LONDON METROPOLITAN ARCHIVES (FORMERLY GREATER LONDON RECORD OFFICE) (LMA)
CLA/002 Court of Orphans' Inventory, no. 2141 Richard Barnes, 1690

THE NATIONAL ARCHIVES (TNA): RESEARCH, EDUCATION AND ONLINE LEARNING
Tudor Hackney http://193.132.104.70/tudorhackney/localhistory/lochhy2.asp

THE NATIONAL TRUST: PHOTOGRAPHIC ARCHIVE
Still Room, basement, Rainham Hall, The Broadway, Rainham, RM13, Havering, Essex, 1989 John Bethell, negative; F Scoones, negative nos F21, F29, F33, L22

ST BARTHOLOMEW'S HOSPITAL ARCHIVES AND MUSEUM, LONDON
Details of tiles including catalogued designs **499–505**

SITES AND MONUMENTS RECORD, MOL, LONDON (SMR)
Hayes Manor, Church Road, Hayes, Hillingdon (Middlesex) 050514/00/00

TOLLEMACHE ARCHIVE, BUCKMINSTER PARK, GRANTHAM NG33 5SD (TM)
Account nos 436, 437

PRINTED AND OTHER SECONDARY WORKS

Aguado Villalba, J, in prep *A corpus of Toledo* arista *tiles*
Anon, 1876 Art tiles, *The Furniture Gazette* 22 April, 254
Archer, M, 1976 Pyramids and pagodas for flowers, *Country Life* 22 January, 166–9
Archer, M, 1997 *Delftware*, London
Barber, B, and Thomas, C, 2002 *The London Charterhouse*, MoLAS Monogr Ser 10, London
Barber, B, Chew, S, Dyson, T, and White, B, 2004 *The Cistercian abbey of St Mary Stratford*

Langthorne, Essex: archaeological excavations for the London Underground Limited Jubilee Line Extension project, MoLAS Monogr Ser 18, London

Barron, C, Coleman, C, and Gobbi, C (eds), 1983 The London Journal of Alessandro Magno 1562, *London J* 9(2), 136–52

Baxter, M, 1994 *Exploratory multivariate statistics in archaeology*, Edinburgh

Berendsen, A, 1967 *Tiles: a general history*, London

Betts, I M, 1991 Billingsgate Fish Market car park, Lower Thames Street: building material (BIG82), unpub MOL rep

Betts, I M, 1994 Tin-glazed wall tiles: 12 Colosseum Terrace, Albany Street (CTA94), unpub MOL rep

Betts, I M, 1998 Benbow House, Bankside, Southwark (BAN95): building materials, unpub MOL rep

Betts, I M, 1999 Early tin-glazed floor tile production in London, in Gaimster 1999, 173–4, pls 7–12

Betts, I M, 2002 Ceramic and stone building material, in Barber and Thomas 2002, 97–9

Betts, I M, 2004 Tin-glazed tiles, in Barber et al 2004, 146

Betts, I M, 2005 The building materials, in Schofield and Lea 2005, 219–24

Betts, I M, 2007a Finds recovered from the Great Fire debris: tiles, in Blair and Sankey 2007, 35–40

Betts, I M, 2007b The tin-glazed wall tiles, in Lyon 2007, 150–63

Betts, I M, 2008a *The delftware tiles of Nonsuch mansion*, London

Betts, I M, 2008b Spanish tin-glazed tiles from Woking Palace and other sites in south-east England, *Surrey Archaeol Collect* 94, 53–69

Black, J, 2001 From maiolica to delftware: tin-glazed earthenware in London and the Low Countries, 1570–1630, *Medieval Ceram* 25, 66–71

Blair, I, and Sankey, D, 2007 *A Roman drainage culvert, Great Fire destruction debris and other evidence from hillside sites north-east of London Bridge: excavations at Monument House and 13–21 Eastcheap, City of London*, MoLAS Archaeol Stud Ser 17, London

Blake, A, 1985 Lesnes Abbey: an assessment of the archaeological finds from the site, unpub Bexley Council rep

Blake, H, Hughes, M, Mannoni, T, and Porcella, F, 1992 The earliest Valencian lusterware? The provenance of the pottery from Pula in Sardinia, in *Everyday and exotic pottery from Europe* c *650–1900: studies in honour of John G Hurst* (eds D Gaimster and M Redknap), Oxbow Monogr 23, 202–24, Oxford

Blanchett, C, 2000 The floor tiles at The Vyne, Hampshire, England, *Glazed Expressions: Mag Tile Architect Ceram Soc* 41, spec edn

Blatherwick, S, and Bluer, R, 2009 *Great houses, moats and mills on the south bank of the Thames: medieval and Tudor Southwark and Rotherhithe*, MOLA Monogr Ser 47, London

Bloice, B, 1971 Norfolk House, Lambeth. Excavation at a delftware kiln site, 1968, *Post-Medieval Archaeol* 5, 91–159

Bowsher, D, Dyson, T, Holder, N, and Howell, I, 2007 *The London Guildhall: an archaeological history of a neighbourhood from early medieval to modern times*, 2 vols, MoLAS Monogr Ser 36, London

Bowsher, J M C, 2007 Encounters between actors, audience and archaeologists at the Rose Theatre, 1587–1989, in *Contemporary and historical archaeology in theory* (eds L McAtackney,

M Palus and A Piccini), BAR Int Ser 1677, 63–6, Oxford
Britton, F, 1987 *London delftware,* London
Britton, F, 1990 The Pickleherring potteries: an inventory, *Post-Medieval Archaeol* 24, 61–92
Brown, J, 2005 The ceramic building materials, in *Saxons, templars and lawyers in the inner temple* (ed J Butler), Pre-Construct Archaeol Ltd Monogr Ser 4, 79–84, Durham
Brown, P, and Brown, D, 1992 Spanish flavour in church tiles, *Glazed Expressions: Mag Tile Architect Ceram Soc* 25, 9–10
Brown, P, and Brown, D, 1993 *Cuenca* tiles and Frederick Garrard, *Glazed Expressions: Mag Tile Architect Ceram Soc* 26, 10–11
Burton, A, 1986 *Bethnal Green museum of childhood,* Victoria and Albert Museum, London
Campbell, I, 1992 *Carlyle's House* [guidebook], The National Trust, London
Casamar, M, 1983 *Catálogo de azulejos del museo de Pontevedra: azulejos sevillanos, toledanos y aragoneses,* Pontevedra
Cherry, B, and Pevsner, N, 1983 *The buildings of England, London: Vol 2, South,* London
Cherry, B, and Pevsner, N, 1991 *The buildings of England, London: Vol 3, North west,* London
Cherry, B, and Pevsner, N, 2002 *The buildings of England, London: Vol 4, North,* London
Cherry, B, O'Brien, C, and Pevsner, N, 2005 *The buildings of England, London: Vol 5, East,* London
Clarke, P A, 1999 Eastcote Cottage: the structure, *Ruislip, Northwood and Eastcote Local Hist Soc J,* 21–4
Cockell, D, 1974 Some finds of pottery at Vauxhall Cross, London, *Engl Ceram Circle Trans* 9(2), 221–49, pls 119–43
Coll Conesa, J, 2009 The Museo Nacional de Cerámica 'González Marti' and ceramic tile collection in Valencia, *J Tiles Architect Ceram Soc* 15, 38–44
Cowie, R, 2008 Lost and found: the great gate of Stratford Langthorne Abbey, *Friends News* [Friends of Museum of London quarterly magazine] 33, 10–11
Currie, C K, 1996 Horticultural wares from Ham House, Surrey, *Post-Medieval Archaeol* 29, 107–11
Currie, C K, 2003 Archaeological excavations at Upper Lodge, Bushy Park, London borough of Richmond, 1997–9, *Post-Medieval Archaeol* 37, 90–125
Dam, J D van, 1991 *Nederlandse tegels,* Amsterdam
Dawson, G J, 1966 Southwark and the origin of delftware, *Guy's Hospital Gazette* 5 March, 121–4
Dawson, G J, 1971 Two delftware kilns at Montague Close, Southwark: Part 1, *London Archaeol* 1, 228–31
Dawson, G J, and Edwards, R, 1974 The Montague Close delftware factory prior to 1969, *Res Vol Surrey Archaeol Soc* 1, 47–63, Guildford
Defoe, D, 1727 *The complete English tradesman in familiar letters: directing him in all the several parts and progressions of trade,* London
Dickens, C, 1886 *A Christmas carol,* London
Draper, W H, 1923 *Chiswick,* London
Dumortier, C, 1999 Maiolica production in Antwerp: the documentary evidence, in Gaimster 1999, 107–11, pl 1
Dumortier, C, 2002 *Ceramique de la renaissance à Anvers,* Brussels
Eames, E S, 1992 *English tilers,* London
Edwards, R, 1974 London potters circa 1570–1710, *J Ceram Hist* 6, 1–141

Edwards, R, 1981 The Vauxhall pottery: Part 1, History and background to 1977–81 excavations, *London Archaeol* 4, 130–6

Edwards, R, 1984 An early 18th-century waste deposit from the Vauxhall pottery, *Engl Ceram Circle Trans* 12(1), 45–56, pls 47–56

Fries Museum, 1971 *Antwerps plateel*, Tentoonstelling Fries Museum, Leeuwarden

Gaimster, D (ed), 1999 *Maiolica in the north: the archaeology of tin-glaze earthenware in north-west Europe* c *1500–1600*, Brit Mus Occas Pap 122, London

Gaimster, D, and Hughes, M, 1999 South Netherlands maiolica floor tiles from Broad Arrow Tower, Tower of London, in Gaimster 1999, 175–9, pl 13

Gaimster, D, and Nenk, B, 1997 English households in transition 1450–1550: the ceramic evidence, in *The age of transition, the archaeology of English culture 1400–1600* (eds D Gaimster and P Stamper), Soc Medieval Archaeol Monogr 15, 171–95, Oxford

Gapp, E, and Willey, C, 2005 Brick and tiles: the fabric of the building, in Pearce 2005, 68–71

Garnett, O, 2003 *Red House*, National Trust, London

Gerrard, C M, Gutiérrez, A, and Vince, A G (eds), 1995 *Spanish medieval ceramics in Spain and the British Isles*, BAR Int Ser 610, Oxford

Gestoso y Pérez, J, 1995 (1903) *Historia de los barros vidriados sevillanos*, repr with introduction by A Pleguezuelo, Seville

Goggin, J M, 1968 *Spanish maiolica in the new world*, New Haven

González Martí, M, 1952 *Cerámica del levante español, siglos medievales: Vol 2, Alicatado y azulejos*, Barcelona and Madrid

Grainger, I, and Phillpotts, C, 2010 *The Royal Navy victualling yard, East Smithfield, London*, MOLA Monogr Ser 45, London

Grainger, I, and Phillpotts, C, in prep *The abbey of St Mary Graces, East Smithfield, London*, MOLA Monogr Ser

Graves, A, 2002 *Tiles and tilework*, London

Gray, M, 1997 *Sutton House*, London

Hinton, P, Orton, C, and Yule, B, 1988 Mark Brown's wharf, in *Excavations in Southwark 1973–6, Lambeth 1973–9* (ed P Hinton), Joint Publ London Middlesex Archaeol Soc/Surrey Archaeol Soc 3, 133–56, 307–47, London

Horne, J, 1989 *English tin-glazed tiles*, London

Horne, J, 1999 *A collection of early English pottery: Part 19*, London

Horne, J, 2005 *English pottery and related works of art*, London

Hughes, M J, 1991 Provenance studies of Italian maiolica by neutron activation analysis, in Wilson 1991, 293–7

Hughes, M J, 2002 Report on ICP-AES analysis of ten tin-glazed decorated floor tiles of probable Low Countries origin in the collections of the Guildford Museum, unpub Guildford Museum archive rep

Hughes, M J, 2005a The analysis by inductively coupled plasma-atomic emission analysis (ICP-AES) and -mass spectrometry analysis (ICP-MS), in Spanish tin-glazed tiles from Woking Palace and other sites in south-east England (ed I M Betts), unpub Friends of Woking Palace rep, 9–14

Hughes, M J, 2005b The analysis of medieval mosaic and other floor tiles from Yorkshire by inductively coupled plasma atomic emission spectrometry, in Stopford, J, *Medieval floor tiles of northern England*, 352–60, London

Hughes, M J, 2007a Neutron activation analysis at the British Museum, *Archaeometry* 49, 255–70

Hughes, M J, 2007b Report on the ICP analysis of stoneware and tin-glazed ware from Lavington Street/Great Suffolk Street SE1 (GLS06), unpub MOL rep

Hughes, M J, 2008 Inductively coupled plasma analysis of tin-glazed tiles and vessels produced at several centres in London, in Tyler et al 2008, 120–31

Hughes, M J, 2009 Inductively coupled plasma analysis (ICP) of six tin-glazed tiles found in London, unpub MOL rep

Hughes, M J, and Gaimster, D, 1999 Neutron activation analysis of maiolica from London, Norwich, the Low Countries and Italy, in Gaimster 1999, 57–91

Hughes, M J, and Gaimster, D R M, 2002 Neutron activation analyses of majolica by the British Museum, in *Majolica and glass from Italy to Antwerp and beyond: the transfer of technology in the 16th and early 17th century* (ed J Veeckman), 215–41, Antwerp

Hughes, M J, and Vince, A, 1986 Neutron activation analysis and petrology of Hispano-Moresque pottery, in *Proceedings of the archaeometry symposium, Washington 1984* (eds J S Olin and M J Blackman), 353–67, Washington, DC

Hughes, M J, Cowell, M R, and Hook, D R, 1991 Neutron activation analysis procedure at the British Museum research laboratory, in *Neutron activation and plasma emission spectrometric analysis in archaeology* (eds M J Hughes, M R Cowell and D R Hook), Brit Mus Occas Pap 82, 29–46, London

Hughes, M, Blake, H, Hurst, J, and Wilson, T, 1997 Neutron activation analysis of Italian maiolica and other medieval Italian ceramics, in *Archaeological sciences 1995* (eds A Sinclair, E Slater and J Gowlett), Oxbow Monogr 64, 77–81, Oxford

Huijg, A, 1978 *De bijbel op tegels*, Boxtel

Hurst, J G, 1999a Maiolica floor tiles, in Thurley 1999, 146–7

Hurst, J G, 1999b Sixteenth-century south Netherlands maiolica imported into Britain and Ireland, in Gaimster 1999, 91–106

Hurst, J G, and Le Patourel, J, 1999 Imported maiolica floor tiles from Whitehall Palace, London, in Gaimster 1999, 181–3

Jackson, S, 1989 Report on the archaeological excavation at 113–129 Lambeth Road SE1: Norfolk House, unpub MOL rep

James, P D, 2004 *The murder room*, London

James, T B, 1995 Southampton and Spain in the 16th century, in Gerrard et al 1995, 41–9

Lane, A, 1960 *A guide to the collection of tiles*, 2 edn, Victoria and Albert Museum, London

Lang, G, 2004 *1000 tiles*, San Francisco

Lemmen, H van, 1986 *Delftware tiles*, Shire Album 179, Princes Risborough

Lemmen, H van, 1990 Children's games on Dutch delftware tiles, *J Tiles Architect Ceram Soc* 3, 22–7

Lemmen, H van, 2000 *Victorian tiles*, 2 edn, Princes Risborough

Lemmen, H van, 2004 P Martin van Straaten: importer of Dutch tiles, *Glazed Expressions: Mag Tile Architect Ceram Soc* 49, 6

Lemmen, H van, 2005 *Delftware tiles*, 2 edn, Shire Album 179, Princes Risborough

Lins, P A, 1984 Technical notes, in Schaap 1984, 178–81

Lorenzo Morilla, J, 1987 Intervención arqueológica en c/Pureza no. 44 de Sevilla, in *En anuario arqueológico de Andalucía*, 574–80, Seville

Lunsingh Scheurleer, D F, 1986 *Tegels en tegeltableaus in het museum Mr Simon van Gijn te Dordrecht*, Dordrecht

Lyon, J, 2007 *Within these walls: Roman and medieval defences north of Newgate at the Merrill Lynch Financial Centre, City of London*, MoLAS Monogr Ser 33, London

Macfarlane, B, 2005 The Bedford Park chunks, *Glazed Expressions: Mag Tile Architect Ceram Soc* 53, 16–17

Mackinder, A, and Blatherwick, S, 2000 *Bankside, excavations at Benbow House, Southwark, London SE1*, MoLAS Stud Ser 3, London

Marsden, P, 1969 Archaeological finds in the City of London, 1966–8, *Trans London Middlesex Archaeol Soc* 22(2), 1–26

Martin, A R, 1926 On the topography of the Cluniac abbey of St Saviour at Bermondsey, *J Brit Archaeol Ass* 2 ser 32, 192–228

Martínez, C, 1991 *Balbina cerámica hispanomusulmana*, Madrid

Melville Balfour, M, 1929 'Judge' Jeffreys' house in Aldermanbury: an historic city mansion, *Trans London Middlesex Archaeol Soc* 6(1), 177–98

Metcalf, P, 1984 Living over the shop in the City of London, in Design and practice in British architecture: studies in architectural history presented to Howard Colvin, *Architect Hist* 27, 96–103

Mills, J, 1984 Excavations in Uxbridge, 1982–3, *London Archaeol* 5, 3–11

Milward, R, 2001 *Eagle House: a short history*, Al-Furqān Islamic Heritage Foundation, no place

Moore, C, Rowell, C, and Strachey, N, 1995 *Ham House*, The National Trust, London

Noël Hume, I, 1977 *Early English delftware from London and Virginia*, Colonial Williamsburg Occas Pap Archaeol 2, Williamsburg

Norton, C, 1984 Medieval tin-glazed painted tiles in north-west Europe, *Medieval Archaeol* 28, 133–72

Opie, I, and Opie, P, 1984 *Children's games in street and playground*, Oxford

Orton, C, 1980 *Mathematics in archaeology*, London

Parry, S J, 1991 *Activation spectrometry in chemical analysis*, Chichester

Le Patourel, J, 1999 Picture tile, in Thurley 1999, 147–8

Pearce, J (ed), 2005 *The last Hendon farm: the archaeology and history of Church End Farm*, Hendon

Pearson, L, 2005 *Tile gazetteer: a guide to British tile and architectural ceramics locations*, Shepton Beauchamp

Pleguezuelo Hernández, A, 1989 *El azulejo servillano: diseño y producción (siglos XV–XVIII)*, Seville

Pleguezuelo Hernández, A, 1992 Francisco Niculoso Pisano: datos arqueológicos, *Faenza* 78(3–4), 171–91

Pleguezuelo Hernández, A, 1996 *Cerámicas de Triana: colección Carranza*, Seville

Pluis, J, 1997 *The Dutch tile: designs and names*, Leiden

Rackham, B, 1926 *Early Netherlands maiolica*, London

Rackham, B, 1959 Floor tiles, in Biddle, M, Barfield, L, and Millard, A, Excavation of the manor of the More, Rickmansworth, *Archaeol J* 116, 186–8

Ray, A, 1973 *English delftware tiles*, London

Ray, A, 1991 Francisco Niculoso called Pisano, in Wilson 1991, 261–6

Ray, A, 1994 *Liverpool printed tiles*, London

Ray, A, 2000 *Spanish pottery 1248–1898*, London

RCHM(E), 1930 Roy Comm Hist Monuments (Engl), *An inventory of the historical monuments in London: Vol 5, East London*, London

Reid, A, 2003 7 Hammersmith Terrace, W6, *Country Life* 197, no. 44, 70–3

Robbins, D, Suleman, R, and Hunter, P, 2003 *Linley Sambourne House, 18 Stafford Terrace, Kensington*, Royal Borough of Kensington and Chelsea

Rocque, J, 1746 Exact survey of the City of London Westminster and Southwark and the country 10 miles round, reproduced in Margary, H, 1971 *'Exact survey of the City of London Westminster and Southwark and the country 10 miles round'* by John Rocque, 1746, Margary in assoc Guildhall Library, Kent

Ruger, A, 2001 *Vermeer and painting in Delft*, London

Sabben, C van, and Hollem, J, 1987 *Antieke tegels*, Rockanje

Sancho Corbacho, A, 1953 *La cerámica andaluza: azulejos sevillanos del siglo XVI – la casa de Pilatos*, Seville

Schaap, E, with Chambers, L H, Hendrix, M L, and Pierpoline, J (eds), 1984 *Dutch tiles in the Philadelphia museum of art*, Philadelphia

Schofield, J, 1994 Saxon and medieval parish churches in the City of London: a review, *Trans London Middlesex Archaeol Soc* 45, 23–145

Schofield, J, 1995 *Medieval London houses*, London

Schofield, J, and Lea, R, 2005 *Holy Trinity Priory, Aldgate, City of London: an archaeological reconstruction and history*, MoLAS Monogr Ser 24, London

Schofield, J, with Maloney, C (eds), 1998 *Archaeology in the City of London, 1907–91: a guide to records of excavations by the Museum of London and its predecessors*, MOL Archaeol Gazetteer Ser 1, London

Schofield, J, and Pearce, J, with Betts, I, Dyson, T, and Egan, G, 2009 Thomas Soane's buildings near Billingsgate, 1640–66, *Post-Medieval Archaeol* 43, 282–341

Sharp, T, 2004 The mantelpiece in the courthouse of St Andrew's Holborn: a possible donor identification by the attribution of a coat of arms, *The Coat of Arms* ns 15(205), 193–203

Shennan, S, 1997 *Quantifying archaeology*, 2 edn, Edinburgh

Shepherd, J (ed), 1998 *Archaeology in the City of London, 1946–72: a guide to records of excavations by Professor W F Grimes held by the Museum of London*, MOL Archaeol Gazetteer Ser 3, London

Skelton, A, 1998 The Carshalton water tower tiled bath – a study in Anglo-Dutch tiles, *J Tiles Architect Ceram Soc* 7, 31–6

Skelton, A, in prep *The Hermitage and the development of the Carshalton House landscape garden*, Carshalton House Estate Rep 2

Sloane, B, in prep *Excavations at the nunnery of St Mary de fonte clericorum, Clerkenwell, London*, MOLA Monogr Ser

Sloane, B, and Hoad, S, with Cloake, J, Pearce, J, and Stephenson, R, 2003 *Early modern industry and settlement: excavations at George Street, Richmond, and High Street, Mortlake, in the London borough of Richmond upon Thames*, MoLAS Archaeol Stud Ser 9, London

Smith, T P, 1999 Tin-glazed wall tiles, in Tyler 1999, 153–5

Smith, T P, 2002 The Flemish connection: cautions regarding some building materials terminology, *J Brit Archaeol Ass* 155, 272–7

Smith, T P, 2003 Report on building materials from Bromley Hall, 43 Gillender Street, London, E14, unpub archive rep

Steele, A, Samuel, M, and Dyson, T, in prep *The Cluniac priory and abbey of St Saviour Bermondsey, Surrey: excavations 1984–95*, MOLA Monogr Ser

Stephenson, R, 2003 Mortlake: specialist appendix, in Sloane and Hoad 2003, 69–79

Survey of London, 1900 *Parish of Bromley-by-Bow* (ed C R Ashbee), Survey of London 1, London

Survey of London, 1957 *Spitalfields and Mile End New Town*, Survey of London 27, London

Survey of London, 1960 *Parish of Hackney: Part 1, Brooke House*, Survey of London 28, London

Survey of London, 1963 *Parish of St James, Westminster*, Survey of London 31, London

Survey of London, 1975 *The museums area of South Kensington and Westminster*, Survey of London 38, London

Survey of London, 1986 *Southern Kensington: Kensington Square to Earl's Court*, Survey of London 42, London

Survey of London, 2000 *Knightsbridge*, Survey of London 45, London

Sygrave, J, 2005 Development and industry in Whitechapel, excavations at 27–29 Whitechapel High Street and 2–4 Colchester Street, London E1, *Trans London Middlesex Archaeol Soc* 56, 77–96

Thomas, C, Sloane, B, and Phillpotts, C, 1997 *Excavations at the priory and hospital of St Mary Spital, London*, MoLAS Monogr Ser 1, London

Thompson, A, Westman, A, and Dyson, T (eds), 1998 *Archaeology in Greater London 1965–90: a guide to records of excavations by the Museum of London*, MOL Archaeol Gazetteer Ser 2, London

Thurley, S, 1999 *Whitehall Palace: an architectural history of the royal apartments 1240–1698*, London

Toppin, A J, 1937 The China trade and some London 'chinamen', *Trans Engl Ceram Circle* 3, 37–56

Tyler, K, 1999 The production of tin-glazed ware on the north bank of the Thames: excavations at the site of the Hermitage pothouse Wapping, *Post-Medieval Archaeol* 33, 127–63

Tyler, K, Betts, I, and Stephenson, R, 2008 *London's delftware industry: the tin-glazed pottery industries of Southwark and Lambeth*, MoLAS Monogr Ser 40, London

VCH, 1971 *The Victoria History of the county of Middlesex: Vol 4*, London

Veeckman, J, 1999 Maiolica in 16th- and early 17th-century Antwerp: the archaeological evidence, in Gaimster 1999, 113–23

Wageningen, R van, 1988 Cerameikimporten in Amsterdam: een mineralogische herkomstonderzoek, unpub PhD thesis, Univ Amsterdam

Wallis, H, 1902 *Italian ceramic art: the maiolica pavement tiles of the 15th century*, London

Weinreb, B, and Hibbert, C (eds), 1993 (1983) *The London encyclopaedia*, rev edn, London

Williams, B, 1995 Survey of Spanish tiles imported into England: an interim note, in Gerrard et al 1995, 335–7

Willis, C S, 1949 Old houses in Epsom, Ewell and Cuddington, *Surrey Archaeol Collect* 51, 110–33

Wilson, T (ed), 1991 *Italian renaissance pottery*, London

Wilson, T, 1999 Italian maiolica around 1500: some considerations on the background to Antwerp maiolica, in Gaimster 1999, 5–21

INDEX

Compiled by Susan Vaughan

Page numbers in **bold** indicate illustrations
Modern London boroughs follow London site names
County names within parentheses refer to historic counties

Abbey, Richard, tilemaker 62; *see also* Liverpool
1–7 Albion Place, Islington 52
Aldgate pothouse, City of London 4, 14–16, 48, 67
Alhambra, Granada (Spain) 9
All Hallows church, City of London **10**, 11, 21–2, 25
Andries family, potters and tilemakers
  Guido di 9, 11, 13
  Jasper 13, 14
  Joris (George) 13, 19
Antwerp (Belgium) 11–13, 23, 44–8

Barston, James 29; *see also* Norfolk House pothouse
Baxter's Coffee House, Tower Hamlets 41
Bear Garden pothouse, Southwark 28
Bermondsey House, Southwark 20, 23, 24
Bingham, Henry, potter and tilemaker 33; *see also* Glasshouse Street pothouse
Blackfriars, City of London 20, **20**
99 Borough High Street, Southwark 52
Bradshawe, Edmund, tilemaker 16; *see also* Montague Close pothouse
Bristol (Glos) 8, 10, 29, 34
Bromley Hall, Tower Hamlets 67
Brooke House, Hackney (Middx) 6, 24, 40, 67–8, **67**
Bushey Park, Upper Lodge, Richmond upon Thames (Middx) 25

1 Cadogan Gardens, Kensington and Chelsea 52, **53**
Campion, John, tilemaker 29; *see also* Hermitage pothouse
Carew Manor, Beddington (Surrey) 12, 23
Carshalton, Sutton (Surrey)
  Carshalton House water tower 40, 68–9, **68**, **69**
  St Philomena's School 82

Cedar House, Hillingdon (Middx) 69–70, **69**, **70**
Charlton House, Greenwich (Kent) 20–1, 34, 43, 71–3, **71**, **72**, **73**
Charterhouse, Islington 23
Chatham (Kent), Commissioners House 42, **42**
2 Chenies Street Chambers, Camden 43, 53
24 Cheyne Row, Kensington and Chelsea 42, 53
Chiswick Manor, Hounslow 19–20
Church End Farm, Barnet (Middx) 73
Cock and Bottle Inn sign, City of London 41
Coimbra Cathedral (Portugal) 9
9 Collingham Gardens, Kensington and Chelsea 54
12 Colosseum Terrace, Camden 42, 54
Copthall pothouse, Lambeth 1, 27–8
Court House of St Andrew's, City of London 54
Cressey, Hugh, tilemaker 16; *see also* Montague Close pothouse

Daun and Vallentin's distillery, Lambeth 31, 41
Delft (Neths) 1, 5, 18, 38
Dora House, Kensington and Chelsea 42, 54–5, **55**
Duke's Place, Aldgate, City of London 13, 14
Dutch tiles
  1500–1666 19–20
  1666–1930 34–7
  see also Delft; Haarlem; Harlingen; Makkum; Middelburg; Rotterdam; Utrecht

Eagle House, Wimbledon (Surrey) 42, 74, **74**
Eastcote Cottage, Harrow (Middx) 74
Elsley, Thomas 43, 78
English tiles
  1500–1666 13–19
    London pothouses *see* Aldgate; Montague Close; Pickleherring; Rotherhithe; Still Stairs
  1666–1930 27–34
    London pothouses *see* Bear Garden; Copthall; Glasshouse Street; Gravel Lane; Hermitage; Lambeth High Street; Montague Close; Mortlake; Norfolk House; Pickleherring; Vauxhall
  production outside London *see* Bristol; Liverpool

Fastolf's Place, Southwark 23
Flemish tiles 11–13; *see also* Antwerp
Forster, Henry 32; *see also* Lambeth High Street pothouse
3 Fournier Street, Tower Hamlets 56, **56**
12 Fournier Street, Tower Hamlets 40, 56–7, **56**, **57**
21 Fournier Street, Tower Hamlets 58
French tiles *see* Lyons; Rouen
Fry, William 17, 18; *see also* Rotherhithe pothouse; Still Stairs pothouse
40–41 Furnival Street, City of London 42, 58–9, **58**

Garrard, Frederick, tilemaker 11, 22, 43, 53, 71; *see also* Millwall tile factory
Glass Sellers' Company 28, 35, 37
Glasshouse Street pothouse, Lambeth 32–3, 48, 49
Gorhambury (Herts) 13
Gravel Lane pothouse, Southwark 31–2, 41, 49, 52
Green, Guy, tilemaker 62; *see also* Liverpool
Greene, John, glass and tile seller 37, 38
Greenwich Palace, Greenwich (Kent) 11, 22
Griffith, William 41; *see also* Lambeth High Street pothouse

Guijarro, Fernán Martínez, tilemaker 10, 11

Haarlem (Neths) 44, 47
Hailes Abbey (Glos) 8
Ham House, Richmond upon Thames (Surrey) 21, 25, 37, 38, 40, 74–6, **75**, **76**
Hamme, Jan Ariens van, potter and tilemaker 1, 5, 27, 28; *see also* Copthall pothouse
7 Hammersmith Terrace, Hammersmith and Fulham (Middx) 76
Hampton Court Palace, Richmond upon Thames (Middx) 38, 76–7
Harlingen (Neths) 34, 43, 72
39 Harrington Gardens, Kensington and Chelsea 59
Hayes Manor, Hillingdon (Middx) 77
Herkenrode Abbey (Belgium) 12
Hermitage pothouse, Wapping 29, 37, 48, 49
21 Highgate High Street, Haringey (Middx) 36, 77–8, **77**
Hodgson, Henry 32; *see also* Lambeth High Street pothouse
Holding, Henry 37; *see also* Hermitage pothouse
Hulst, van, tile manufacturer, Harlingen (Neths) 43

Jansen, Jacob, tilemaker 13, 14; *see also* Aldgate pothouse

12 Kensington Square, Kensington and Chelsea 59
33 Kensington Square, Kensington and Chelsea 36, 59–61, **60**, **61**
2 King Edward Street, City of London 27, 37, 62

Lam, Charles, tile importer 43
Lambeth High Street pothouse, Lambeth 32, 41
Leadenhall Street, City of London 39–40
Lesnes Abbey, Bexley (Kent) 23
Lewisham High Street, Lewisham (Kent) 78, **78**
Liberty (Store), Westminster 62–3, **62**
Linley Sambourne House, Kensington and Chelsea 43, **43**, 63, **63**
Liverpool (Lancs), tiles 29, 34, 42, 58, **58**, 61, 62, 78
Load of Hay public house, Barnet (Herts) 51, 78
Lombards Place, City of London 19, 22, 25
Lyons (France) 12

Makkum (Neths) 43, 54, 65
Manor of the More, Rickmansworth (Herts) 22
Marks, Charles, tile importer 43
1 Marlborough Crescent, Ealing (Middx) 43, 78
Meredith, Howard W, tile importer 43
Middelburg (Neths) 19

Millwall tile factory, Tower Hamlets 11, 43
Mitre Hotel, East Molesey (Surrey) 59
Montague Close pothouse, Southwark 16, 28–9
Mortlake pothouses, Richmond upon Thames (Surrey) 33
Moss Brothers 33; *see also* Glasshouse Street pothouse
Mychele, Henry, tile importer 22

Newcastle House, Islington 23–4
Newgate Street, City of London 43
Niculoso Francisco (Pisano), tilemaker 10, 11
Nonsuch Mansion, Cheam (Surrey) 41
Norfolk House, Lambeth 24, 30
Norfolk House pothouse, Lambeth 27, 29–30, 37, 41, 48, 49
North London Collegiate School, Barnet (Middx) 43, 79, **79**

Oade, Nathaniel 31, 36; *see also* Gravel Lane pothouse
Osbaldson, Edward 18; *see also* Still Stairs pothouse

Pether, Henry 33; *see also* Glasshouse Street pothouse
Pickleherring pothouse, Southwark 16–17, 28, 37, 48, 49
Place Farm, Bletchingley (Surrey) 13
pothouses *see* English tiles, London
Pulido brothers, tilemakers 9, 10, 11

Rainham Hall, Rainham (Essex) 42, 79–82, **80**, **81**, **82**
Ravesteijn (Westraven), Utrecht (Neths) 43, 63, 66
Red House, Bexleyheath (Kent) 82, **82**
Red Lion Inn, City of London 25
Rickard's distillery, Piccadilly 41
Robins, John 28, 37; *see also* Pickleherring pothouse
Rose Theatre, Southwark 25
Rotherhithe pothouse, Southwark 4, 17–18, 48, 49, 67
Rotterdam (Neths) 34, 82
Rouen (France) 45, 46

Sadler, John, tilemaker 62; *see* Liverpool
Saffron Walden (Essex), Old Sun Inn 41
St Bartholomew's Hospital, City of London 64–5
St George the Martyr church, Southwark 65, **65**
St John the Evangelist's church, City of London 25
St Mary Clerkenwell nunnery, Islington 23
St Mary Graces Abbey, Tower Hamlets 24
St Mary Spital, Tower Hamlets 23, 24

St Matthew's church, City of London 25
St Philomena's School, Carshalton, Sutton (Surrey) *see* Carshalton
Savino (Andries), Guido di, potter and tilemaker *see* Andries, Guido de
Seville (Spain), tiles 1, 8–11, 22, 52, **53**
Sibley *see* Sybley
Singer, Alfred 33; *see also* Glasshouse Street pothouse
Southbridge House, Southwark *see* Rose Theatre
Spanish tiles 1, 8–11; *see also* Seville; Toledo; Valencia; Valencia region tiles
30 Spital Square, Tower Hamlets 66
Steam Engine public house, Lambeth 34, 42, 43, 66, **66**
Still Stairs pothouse, Southwark 18–19
Straaten, Martin van, tile importer 43
Stratford Langthorne Abbey (Essex) 24
Sutton House, Hackney (Middx) 8, 24–5, 40, 83
Sybley (Sibley), James, glass and tile seller 4, 28, 37

Taye, Martin, tile-painter 14; *see also* Aldgate pothouse
Temple church, City of London 11, 23
Tichelaar, Makkum (Neths) 43
Titchfield Abbey (Hants) 23
Toledo (Spain) 9, 52, 73
Tower of London, Tower Hamlets 12, 22
Townsend, John 17; *see also* Rotherhithe pothouse

Utrecht (Neths) 34, 42–3, 44, 47, 63, 66

Valencia (Spain) 1, 9, 62, 63
Valencia region tiles 8, 11
Vauxhall pothouse, Lambeth 5, 30–1, 37
Vullens, Jan Jansz, tile-painter 18
The Vyne (Hants) 11–12, 23

Wagstaff, William 33; *see also* Mortlake pothouses
Warwick Inn, City of London 13, 24
Waxwell Farm, Harrow (Middx) 83, **83**
Westminster Abbey, Westminster 51
Westminster Synagogue, Kensington and Chelsea 66
Whitehall Palace, Westminster 12
Wilhelm, Christian, potter and tilemaker 16; *see also* Pickleherring pothouse
2–3 Windsor Street, Uxbridge (Middx) 41
Woodland, Joseph 37; *see also* Pickleherring pothouse

York Place, Westminster 22